HOW GERTRUDE TEACHES HER CHILDREN; AN ATTEMPT TO HELP MOTHERS TO TEACH THEIR OWN CHILDREN; AND AN ACCOUNT OF THE METHOD

Published @ 2017 Trieste Publishing Pty Ltd

ISBN 9780649607969

How Gertrude Teaches Her Children; An Attempt to Help Mothers to Teach Their Own Children; And an Account of the Method by Johann Heinrich Pestalozzi

Edited by Trieste Publishing Pty Ltd.
 Cover @ 2017

www.triestepublishing.com

JOHANN HEINRICH PESTALOZZI

HOW GERTRUDE TEACHES HER CHILDREN; AN ATTEMPT TO HELP MOTHERS TO TEACH THEIR OWN CHILDREN; AND AN ACCOUNT OF THE METHOD

Trieste

HOW GERTRUDE
TEACHES HER CHILDREN

HOW GERTRUDE
TEACHES HER CHILDREN

An Attempt to Help Mothers to Teach their own Children

AND

AN ACCOUNT OF THE METHOD

A Report to the Society of the Friends of Education, Burgdorf

BY

JOHANN HEINRICH PESTALOZZI

TRANSLATED BY

LUCY E. HOLLAND AND FRANCIS C. TURNER

AND EDITED, WITH INTRODUCTION AND NOTES,

BY

EBENEZER COOKE

London

SWAN SONNENSCHEIN & CO., LIM.

SYRACUSE, N.Y.: C. W. BARDEEN

1900

First Edition, *June 1894.*
Second Edition, *March 1900.*

CONTENTS.

EDITOR'S PREFACE.

The Method in time and thought precedes *How Gertrude Teaches*. It may be read after Letter I., for in this letter Pestalozzi gives the history and circumstances which led him to those principles he first definitely stated in *The Method*. The *First Letter from Stanz* also belongs to this period. It will be found in De Guimps' Life and in Quick's *Essays on Educational Reformers*. These works form a complete group, and are his most important educational works. They are undoubtedly his own; of later works this cannot be said until we come to the *Swan's Song* and *My Experiences*.

The portions of *How Gertrude Teaches* in Biber's *Life of Pestalozzi* are all that have been translated. Its peculiar terms, such as "Anschauung," may partly account for this neglect. These terms are difficult, for apparently we do not grasp Pestalozzi's thought. We neither read nor follow him. If we walk in his ways, we may see what he saw; if we repeat his experiments, we may in some measure share his thought. Doing leads to knowing. He has been blamed for not defining his terms. He gives instead the history of his conception, the circumstances which led to it, its development, and his schemes founded on it. " There are two ways of instructing," he said; "either we go from words to things, or from things to words. Mine is the second method." His meaning may become clearer if the reader will substitute "Anschauung" for "sense impression" and for all other equivalents throughout the work. It has, and can have, no equivalent in English. We may partly learn its meaning, as we have learned that of some other words, from its use. If definitions are desired, the most helpful will be found at the beginning of Kant's *Critique of Pure Reason.* Kant's method is to begin with definitions.

We have tried to translate this work literally, without paraphrase and without omissions: no difficult passage has been left out. Much might be improved. The more we learn from him the more evident this is. Any help which will make his thought still clearer will be gladly and thankfully received.

For my part, I heartily wish it had been in abler hands, but the work seems to me as much needed here and now as ever. This is in part my apology for rushing in where more competent beings have feared to tread. It has not been done without much help, and in recording my obligations for this other circumstances will intrude.

To one, first and foremost, my gratitude is due. Of him I have known nothing for more than forty years. Between 1845–1850 the transition from the old school of our forefathers—very similar to that of Samuel Dysli, of Burgdorf—to the new school of trained teachers took place in our retired parish. The old dame and the severe schoolmaster passed away, and among the new teachers came one from Bristol—Mr.

Wm. B. Morgan—with a new method—Pestalozzi's. He stayed only one year, and returned. We heard of him no more. In a small way we had our Stanz. The school was transformed, its tediousness vanished, and unknown powers awoke. He joined us at play, and so extended his master's principles naturally, at a time when Froebel was doing the same.—The first kindergarten had been established but seven or eight years, and this was six or seven years before it was introduced into England.—He gave too a memorable lecture on the new method, illustrated by a grammar and a " moral " lesson. By " Socratising " he obtained the material from us, and taught us to think and to learn from our own thought. It was a revelation, and the impression of it lives still an example of what a teacher may do who enters into the thought of the child, and sets what Buss calls the " fly-wheel in motion, that needs only to be set going to go on by itself." Many years later I was driven back on this teaching, needed help, but found none ; hence this attempt.

Pestalozzi foresaw, on its first morning, when he began *How Gertrude Teaches*, the nature of the coming century: " The whole earth the beauty wore of promise." We have entered into it. From Wordsworth's *Prelude*, " dedicate to Nature's self and things that teach as Nature teaches," written at exactly the same time, and in the same spirit, as *How Gertrude Teaches*, to our latest schemes of technical education, we have been thinking and working in the same ways, with but little of his direct influence. Education generally ; the doctrine of development ; the culture and knowledge of the body, practically by exercise, theoretically by physiology; science and art, both included in his elementary means—form, both founded on Anschauung; the training of teachers, based on psychology; our social schemes for the welfare of the people—are all and more to be found in this work.

In other minds similar ideas germinated independently. Portions of the truth Pestalozzi perceived were seen by many. Soon after the middle of the century much of it was re-embodied by the Rev. F. D. Maurice in the Working Men's College. His faith in both "learning and working" are in the name. In his deep religious feeling and human sympathy, his perception of principles in the common facts of every-day life, the unity of all studies, their relation to work, in his desire to educate, exercise, and develop the whole being, and in many other ways he resembled Pestalozzi. At a time when the "mutual instruction" of Stanz had been twisted here to support the monitorial system, the reality itself reappeared in the conversational teaching—allied to socratising—which was generally adopted at the College. Men taught men in a non-professional way, for the social and human elements were considered as important as learning. In this direct action of mind on mind was to be found something of the "mutual self-vification" of Stanz.—The unselfish devotion of Mr. Maurice's fellow-workers to a common purpose is a significant contrast to the divisions at Yverdun.

Among his associates, Mr. Ruskin, who may have been influenced by Rousseau, maintained the supremacy of Nature, and insisted as strongly as Pestalozzi himself on learning to "see" and on "seeing" as the beginning of art and thought. He claimed for form sense-impression and doing, a place in education. "Every youth should learn to do something thoroughly with his hands to know what touch means," he said. In many other ways he continued Pestalozzi's thought. Another associate, Rossetti, restored to form its old power of expressing thought, and unconsciously illustrated—as did all the Pre-Raphaelities—the Pestalozzian principle;—the development of the individual follows that of the race. The College was perhaps at its best nearly twenty years before Payne's lecture on Pestalozzi.

The privilege and duty of continuing Mr. Ruskin's teaching in one class fell to me, and after several years this attempt to teach from nature naturally led me to Mr. C. H. Lake. He watched with much sympathy my attempts to teach drawing and natural science. Of these things he professed to know nothing, but his profound knowledge of psychology, educational principles, and of Pestalozzi's spirit—he had been friend and fellow-worker with Payne for many years—made him the best guide and critic possible, perhaps the only one. He entered into the work with great interest, for he delighted in experiments, and to bring actual school work to the test of principles. He was a master of socratising, believed in inductive teaching, and, with Pestalozzi and Maurice, in that "mutual instruction" which brings minds into direct contact by conversation. To him I am much indebted. I was compelled to fall back on the unforgotten lessons of my boyhood, and I expected to find the methods and principles of Pestalozzi established, well known, even extended, and his own work easily accessible; but only Biber's fragments were available. Blind to its difficulties, I long failed to induce friends to translate *How Gertrude Teaches*, until, trying for myself, help was for the first time offered; Miss L. E. Holland not only translated this work, but several others which threw light on it. There were difficulties, and the late F. C. Turner revised the whole work, and reduced the number. He sought in both French and German literature to verify passages and for help generally, even during his long and painful illness. The amount and kind of help of these friends could only have been given by those who fully sympathised in the work.

Some doubtful passages remained; for these several friends were consulted, and the various readings compared. In this way we had help from Mme. Michaelis, Miss F. Franks, Fraulein H. Seidel, Mr. A. Sonnenschein, and others. We have added the index.

April, 1894.

INTRODUCTION.

Biographical.

JOHANN HEINRICH PESTALOZZI was born January 12th, 1746. He gives in this book some account of his life in relation to his work; a few other facts of a similar nature may be useful. "In the years of my childhood," he says, "I lived out of touch with the world, at least, so far as this gives one power, skilfulness, and a good bearing in the intercourse and business of life. I lost my father early; this caused defects in my education which have been a disadvantage to me throughout my life; but it was mixed with good. I cannot say, I would it had been otherwise. My father, on his death-bed, said to a poor maidservant who had been hardly six months with us, 'Do not forsake my wife if I die, or my poor children will be lost.' She gave him her hand and her word, and remained more than thirty years in my mother's service, and did not forsake her till she herself quitted this earth. If she had not stayed, we should have lost both mother and home. My mother instilled into us respect and gratitude to her which will never be extinguished. She sacrificed herself for us completely. From the roughest work of the meanest servant to the highest, she did everything the whole time of her service. While economising every

penny, she watched over our honour with incredible
tenderness; nothing escaped her. But she put no
value on this. If any one said, ' You do a great deal
for the household,' her answer was, 'I promised it,
and I must keep my promise.' She rejected any
offer of a better place with these words, ' What do you
think of me?' every offer of marriage with 'I must
not.' Gessner, such fidelity is rare in this world; for
anything like it you must go back to the noblest days
of our country, to the noble deeds of our forefathers.
The spirit of their high power of sacrificing self for
Fatherland, religion, freedom, truth, and right, with
which they saved their country, was in no wise
different from the power of self-sacrifice of our maidservant, by which she saved and raised our household.
Just as I was sensible of this fidelity throughout my
life, just as it influenced me with a real life-giving
satisfaction from early morn to latest eve, just as I felt
cared for by her every hour while I was growing, so
the people in the good old days were ever sensible
of the fidelity of their noble forefathers, during the
whole of their lives it influenced them with a life-
giving satisfaction, and they felt they were cared for.
This sacred fidelity exercised its influence especially
on widows and orphans and on the poor and lowly in
the land. Sacrifices for fidelity and faith, paternal
feeling and love for the people, heartfelt pity for the
wants of the oppressed and courageous deeds to protect
them against injustice, came naturally to our ancestors,
and was part of the morality of their time."[1] This

---

[1] *Pestalozzi-Blätter*, Dec., 1889, Zurich. For another account
of her in a letter to Prof. Ith, 1802, see De Guimps, pp. 3, 4.

abbreviated extract from what he intended for a new version of *How Gertrude Teaches* will help to answer a question often asked, What has the book to do with Gertrude? as well as give some idea of one of the deepest influences of his childhood. The title does not perhaps clearly express the contents. Some critics say that the contradiction in the title-page is characteristic of the book.

In 1760 Pestalozzi became a student at the University of Zurich. He entered fully into the movements and thoughts of his time. "Living in a time and country in which well educated young men eagerly enquired into the causes of the evils in the land, and were zealous to oppose them wherever they were, I too, like all the students of Bodmer and Breitinger, sought the sources of those evils which crushed the people of our Fatherland " (*Ein Blick*, etc.).

In 1762, when he had been at Zurich two years, he was very deeply impressed by one of the most powerful influences of the pre-revolutionary period—Rousseau. The Government of Geneva condemned Rousseau. The people supported him, and asked that the decree might be repealed, as unjust and ill-advised. These doings caused a great stir in Zurich. (See De Guimps, page 13.)

The Revolution began a new epoch, and with it a new education. The Renascence revived ancient literature, and set up the book as the regenerator of the world, and exalted book-learning. Instruction meant the study of Latin and Greek, words and dead languages. The Revolution in many ways opposed this, and the conditions and institutions that had been brought about by it, in conjunction with the mediæval religious system. "Do the opposite of what is usually done, and you will be right," is Rousseau's maxim in education. "All is artificial; we must return to nature. Man is bad by institutions, not by nature." The old religious system had insisted on blind faith, on authority, and tradition. The Revolution demanded free investigation of facts, free thought, and free speech, culture of reason and intelligence, and the natural claims of all to justice and education. The mediæval religious system had taught that the natural instincts of the body were to be suppressed, that human nature was utterly depraved, and all nature was gross and impure. The Revolution again set the little child in the midst, a study for mankind, and pronounced nature itself very good.

"Directly Rousseau's *Emile* appeared," Pestalozzi says, "my visionary and highly speculative mind was enthusiastically seized by this visionary and highly speculative book." Rousseau's influence also increased in him the desire for a more extended sphere of activity for the happiness of the people, and induced him to give up the idea of the clerical profession for that of law. In 1762, when the Government of Geneva, following the example of the Paris Parliament, condemned the author of *Emile* and *The Social Contract*,[1] the people of Geneva warmly remonstrated. The patriotic students at Zurich sympathised with Rousseau and also protested against the action of the government of Geneva. Pestalozzi was one of the most enthusiastic.

[1] See *Rousseau.* Note 1, Letter IV.

His sympathies brought him into conflict with the authorities and injured his prospects for life. He too was condemned, fined, and confined several times ; he was considered a dangerous revolutionist. The people he earnestly wished to serve misunderstood him. They even threatened him with death more than once. The effect of this was deeply wrought into his life.

Of his powers at this time he says: " I was far behind my fellow-students in some things, in others I often surpassed them in an unusual degree. This is so true that once when my professor, who had a good knowledge of Greek but not the least eloquence of style, translated and published some of the orations of Demosthenes, I had the boldness to translate one myself and give it at the examination." This was published, and was generally admired.

His first serious experiment in life was an attempt to work out his naturalistic principles. He abandoned first the Church and then Law, for which he had studied, and became a farmer (1768) of uncultivated land,—barren, chalky heath, and sheep walk; which was to him unprofitable, although in 1869 the very same land was rich and produced several crops in the year.

The next year, 1769, he married, and in 1771 settled at Neuhof, in Letten, near Birr, in Argau. Farming failed, and for some time before the actual crisis Neuhof became a home for neglected children, orphans and beggars, who were taught to work and learn at the same time. The following memorable passage referring to this period is left out of the second edition of *How Gertrude Teaches:* " Long years I lived surrounded by more than fifty beggar children. In poverty I shared my bread with them, I lived like a beggar in order to learn how to make beggars live like men. My ideal training included work on the farm, in the factory, and the workshop,"—and he never abandoned this ideal. At last when all was spent, both strength and fortune, the farm was closed (1780), leaving him "more than ever convinced of the reality and truth of his principles at the very moment of their apparently entire destruction."

In 1781 he wrote *Leonard and Gertrude*, his greatest success. It was a novel intended to show that the world might be regenerated through education, the mother, Gertrude,[1] being the chief teacher. This work brought him many friends of every class, among them Fichte, who apparently influenced him much.

Fichte lived two years at Zurich, 1788 to 1790, and was intimate with Pestalozzi's circle of friends. He married a niece of Lavater's there, 1793, and stayed some months afterwards. Pestalozzi's psychology and thought after this time alter somewhat; but in *Leonard and Gertrude*—published the same year as Kant's *Critique of Pure Reason*—Fichte found that already "experience had led him to many of the same results as Kant." Fichte's friendship strengthened this tendency, and from it originated his later thought and principles. These remained in a germ-like state in his mind until his experience at Stanz developed them and made them real and living. But if Fichte was able to influence his psychology and thought, he was

---

[1] A character probably inspired by his recollections of the devoted maidservant mentioned above. See note 8, p. 214.

probably less familiar with the subject of development. The union of these is one of Pestalozzi's special characteristics. Evidently Fichte saw the importance of his doctrines; it was by Fichte's advice that he wrote a philosophical treatise, *Inquiries into the Course of Nature in the Development of the Human Race*, which was produced in 1797. His educational works brought him friends in the Swiss Government, and he was working out an official scheme of education when Stanz was burnt down.

The new French Republic wished to improve its neighbour the old Swiss Republic by centralization. Unterwalden, one of the three cantons which founded the Republic, proud of its own self-government, objected, and refused to take the oath of allegiance to the new Unitary Constitution imposed by France. The French army marched on Stanz, its chief town. It was resisted and repelled, but eventually it reached Stanz, and, exasperated by the vigorous and unexpected resistance, massacred the inhabitants and burnt the town, September 9th, 1798. There were 169 orphans, excluding 77 provided for by private charity and 237 other children practically homeless. The central Swiss Government, November 18th, determined to found an Orphans' Home at Stanz, and Pestalozzi was appointed manager, December 5th. He arrived two days later and opened the orphanage January 14th, 1799. "It is a great trouble to all of us," wrote Mrs. Pestalozzi. "If I am worth what I think I am," replied Pestalozzi, "you will soon find me a comfort and support. You have waited thirty years; will you not wait another three months?" He alone can tell the story of

Stanz, and he has told it twice, first in a letter to Gessner directly after he left, and again here.[1] In five months there was war again. The convent was wanted for a military hospital, and on June 8th, 1799, sixty children were sent away, and Pestalozzi, almost dead, went to Gurnigel for a little rest.

The Government, influenced possibly by an unfavourable report from Zschokke, one of the secretaries of the Minister of Education, and Businger, priest at Stanz, did not wish Pestalozzi to return. Stapfer, the minister, alone supported him, and tried to find another field for his experiments. Ever since he had been a minister Stapfer had made attempts to establish a Teachers' Institute. His secretary, Fischer, had submitted plans for such an institute, which he approved. Burgdorf was considered a suitable place for their trial, and in July, 1799, Fischer went there, was lodged in the castle, and superintended the schools which he had organized, but the Normal School was not opened.

To Burgdorf, then, Stapfer directed Pestalozzi, and on July 23rd, 1799, a dwelling in the castle was appointed him near Fischer, and he was sent to the house of Samuel Dysli, shoemaker and schoolmaster, who worked at his trade even during school-time. But Pestalozzi would not object to this. He approved of working and learning together. It was one of his first and last wishes to unite them; but he soon found out they could not agree or work together. His improvements had already transformed the school, and here old and new came into strong contrast and con-

[1] The *First Letter from Stanz* is given entire in De Guimps' Life, pp. 147–171.

flict. The practice of the old schoolmaster had come down from the middle ages, and here was the reforming spirit of the new education overturning all. There were no books, no copying, no learning by rote, no hearing of lessons, no tasks, worst of all, no catechism and no psalter. He spoke aloud, the children repeated, and at the same time drew figures on their slates, just as at Stanz. But not even there, where he was considered a heretic-enemy incapable of teaching, was prejudice stronger than here. The acknowledged fact that he was making experiments showed plainly that he did not know what he was doing, and therefore was not to be trusted. The shocking neglect of catechism and psalter proved that he was quite unfit to teach or to have charge of the young. This first hand-to-hand fight between old and new is a type of many a later struggle. Honest prejudice, with its second-hand and worn-out systems, still opposes the new revelation and drives it from the door. Pestalozzi was soon removed to Miss Stähli's [1] school.

He had gone to Burgdorf at the end of July, 1799, and on March 31st, 1800, a report of the examination of his pupils at Miss Stähli's begins by stating that he had been "teaching the children there for the past *eight* months," therefore he could not have been many days with Dysli, the shoemaker.

Meanwhile another school arose in Burgdorf. At the end of 1799, war in Eastern Switzerland caused distress in the cantons of Sentis and Linth. Fischer at Burgdorf sent for thirty children, and nearly that number

---

[1] For condition of old schools see Note 20, Letter I., p. 219; and Diesterweg, *Old Schools*; H. Barnard's *Pestalozzi*, p. 18.

arrived on the 27th Jan., 1800, and with them their teacher, Hermann Krüsi. At the beginning of February forty-four more came from Appenzel. Krüsi lived with Fischer and Pestalozzi in the castle. The children were placed in different families, but went to the castle to school.

Three days after the favourable report of Pestalozzi's teaching was presented, Fischer left Burgdorf (April 3rd, 1800), and soon after died. "With his death begins for me a new epoch," says Pestalozzi. The teachers' Institute became his charge. In May, 1800, he was appointed to a higher class, but was not so successful. "These young people thought themselves already tolerably well educated, and such simple childish exercises, far from interesting them, only served to wound their vanity. The same thing happened again afterwards," and continues to happen even now if his methods are used. The teacher should use observation while it is still natural to the child that it may never be dropped, but be strengthened and made permanent.

Stapfer had founded the Society of the Friends of Education, and Pestalozzi wrote for it a *Report of the Method*, a work of such importance we have translated and added it here ; it is the foundation of his teaching, and quite distinct from *How Gertrude Teaches*. It is dated June 27th, 1800.

To unite the children under Krüsi with his own scholars more room was wanted, and on July 23rd, 1800, the Council, through Stapfer, granted the necessary room. The commissioners reported,[1] October 1, and

---

[1] For Report, De Guimps, pp. 204-6.

on October 25th Pestalozzi announced the opening of his Institute for Training Teachers. The Society seeing that State help was insufficient, appealed for subscriptions. The newspapers still considered Pestalozzi more revolutionist than educationalist. The Institute was opened January, 1801, and is the best embodiment in this direction of his idea. He was really the head, and his newly-discovered principles were dominant; it only lasted three and a half years, but it carried his fame far and wide.

In October, 1801, *How Gertrude Teaches her Children* was published.

Federalism was re-established in Switzerland February 19th, 1803. The restored government of Canton Bern again took possession of the castle. Although Pestalozzi had favoured the unitary government and was considered revolutionary, he could not now be neglected, and another residence was provided, an old convent at München-Buchsee, near to Fellenburg's agricultural establishment. He went there on June, 1804, but left October 18th for Yverdun.

For twenty years he carried on the Institute at Yverdun under varying fortunes; troubles arose chiefly from differences among his fellow-workers, especially Niederer and Schmidt. Niederer was a Doctor of Philosophy and minister who joined Pestalozzi here, and regarded himself as the philosophical interpreter of Pestalozzi's ideas. Schmidt gained great reputation by his mathematical teaching and business capacity. Here "each disciple interpreted the master's doctrine in his own way," and later each, "after claiming to be the only one who had understood Pestalozzi, ended by declaring that Pestalozzi had not understood himself " (Prof. Vulliemin, De G., p. 256). These disciples had never been at Stanz. While the Institute was in distracted disorder consider Pestalozzi. It had never satisfied him. It was never what he wanted. At Burgdorf as early as 1803 he longed to leave it and follow his own way. He wanted to found another school for poor children, where they might work as well as learn. Again and again he repeated this wish, and made attempts to realize it. At the end of his life he declared that in founding the Burgdorf Institute he had made a mistake. "I was already lost at Burgdorf through my attempts to do what was utterly foolish and absurd " (*My Experiences*).

When the Institute at Yverdun was at its worst, he returned to his favourite scheme, just as he had done when Neuhof was in the same condition. He founded at Clendy in 1818 a school for poor children, and at seventy-two worked with the same energy, love, and complete success as at Neuhof, Stanz, and Burgdorf. Why was he always successful with these schools? With the idea of founding similar schools in which handicraft might be taught, he caused Ramsauer to learn several handicrafts (1807–1816). Does he fail and succeed at the same time? Of his failures much has been said. What of his successes?

The Institute was closed, and he left Yverdun, March, 1825. He went home to his grandson at Neuhof, and on the same spot where his farming had failed fifty years before he again ordered buildings for an industrial school. Here he wrote his last works, the *Swan's Song*, and *My Experiences*. In the latter book he spoke strongly, perhaps with exaggeration, of his old friends who had forsaken him. Niederer was hurt. " His grievances were eagerly taken up by a man named Edward Biber. This man had arrived at Yverdun after Pestalozzi's departure, and stayed but one year there." He then left and wrote a pamphlet in Niederer's justification, which was "little more than a long insult to the venerable philanthropist ending his days in misfortune. . . . No one was more genuinely indignant with this infamous production" than Niederer[1] himself. To Pestalozzi it was a death-blow. He died February 17th, 1827.

historical.

Pestalozzi's work generally is unknown in this country. At times, efforts and enquiry have been made, but he has never been understood or naturalized. He is the follower of Bacon and of Locke; he embodies their principles; and yet their countrymen neither understand nor receive him. At the beginning of the century, Englishmen seem to have believed Bell. " My system includes all this," he said at Yverdun. The common opinion about Pestalozzi now was expressed by the late Mr. E. Coghlan, when he lectured on him at the Education Society in 1880. " We have learned what he had to teach, and we are far beyond him." Erroneous, even false statements

[1] So says De Guimps; but Morf quotes letters from Niederer identifying himself with Biber, and speaking of his pamphlet as " Our Defence."

of his principles and methods are frequently found where we might expect accuracy, and there is no work of his to witness against them. To know what he thought, and how he worked, we must go to the originals, and the foreign biographies, for there is nothing satisfactory in English. Quite recently Roger de Guimps' Life has been translated. We have no translation of such works as those of Morf and Guillaume, and we have but little literature of value on the subject.[1] If the new movement in education which has had world-wide influence, and which he practically began, is the most important of modern times, if it is still growing and developing, this book, the greatest of his educational works, should certainly be known; the selected passages and paraphrased fragments, we have may give a little help, but they are inadequate; they never give his whole thought, but often obscure and misrepresent it. He wants to show how the germ of the idea of popular education was developed in him. To throw light on that is the purpose of this book; not merely to state theories and give details of his teaching. He wants to show how the principle grew in him, how we can follow him in spirit. It is the history of the growth of an Educator's mind, of the conditions under which he worked, the experiments he made, their failure or success, and the method he learned through direct study of nature. He does not —he cannot—separate the events of his life from his

---

[1] Barnard's volume on Pestalozzi contains part of Raumer's life, and nearly all that has been translated of his works; but the account given in it of *Wie Gertrud* is very defective, almost useless; the principles on which the system is founded are not included.

experiments and theories. He has no life, no thought, apart from his one aim. He thinks of nothing else, works for nothing else. From out of his work comes his methods. his theories, and his sympathy. He is represented to us as the most visionary and impractical of men: in some ways he may be, but he is essentially the man of observation and experiment, his knowledge comes from his seeing and doing. He made a foundation for a science of education.

At the beginning of this century, when central Europe was attending to his teaching, and influenced by it, we in England were entirely pre-occupied with Bell and his Madras system. This has kept us back more than half a century. In 1815, or more probably 1816, Bell visited Pestalozzi, but saw nothing in him or his method.[1] Parting from Ackermann, who had acted as his interpreter, he said, "Now I understand the method of your Pestalozzi. Believe me, sir, in twelve years it will not be mentioned, while mine will be spread over the whole world" (*Pest.-Blätt.*, 1886, p. 55). In 1818, when Pestalozzi, returning to his own idea, opened the school at Clendy, several Englishmen were attracted to him, and were very enthusiastic. This gave him great hopes of help from this country, and an

---

[1] This visit was possibly occasioned by the account of an Irish gentleman, Mr. Mills, who visited Yverdun for two hours, and stayed three months in 1815. He wrote *A Biographical Sketch of the struggles of Pestalozzi to establish his System*, by an Irish traveller, Dublin, 1815; and *A Sketch of Pestalozzi's Intuitive System of Calculation*, Dublin, 1815. He introduced the "Tables of the Relations of Numbers" into Model Schools, Dublin, and so influenced the teaching in Irish schools. The same tables were introduced into this country by Sir J. K. Shuttleworth, under the Council of Education later.

appeal was made by him in English.[1] His influence on England is said to have led to the establishment of infant schools everywhere. Prof. Vulliemin says in his *Reminiscences*: "As for infant schools, which now exist everywhere, it was he who originated them, in a manner I myself saw, and will now describe . . . Clendy fell, but there was a man there who had taken part in the short-lived enterprize, a man of Christian spirit and enlightened understanding. This man, who was an Englishman, by name Greaves, carried the ideas he had gathered at Clendy back to England, where they took root, and became the origin of infant schools. From England these schools returned to us, first to Geneva, then to Nyon, then everywhere. We had not understood Pestalozzi, but when his methods came back from England, though they had lost something of their original spirit, their meaning and application were clear."

Mr. J. S. Reynolds and Dr. Mayo were also chief movers here. "Some of his fondest expectations are kindled by our infant schools," says Dr. Mayo. " Pestalozzi was peculiarly solicitous that the *idea* of his method of education should not be confounded with the *form* it might assume. He felt strongly the value of the *idea*, and highly disposed as he was to appreciate the application of it by his disciples, he saw they were at best imperfect, incomplete embodiments of his profound conception " (Dr. Mayo, *Introduction to "Lessons on Objects"*).

In 1831 came the first original and important work,

---

[1] A copy of this Appeal is in the library of the Froebel Society, London.

An Account of Pestalozzi's Life and Writings, by Edward Biber, whose intemperate and abusive pamphlet against Pestalozzi, on behalf of and supported by Niederer,[1] satisfied none. Soon after its publication Biber disappeared from Switzerland and came to this country, first as a schoolmaster, then Vicar of Roehampton till 1872. He was editor of *John Bull* from 1848 to 1856, but we hear no more of Pestalozzi from him. He says, "It would be an endless task to recount, and a hopeless one to refute, all the erroneous and absurd notions which are afloat on the subject " (*i.e.* Pestalozzi's principles and method). Some to gain attention had modified the ideas they had to set forth, so as to render them palatable to intended readers; and had so distorted the original. The regret with which he had for several years past (he was at Yverdun in 1826) witnessed these mistakes induced him to translate *How Gertrude Teaches her Little Ones*, but perceiving that in the confused state of public opinion a mere translation could not clear up the matter, he resolved to embody the most interesting and practical parts in a larger work, which should give an authentic history of Pestalozzi's life, establishments, works, and method. But he fell into the error he wished to correct: like many others, he thought he knew far better than Pestalozzi, so he paraphrased and polished his expressions, but failed to reproduce his thought; if he did not in some cases wilfully misrepresent it, he certainly often missed the main principles. He had never been with Pestalozzi; he was at Yverdun for a

---

[1] A copy of this is in the British Museum : *Beitrag zur Biographie Heinrich Pestalozzi's*, etc.

year, but it was after Pestalozzi had gone. In England he has been credited with being an eye-witness, and he did not correct the mistake. At that time nothing was known of his unenviable reputation in connection with Pestalozzi's death. He was not the missionary Pestalozzi would have sent us. His fragments have hitherto been the only portions of *How Gertrude Teaches* open to those who do not read German. They show clearly that he did not understand Pestalozzi, and that a literal and full translation of that work was necessary. Biber's influence unfortunately has not yet passed away.

Later a truer conception of him arose. Parliament in 1839 was discussing national education, and continued to do so for over thirty years. About the middle of the century a wave of social and political disturbance—like that at its beginning, only less violent—directed attention to education. Brougham said in the House of Lords, 1839, "All parties confess we are far less educated than the people of Central Europe." Pestalozzi's influence there had evidently been divined, for Sir Jas. Kay Shuttleworth, on behalf of the Government, endeavoured to diffuse a knowledge of his method among London teachers without success. He introduced the " Tables of the Relations of Numbers." From the same source originated, I believe, a translation, in 1855, by J. Tilleard, of Raumer's Life of Pestalozzi—an article in his *Geschichte der Pädagogik.* This was not likely to

---

[1] " Biber, writing as an eye-witness, says " . . . *Pestalozzi and his Principles*, p. 141. (Published by Home and Colonial Society, 3rd Edn., 1873.)

promote his teaching; it presents his weakest side strongly, and in some ways entirely misrepresents him. Later it produced more than could have been expected, and fruit after its own kind also.

The translator of Karl von Raumer's [1] work believes it to be most accurate, unbiassed, and truthful; others, carried away by admiration, have too implicitly accepted Pestalozzi's applications; but Raumer's great merit is that he shows how Pestalozzi's principles and practice are diametrically opposed.—Who are these "others"?—Then, Raumer himself says, contradiction is especially characteristic of *How Gertrude Teaches*, and begins on its title-page; this work "contains fundamental principles of the highest importance, side by side with the most glaring blunders and absurdities." It is a difficult work; he will analyse it. In it are three elements—(1) "It is the desire of his (Pestalozzi's) whole life. (2) The second element is a fierce fulminating battle against the sins and education of his time. (3) The education he proposes." This divides into *practical skill*, of which little is said, and *theoretical knowledge*; which is based on "observation. What does Pestalozzi mean by observation? Simply directing the senses to outward objects, and exciting consciousness of the impressions produced on them by these objects." This is Raumer's view of Anschauung. Pestalozzi never limits it to objects, nor to the first simple stage; he includes sound (p. 114). "But just as we begin to think we understand Pestalozzi,"

---

[1] Von Raumer was, I believe, the Minister of Education who prohibited the Kindergarten in Prussia in 1851.

says Raumer, "he leads us again into uncertainty as to the idea he attaches to observation." Then, of course, he will follow Pestalozzi and learn his meaning; not so; Raumer goes no farther. Pestalozzi's conception is not Raumer's, but his own. He asks himself, when he examines the elements of his system, What is the basis of Anschauung? What are its elements? But this "deep psychology" is a thicket of impenetrable thorns, and Raumer turns aside. He brings, as others have done, limited preconceptions to the study, and, instead of learning Pestalozzi's meaning, censures him for offering conceptions different from his own. "Many men glanced at me, but found little of themselves in me," are Pestalozzi's own words. And Raumer sees not the first principles of this work he so severely handles; he puts his "simple" notion of Anschauung for the masters, and all else he knows not.

How Gertrude Teaches rests on development and psychology. All Raumer says of the first is "Pestalozzi repeatedly dwells on intellectual development"; to him it is of no importance, while his psychology shrinks away from the first difficulty. Can there be really accurate, unbiassed judgment, if its fundamental principles are not even recognised or known? Having himself shown that he cannot satisfactorily deal with the principles, he proceeds to their application with the same result. It is in this work the contradictions, blunders, and absurdities exist; they are concentrated about Language. Raumer notices very little else, so that on these errors in language-teaching his whole strength is put forth; these are the materials on which he forms his estimate.

The origin of language Pestalozzi connects with expression, and that with impression and thought, and all with development and psychology. His system is a connected whole from his point of view. His language-teaching consists of lessons in (1) sound; (2) words; (3) language. Raumer selects the extreme errors only, under each division, in support of his position, and says nothing on the other side. He does not indicate how they arose, naturally, out of the thought of that time. In his first attempts to apply the principles he perceived Pestalozzi stumbles and errs; but he learned from his errors. He says at the outset he must lead us through the labyrinth of confusions he had himself to pass through to get light—that is one purpose of the book. There is another great mistake. Nothing is said of Pestalozzi's own criticism and revision. He had abandoned all these glaring blunders and contradictions,—the essential portions of Raumer's case against him,—long before Raumer wrote. It is strange Raumer did not know this. His criticism has had such pernicious influence here, and is so often seriously quoted as if it were true, we will sketch its main details.

(1) *Sound.* Raumer quotes what is said about spelling sounds to the child in the cradle (pp. 90, 91), but *not* the note on the same page. " These attempts were abandoned, owing to deeper knowledge. They were but vague aspirations towards methods of which I was far from clear." (2) *Words.* Here Raumer founds his objections on the Mother's Book. This, Pestalozzi says, never existed; it was abandoned for the same reasons—" erroneous views I then held " (p.

102). To "lists of names" there is reasonable objection, but they are included in the above note. We shall see under "Language" the value of his statement—"it is not even remotely hinted that the children ought to know the things named." (3) *Language.* "Names, mere names," says Raumer, and ignores all Pestalozzi insists on again and again, *e.g.* "this purpose . . . to express ourselves clearly about objects" (p. 98). "I try in no way to lessen the free play of the child's own thought." "I try to make the child, who is in many ways acquainted with objects, still clearer about them so far as they are known to him" (p. 101). It is necessary to exercise thought as well as the senses; to appeal to memory and knowledge as well as to the object. The specimen may be in the hand, and yet ideas about it may be obscure. Pestalozzi is here dealing with "means to clear ideas." "Socratising" is often better without objects. These "means" are another scheme, but it is still founded on Anschauung. He concludes Letter VII. with, "It must be understood throughout the whole teaching, the result is attained not by isolated exercises, but by connecting the whole sequence, by which the mind rises from sense-impression (observation) to clear ideas" (p. 132). In face of this Raumer complains that of observation nothing is said; and he concludes—after referring to the teaching of geography, which had also been abandoned as erroneous—by repeating, "Pestalozzi does not begin with observation, but with words." From Raumer's conception of Anschauung, sound seems excluded. He often puts "words" for "sounds." It was the "sound" teaching at Stanz which led Pestalozzi to sense-impression. So the child and the race begin language. "Sound, however simple, if it expresses an impression, is more than sound." The whole sequence is connected, language and thought are inseparable; thought originates from impression, and so too does language.

Raumer's criticism comes to nothing ; every item of importance is already abandoned, and every application might be withdrawn, and the principles of *How Gertrude Teaches* will remain intact. He patched these cast-off rags into a lifeless scarecrow; at a crisis in the history of education in this country, it frightened our teachers away from Pestalozzi. What else could it do? To parade these rejected errors is not accuracy. Contradictions there may be, for his theory comes from his practice, and his practice from his theory ; so there is constant growth and change. The true system, like true education, is drawn out of the teacher; it is the expression of himself, and grows and changes with his growth.

In direct contrast to Raumer appeared the most important original work which this country has produced in connection with Pestalozzi—*Education*, by Mr. Herbert Spencer, 1861. By this time another Royal Commission had finished its work, and the discussion of Education had extended and included higher teaching. The old fundamental question, words or things, in the modern form, classics or science, had become foremost. The question of real as opposed to book knowledge, which Pestalozzi had worked out half a century earlier, reappeared in our midst ; and science, strengthened by its recent and many victories, demanded recogni-

tion. Among its distinguished champions was Mr.
Herbert Spencer. He had his own scheme, but he had
no doubt where help was to be found for teaching
science. "He would defend in its fullest extent the
doctrine which Pestalozzi inaugurated." Of which
Fichte also had said, "I find in this man's system of
education the true remedy for the ills of humanity, if
not the only means of fitting the mind for scientific
teaching." Philosopher, psychologist, biologist, the ex-
ponent of evolution, Mr. Herbert Spencer was able to
see Pestalozzi from all these sides ; he had another
great advantage—experience, real not book knowledge of Pestalozzi's method. The internal evidence
of this was lost on educators at that time. Prof. J.
Payne, in his first published lecture, *The Curriculum of
Modern Education,*" 1866, says of Mr. H. Spencer's
work : "It is evolved, apparently, out of the depths of
his own consciousness, for he does not profess to have
any practical experience either as teacher or schoolmaster." He did not see that if Mr. Spencer had not
taught others, he had learned to teach himself, and
self-education is a kind of practical experience which
includes the problems of teacher and pupil. That self-
education is "practicable," he says, "we can ourselves
testify, having been in youth thus led to solve the com-
paratively complex problems of perspective." That
was Pestalozzi's, or rather Krüsi's method. We know
now that his father, W. G. Spencer, was a distinguished teacher, possibly a disciple of Pestalozzi also,
for his *Inventional Geometry* stands alone, our most
Pestalozzian school-book : Huxley's *Biology* is similar.
Payne says nothing in this lecture of the Pestalozzian

basis of Mr. Spencer's work—he had hardly begun to study Pestalozzi then; but he does say that at this time —five years after its publication—" he had not a clear idea how science should be taught." Mr. Spencer had.

It is not his primary business to expound Pestalozzi, but he does so incidentally as none beside have done. Unlike Raumer, he insists on principles—on the spirit, not the form. Although he defends his whole doctrine, much evil is likely to arise from uncritical application of his method and from confounding form with spirit. There is but little disproportionate criticism of tentative and rejected experiments. There is some, for he relies on Biber, and adopts his mistakes. *How Gertrude Teaches* seems unknown to him, for he quotes against Pestalozzi the usual passage from the Spelling Book, Biber's version. If he had seen the work itself he would have known it was abandoned. Biber, like Raumer, ignores the notes and revision. There is another proof—he attributes to Comte, with some doubt, the doctrine that the child's development follows that of the race.—Comte's *Positive Philosophy* was published 1830.—If he had read this work of Pestalozzi's, he must have seen the statement at pp. 149–151. Mr. Spencer alone among our exponents perceived any value in this doctrine. Other of his special principles —purely psychological—as the " prototype," are not mentioned. Biber wishes to save his readers the trouble of thinking " they had no predilection for the transcendental," so Mr. Spencer is saved this incomprehensible jargon or deep psychology; he could have shown its relation and value. This has yet to be done; "everything depends on it," so Pestalozzi thought.

d

But Mr. Herbert Spencer adopts Biber's opinions of Pestalozzi as a thinker. He says, "As described even by his admirers, Pestalozzi was a man of impartial intuitions—a man who had occasional flashes of insight, rather than a man of systematic thought.

His admirers—who first said, "If ever he throws out a spark that might lead us to think him capable of something, the next moment it is dark,"—were the people of Stanz, who hated him as enemy and heretic. He reports this (p. 21), and Biber polishes it into "His genius was like the dark summer cloud, pregnant with light, but incapable of emitting it except in sudden flashes" (Biber's Life, p. 51). These are the admirers Mr. Spencer supports. He continues, "Much of his power was due not to calmly reasoned-out plans," but to profound sympathy and quick perceptions of childish needs. Was not this sympathy and power due to knowledge gained from observation of the children and experiments in teaching?—to his own first principles, in fact? He says it was, and at the same time he anticipated Mr. Spencer's and Biber's next point against him, which is, "He lacked the ability logically to co-ordinate and develop the truths he thus from time to time laid hold of; and had in a great measure to leave this to his assistants." Mr. Spencer has apparently the above passage of Biber still in view. It praises Niederer, the bright and shining light, to whom Pestalozzi is but a lamp glimmering in forest gloom. In the Preface of this work Pestalozzi anticipates this. Niederer's deductive, and his own inductive methods are different ways to one end. His way, that of observation and experiment—the only way possible to him

—is one way to truth : " *by it I am what I am, and know what I know* " (p. 6). Is not this the secret of his sympathy and power ? Those who doubt his ability, but cannot deny his sympathy, power, and insight, are driven to attribute them to " inspiration." His own reasonable and sufficient explanation is that they are results of his first principle ; but this is rejected as incredible. Of our exponents, none have such powers of judging him from " many sides "; that Mr. H. Spencer sees him through the medium of Biber is unfortunate, but even with this disadvantage none have pronounced more strongly for him and his system. " The Pestalozzian ideal remains to be achieved," he says; and also " True education is possible only to a true philosopher."

On science and its teaching, there was abundant material awaiting the teacher who could correlate and apply it. Besides Mr. Herbert Spencer, our greatest scientific authorities—Faraday, Forbes, Huxley, Tyndal, and others had contributed to the discussion largely— there was also the evidence given by the Commission on Public Schools. From the discussion, educationalists evolved. Prof. Joseph Payne, " who had always been fond of science," had been thinking of the question for twenty years before his first lecture was published, in 1866, which deals with the claims of classics and science. Liberal, enlightened, and learning all his life,—at twenty-three he published his *Exposition of Jacotot's Method ;*—after years of practical teaching, he retired in 1863, and devoted himself to the study of its principles, just as this question is foremost. His first search is for a method of science teaching. He studies all scientific men have said. "It is very valuable," he says, "but it left the real difficulties of teaching science untouched; but I confess I have not a clear idea of the manner in which science should be taught, never having been enlightened on that point" (p. 275, vol. i., Payne's Works).

Pestalozzi seems unknown to him. Four years later, dealing with "Educational Methods," he is first mentioned, Payne is evidently studying him, and Tilleard's translation of Raumer is his text-book. He had at this time no definite opinions of his own. He quotes Ramsauer's account from Raumer, only making a few comments on it, and accepts without question or surprise Raumer's estimate and decision. But there was one word which arrested him. The translator had used " observation " as an equivalent for " Anschauung." Forbes had said, "The great defect of our education is neglect of the educating of the observing powers—a very different matter, be it noted, from scientific or industrial *instruction*"; and all our best authorities said the same thing. Payne knew this well; he quotes it, he is correlating the ideas of scientific men on science teaching. His *Essay on the Culture of the Observing Powers of Children*, 1872, and his *True Foundation of Science Teaching*, 1873, showed he had now found what he wanted. He had learned how science should be taught; and in 1875, when he lectured on Pestalozzi, we at once see the difference. He has opinions and knowledge of his own; now Pestalozzi "stands forth among educational reformers as the man whose influence on education is wider, deeper, more penetrating than that of all the rest—the prophet and the sovereign of the domain in which he lived and laboured " (p. 98, vol. ii., Payne's Works).

But by the side of this enthusiastic recognition, founded on his own knowledge of the Method — for he now used it—he yet repeats Raumer's mistakes, and is led by him into confusion. He mixes what he knows with inferences from what he is told by one who understands not, with this result: he attributes to Pestalozzi exactly the opposite of what he says and means, and is surprised.

Here is one example. Pestalozzi applied his doctrines of development and psychology to language—a difficult subject. He may be right or wrong ; but before we can understand or judge, we must get some idea, however vague, of *his* meaning. We must at least try to read his thought, not put ours in its place, and then condemn him. He says, " Every word is evolved, as ideas are, from sense-impression, or by observation. ' Man first observed the characteristics of objects, and then named them.' In language is reflected all impressions man received from nature." To this Raumer replies, " Language has nothing to do with observation. Why should I not be able to form a perfectly correct notion of an object that has no name—for instance, a newly-discovered plant ? Language only gives us the expression for the impression of the senses." [1]   Here

---

[1] Raumer continues : " In it is reflected the whole world of our perceptions. It is, as Pestalozzi rightly observes, the reflex of all the impressions which nature's entire domain has made on the human race. But what does he go on to say? Therefore I make use of it, and endeavour by the guidance of its uttered sounds to reproduce in the child the self-same impressions which,

Raumer does not understand Pestalozzi. The whole passage is given below for comparison. He changes the thought entirely into his own, and puts it in place of Pestalozzi's, and then easily convicts him of contradiction and incapacity. Later in the same passage he changes " sound " to " word," and gets into deeper confusion. Then Payne follows him—" Raumer shows," he says, " that Pestalozzi erred against his own principles. . . . No doubt he is continually tending to put (words) into the place of things. In one passage he says, 'Great is the gift of language; it gives the child in one moment what nature required thousands of years to give to man.' The only meaning of which is, that if you give the words you give the knowledge. A wonderful principle, certainly, to come from the pen of one who maintains that observation—personal exercise of the senses—is the true and essential basis of knowledge " (Works of J. Payne, vol. ii., p. 106).

But it is still more wonderful that Payne did not consult Pestalozzi himself. He insists from his first

---

in the human race, have occasioned and formed these sounds. Great is the gift of language. It gives in one moment what nature required thousands of years to give to men.

In that case every child will be a rich heir of antiquity without the trouble of acquisition. Words (Pestalozzi says *sounds*), would be current notes for the things they designate. But both Nature and History protest against payment of such currency, and give only to him that hath.

Pestalozzi's further treatment of language clearly proves that, contrary to his own principles, he really ascribed a magical power to words, that he put them more or less in the place of observation, that he made the reflected image of a thing equal to the thing itself " (Raumer's Life, translated by J. Tilleard, p. 30). Compare pp. 111, 112; also pp. 149–151, *How Gertrude Teaches.*

lecture on the difference between *knowing a thing* and *knowing something about it*, between knowledge and information.

"If you want to know a thing, go to it and learn," he says ; and yet he goes to Raumer, not to Pestalozzi, and that, too, after he has by his own experience and knowledge come to a clearer, more accurate conception of him than Raumer's book about him presents. From one imperfect medium to another Pestalozzi's ideas are transmitted, until they are distorted beyond recognition or are quite reversed. In the whole history of his teaching here, now extending over nearly a century—while his doctrine of real knowledge is preached, and readers are advised to go to his works—no one goes. There is not one, so far as I see, even of our best expositors, who have read, in Herbart's sense, *How Gertrude Teaches*, his greatest educational work, or *The Method*.

Pestalozzi himself, as a whole, is unknown. By his own work he should be judged, not by the street gossip of Stanz, however much improved ; nor by authority and opinion which led even Payne to conclude that he was "incapable of controlling his conceptions." His powers and his thought may not be extraordinary, but let us see him as he is. He is obscured by all kinds of obstructions. Those who might know him, who read his own language, avoid fairly facing his thought. We have shut our eyes to it so long that now we maintain it does not exist. Petty details, unimportant by-matters, and tentative experiments which he had abandoned, are overloaded with criticism and comment, while fundamental principles on which he says "everything depends," such as the "prototype," first form, or "pure intuition," are passed by literally without a word. This is wonderful. We have not learned that first lesson of Stanz—the value of real knowledge as opposed to book-knowledge and hearsay.

Payne relies on Raumer, an eyewitness, Minister of Instruction, author of a *History of Education.* If he is not to be relied on, who is? Payne follows wondering; he never suspects his leader. Raumer is not surprised; for Pestalozzi "often contradicts himself." But time has its revenges, Raumer dismisses development with one sentence. Fifty years before Darwin, Pestalozzi applied the doctrine of development to language. Raumer's inability to comprehend it led to misrepresentation, which has been freely transmitted to us; and yet just as Pestalozzi's doctrine of development is supported by Darwin, his application of it to language is stated again in almost his own words, and supported by the profound knowledge of Professor Max Müller. He was a psychologist, and that alone to common-sense people was enough proof that he was impracticable. We are all psychologists now; but his psychology is as incomprehensible to us as it was to Raumer. We have not penetrated the mist of his confused thought, and yet if Fichte and Herbart are to be trusted, the mist and confusion are in us, not in the psychology of Kant as conceived and modified by him.

It is natural to ask, Is this the kind of evidence and authority on which the ignorance and incapacity of Pestalozzi rest? Other misrepresentations can be traced back, till they become inverted. We want just judgment. Let us have all evidence the Raumers and Ramsauers can give, but why exclude Pestalozzi himself? In working out his scheme contradictions necessarily appear. But if he was so ignorant, how did he improve his Professor's Greek translation of Demosthenes? Is it possible that he can forget his studies at the university, and those also for Church and Law? It is strange he can not only write *Leonard and Gertrude*, but revise his reviser. Stranger still, that Fichte and Herbart did not discover his ignorance. They study and follow him. Of this work *How Gertrude Teaches*, Herbart says it is not easy enough to read.—Herbart's own books are not light reading; he has read and understood this, he says nothing of the absence of logical ability to co-ordinate and develop truths, nor the want of systematic thought, but the reverse.[1]—Impractical he was, beside being a psychologist. He gave his silver shoebuckles to a beggar when his pocket was empty; but when searching into the nature of teaching, he is practical and even scientific. It will be objected that he is always going wrong. But what science was ever gained without thousands of faulty and fruitless experiments? The real worker knows this, especially if his method is by observation and experiment.

He is honest and open; we see his work in the rough

[1] Herbart says, "It was the discovery of this sequence, of the arrangement and co-ordination of what was to be learned contemporaneously and what consecutively, which formed, as I understood it, Pestalozzi's chief aim. Granted he had found it, or at least was on the road to it. . . . There was no deviation from the true course." (Quoted in Introduction to Herbart's *Science of Education*, H. M. and E. Flelkin, pp. 11, 12.)

state, the vague thought growing clear. If we are accustomed to observe the course of thought, and have travelled this same road, we shall need no directions to follow him. Authors usually hide their errors and ignorance; we see only their knowledge, not the materials nor the mental action by which they form it; we may see the finished statue, but are not allowed into the studio. He reveals all, and for some that is too much.

Another proof of his lack of practical ability constantly urged is Yverdun, but compare it with Stanz. There the facts are simple, no one disputes them; this cannot be said of Yverdun. By his own power alone, absolutely without means or materials, under the most difficult circumstances, with most troublesome children, out of chaos, in a few weeks he evolved order. "If ever there was a miracle, it was here." This success was repeated wherever he alone had free play. We want more equally balanced accounts of him; we may get nearer than any eye-witness, but we rely on one who rests on another. We prefer to read the book about him rather than his own thought in this book, which is "not easy enough to read."

In his "Essays on Educational Reformers," the Rev. R. H. Quick, one of the many friends and fellow-workers with Payne, takes us into other regions, and gives later views. Pestalozzi, he says, "proved great both as thinker and doer. He not only thought out what should be done, but made splendid efforts to do it." Payne's estimate rests partly on his own knowledge. He verified by experiment; his sympathy is with science. Quick verifies his quotations; his sympathy

is literary rather than scientific. With less knowledge of the fundamental principle than Payne, he
is not led so far astray, for he has a better guide.
His estimate and criticism are, as a whole, more
equal. He sought carefully and long to answer a
question which, shortly before the second edition of
his " Essays " appeared, he proposed for discussion at
the Education Society, " Why is Pestalozzi so highly
esteemed on the Continent and so little valued here ? "
He never quite answered this to his own satisfaction,
although he acquiesced in the decision. Pestalozzi is
many sided. The well-defined stages in his development have each representatives and corresponding
expression in his works. *The Method* and Letter 1 of
How Gertrude Teaches contain his account of Anschauung, and of this first stage Payne is represen-
tative. Thought follows observation, he analyzes the
first principle into its elements ; this results in " means
of making ideas clear." *How Gertrude Teaches* is
chiefly concerned with this second phase : with it Quick
is more directly associated. " The art of teaching in
Pestalozzi's system consists in analyzing the knowledge
the children should acquire about their surroundings,
arranging it in a regular sequence, and bringing it to
the child's consciousness gradually, and in a way in
which their minds will act upon it." But generally
he too rests on another, Roger de Guimps, whose *Life
of Pestalozzi*, recently published, is the best we have.
De Guimps' criticism and conclusions are of a kind
quite different from that of Raumer and Biber. For
the first time we have copies of original documents,
uncoloured, not partial hearsay. We have the

materials to form our own opinions. There is, too, a rational basis for his educational principles.

Quick's essay is very appreciative, but his treatment of fundamental principles—like that of Anschauung, —is characteristic. "We English," he says, "have troubled ourselves so little about Pestalozzi, or rather about the theory of education, we have not cared to get equivalent words for *Anschauung*. 'Intuition,' which some borrow from the French, was taken (first, I believe, by Kant) from the Latin;"—but intuition is used by South and Dryden. This one reference to Kant indicates association, but it does not occur to him that Kant uses it to express a new conception. No; he thinks we shall be wise in following those writers who borrow from the French. "If the Germans find the French can express their own thoughts more clearly than they can themselves, we may think ourselves fortunate that we have French interpreters." "I therefore gladly turn to M. Buisson, and translate what he says about intuition" (p. 361, E.R.). Then he goes to Jullien. Again our guides turn aside and go not to Pestalozzi himself, from whom alone we can learn, not even to his contemporaries and allies in thought. "No Englishman," Quick says, "may have found a good word to indicate *Anschauung*, but one Englishman at least had the idea of it long before Pestalozzi—Locke." "Thus in theory Pestalozzi was, however unconsciously, a follower of Locke." Quick had not read the principles on which this scheme rests, pp. 84, 85. What is there in Locke of "the prototype on which all depends"? Of "the *form* in which the culture of mankind is determined"? or "every word is a result of the understanding evolved from ripened sensuous impressions"? (See Locke, *Understanding*, Bk. iv., ch. 4).

The difficulty is not in the word, but in the thought. Pestalozzi's conception will not be found in the dictionary; we may seek it in vain in Buisson and Jullien. His psychology is not that of Locke. Fichte, the most competent authority, says that even in *Leonard and Gertrude*, which was published the same year as the *Critique of Pure Reason*, "Pestalozzi had been led to many of the same results as Kant." Kant analyzed experience; Pestalozzi, in this work, seeks the elements of Anschauung, the basis of all education. When his ideas become clear about it, when he has found its elements, other difficult terms are used, of which this is the parent, such as "form" and "prototype" (*Urform*), which might be translated "pure form," or "pure intuition," and this, again, is Kant's term. These terms, the nature of the inquiry, its psychological basis, his intimacy with Fichte, all indicate the direction in which we might search, if we go beyond Pestalozzi himself.

His deep psychology has been the source of much error. Biber, our authority, not Pestalozzi, following the fashion of his time, ridicules Kant's philosophy. He represents these principles of Pestalozzi as "incomprehensible jargon;" but when we remember that it was against this same Biber's misrepresentations that Pestalozzi died protesting—to answer them he longed for a few more weeks of life—to this attack on him we may owe Biber's refuge here—we may be allowed to think for ourselves, and if we know nothing of these depths, we may at least weigh against Biber the testi-

mony of Fichte and Herbart. Pestalozzi believes that
this deep psychology connects his whole scheme, and
it is only fair we should see it from his position. If
we do not agree with him then, we shall talk less of
disconnected thought and incapacity. Let us at least
follow Pestalozzi, not Biber. The "deep" psychology
may be put aside, and much of his work remains. Mr.
H. Spencer, who is of another school of thought, never
recognises it, and yet defends the system to its fullest
extent. Neither Quick nor De Guimps mention it. How
far it is essential, what imperfection there may be on
his part, how far it differs from Kant, Fichte and
Herbart, its relation to his system and teaching,
authority greater than Biber must determine. Unfortunately, it is Biber who obscures the view of Mr.
Herbert Spencer, who might have done him justice.

Another doctrine of Pestalozzi Quick dismisses very
curtly the parallel development of child and race. He
does not even attribute it to Pestalozzi, but to Mr.
Herbert Spencer, and his only comment on it is, "This
is the thesis on which I have no opinion to offer."

We see that our ablest exponents of Pestalozzi do
not study him directly ; they are each supported by an
attendant spirit, who in turn is supported by them.
Mr. Herbert Spencer has Biber, Payne relies on Raumer, and Quick has De Guimps. When Mr. Herbert
Spencer says Pestalozzi was a man who had occasional
flashes of insight rather than a man of systematic
thought, and that he lacked logical ability to develop
his thought, he is following Biber. We cannot accept
this as his own final judgment on the subject, for he had
evidently not the facts before him. When Payne says,
"If he means anything," implying that Pestalozzi,

even when most definitely stating his principles, uses words that mean nothing, he is following Raumer. Payne's own teaching is often nearer Pestalozzi's than the erroneous teaching he attributes to him. He has not the facts, either. Quick has a more genial and truer guide, and this is reflected in his work. De Guimps is free from the grave defects of Raumer and Biber.

The authority of Mr. H. Spencer and Payne is strengthened by their undoubted knowledge. This gives weight to the information and opinions they transmit; but those who rely on them, and repeat truth and error without real knowledge, confuse, degrade and sometimes reverse the words, thought and teaching of Pestalozzi. His influence and power are destroyed by unduly insisting on what he calls his " tentative and erring means," and his incapacity. Common-sense people will have nothing to do with him. In vain did Raumer's book appeal to London teachers. "Separate my doubtful statements from those that are indisputable," he said, but he never expected the doubtful statements would be collected and selected, while the indisputable were excluded or neglected.

It seems clear, that it is most difficult for the best of us to follow always that simple principle of observation, or sense-impression which we hold so easy. We say we have learned all he had to teach, and are far beyond him; we have not begun our A B C of Anschauung ; even those of us who know it and hold to it most firmly are liable to fall. Personal observation, personal thought, and the expression of our own ideas, are still chiefly matters of theory. We have not learned enough of his first principles to apply them to himself. Truly, " the ideal of Pestalozzi remains to be achieved."

How Gertrude Teaches Her Children.

PREFACE.[1]

IF these letters may be considered in some respects, as already answered and partly refuted, by time, and thus appear to belong to the past rather than to the present, yet if my idea of elementary education has any value in itself and is fitted to survive in the future, then these letters, so far as they throw light on the way in which the germ of the idea was developed in me, may have a living value for every man who considers the psychological development of educational methods worthy of his attention. Besides this general view of the matter, it is certainly remarkable that this idea, in the midst of the simplicity and artlessness of my nature and life, came forth from the darkness within me as from the night. In its first germ it burnt within me like a fire that showed a power of seizing on the human mind; but afterwards, when men looked upon it and spoke of it as a matter of reason in its deeper meaning, it did not maintain its first vitality, and even seemed for a time, to be quenched. Even in this early stage Ith, Johannsen, Niederer,[2] and others gave a significance to my own expression of my views, which went far beyond that which I gave them myself, but which therefore stimulated public attention in a way that could not be sustained. Gruner, von Türk, and Chavannes [3] about the same time took up the actual results of our experiments in just as marked a way, and brought them before the public in a

manner which went far beyond my original view of the subject and the power that lay at the basis of my efforts. It
is true there lay deep in my soul's consciousness a prevision
of the highest that might and should be aimed at, through a
deeper insight into the very nature of education; and it is
indisputable that the idea of elementary education was implied in the view I took in its full significance, and shimmered
forth in every word that I spoke. But the impulse within
me to seek and find for the people simple methods of instruction, intelligible to every one, did not originate in the prevision that lay in me of the highest that could come from
the results of these methods when found; but on the contrary this prevision resulted from the reality of the impulse
that led me to seek these methods. This soon led me naturally and simply to see that intelligible methods of instruction must, as a general principle, start from simple beginning
points; and that if they are carried on in a continuous graduated series the results must be psychologically certain. But
this view of mine was far from being philosophically and
clearly defined and scientifically connected. As I was unable
by abstract deductions to arrive at a satisfactory result, I
wanted to prove my views practically, and tried originally by
experiments to make clear to myself what I really wished
and was capable of doing, in order by this path to find the
means of accomplishing my purpose. All that I strove for
then, and strive for now, is closely connected in my mind
with that which twenty years before I had tried on my
estate.

But the higher significance that was given to my views, so
loudly, so variously, and I must say, so carelessly and hastily,
gave a direction to the form and method of carrying them
out in my Institute, that was not really the outcome of my
own soul, nor that of the people round me, nor that of my
helpers, and I was in this way, led away from myself, into

a region strange to me, which I never trod before. Certainly this visionary world, into which we fell as from the clouds, was not only quite new ground to me, but with my eccentricity, with my want of scientific culture, in the singularity of my whole being, as well as my age at that time,—in these things there were reasons why I could scarcely expect even a half-lucky star to shine upon this course. Insurmountable difficulties seemed to obstruct the hope of being able to advance in this region to happy results. These lay in the peculiarities of my assistants, who, though they were in part quite helpless themselves, should have stretched out helping hands to me in my efforts on this new ground. Meanwhile a lively impulse to tread this region was roused in our midst. But the cry "We can do it" before we could, "We are doing it" before we did it, was too loud, too distinct, too often repeated, partly by men whose testimony had a real value in itself, and deserved attention. But it had too much charm for us; we made more of it than it really said or meant. Briefly, the time as it was, dazzled us; yet we still worked actively, in order practically to approach our end. We succeeded in many respects in the way of bringing a few beginning subjects of instruction into better order and to a better psychological foundation; and our efforts on this side might have had really important results; but the practical activity, which alone could secure the success of our purpose, was gradually lost in our midst in a lamentable manner. Matters strange and far removed from our duty soon absorbed our time and powers, and gave a mortal blow to the simplicity, the progress, the concentration, and even the humanity of our original efforts. Great ideas for improving the world, which arose out of elevated views of our subject, and which soon became exaggerated, filled our heads, confused our hearts, and made our hands careless of the needs of the Institute that lay before our eyes. In this state of things the loss of the lofty spirit of our first union was inevitable; our old love could be the same no more. We saw more or less all the evils under which we suffered, but no one sought for them enough and saw them where he ought,—in himself. Every one blamed the other more or less; every one required of the other what he himself neither did, nor could do; and our greatest misfortune in this condition was that our very efforts, special and one-sided, led us to seek help against the evils of our house in deep philosophical researches. We were, in general, unfit to find in this way what we sought. Niederer alone felt his own strength in this region in which we now ventured, and since in this power he had for many years stood alone in our midst, he gained such an overwhelming influence, not only over those around me, but also over me, that I actually lost myself in myself; and against my nature, and against all possibility of success, I tried to make myself and my house that which we ought to have been, in order to make any progress in this region. This preponderance that Niederer gained in our midst, and the views he laid down on this subject, so caught hold of me and led me on to such a resigned subjection and complete sacrifice and forgetfulness of myself, that I, as I know myself, can and must now say clearly, it is quite certain if he had been with us when I wrote these letters, I should have considered their whole contents, and consequently the idea of elementary education as it then lay before me, like a vision glimmering in the clouds, as coming from him and carried from his soul into mine. In order to believe this statement and look upon it as naturally and innocently as it comes from me you must really know me more; you must distinctly know how I am, on the one side, animated by the conviction of how much I was and still am wanting in clear, philosophical, definite ideas on this subject; and on the other side, the degree of my trust in the lofty views of my friend, and the weight which he would necessarily have upon those ideas lying dim within me, vague and limited. That Herr Niederer was not with us when I wrote these letters, is the only circumstance that makes it possible for me to see clearly what was Herr Niederer's service in our efforts in elementary instruction, and what I may consider as coming from myself. I know how little this is, and how much and what it still requires if it is not to be a mere nothing, or at least if something is to come out of it. In the last respect my reward is greater than my merit. In any case it is quite clear to me that the deductive view of our efforts, advancing in front of the practical performance, far surpassing it, and leaving it behind, was Herr Niederer's view; and that my view of the subject came out of a personal striving after methods, the execution of which forced me actively and experimentally to seek, to gain, and to work out what was not there and what as yet I really knew not. These two efforts opened the ways on which each of us must go to reach the common end, and for which each of us felt in himself a special power. But we did not do this, and hindered one another, because we forced ourselves long, too long, to go with him hand in hand, I might say in the same shoes, and at the same pace with him. Our end was the same, but the road, which we should take to get to it, was marked out for each of us differently by Nature, and we ought to have recognised sooner, that each of us would reach his end with more ease and certainty, if he would step and go along it in perfect freedom and independence. We were too different. The crumb lying on the road arrested me if I thought it would afford the least bit of nourishment to my effort and further it. I must pick it up. I must stop at it and examine it, and before I know it enough in this way I cannot possibly consider it critically and look upon it as instructive for me, in universal connection and combination with all the relations, which as a single thing, it bears to our efforts. My whole manner of life has given me no power, and no inclination, to strive hastily after bright and clear ideas on any subject, before, supported by facts, it has a background in me that has awakened some self-confidence. Therefore to my grave I shall remain in a kind of fog about most of my views. But I must say, if this fog has a background of various and sufficiently vivid sense-impressions, it is a holy fog for me. It is the only light in which I live, or can live. And in this peculiar twilight of mine I go on towards my goal in peace and content so long as I go in peace and freedom, and at the point I have reached, in striving after my ideal, I stand firm to my conviction, that while I have done very little in my life to reach ideas that can be defined with philosophical certainty by words, yet in my own way I have found a few means to my end, which I should not have found by such philosophical inquiries after clear ideas of my subject, *as I was capable of making.* Therefore I do not entirely regret my backwardness. I ought not. I ought to pursue my way of *experiments,* which is the way of my life, willingly and gladly, without desiring the fruit of a tree of knowledge that for me and for the idiosyncrasy of my nature, is forbidden fruit. If I pursue the road of my experiments, however limited, honestly, faithfully, and energetically, I think by doing so I am what I am, and know what I know, and my life and action, though imperfect, is not merely a blind groping after experiments not really understood—I hope it is more. I hope in my way to make some few points of my subject philosophically clear, that could not so easily be made equally clear in any other way. The idiosyncrasies of individuals are, in my opinion, the greatest blessing of human nature, and the one basis of its highest and most essential blessings; therefore they should be respected in the highest degree. They cannot be where we do not see them, and we do not see them when every-thing stands in the way of their showing themselves, and every selfishness strives to make its own peculiarity rule, and to make the peculiarities of others subservient to its own. If we would respect them it is necessary that we should not sunder that which God hath joined together, and also that we should not join together that which God hath put asunder. Every artificial and forced joining together of heterogeneous things has according to its nature, the result of checking individual powers and qualities; and such unsuitably joined, and there-fore checked and confused, individual powers and qualities express themselves then in every case as unnatural, forcibly brought forward, and work upon the whole mass, in whose interest they were thus brought together, in a destructive, confusing, and distorting manner. I know what I am not, and therefore may honestly say I would not be more than I am. But in order to use the powers that may fall into my hands as I am, I must use my powers freely and indepen-dently, however little they may be, that the words "To him that hath, shall be given," may be true for me, and the others, "He that hath not, from him shall be taken away even that which he hath," may not be too depressingly ful-filled in me.

As I now look in this way upon the value that this book may have for me and the world, I must let it appear exactly in the shape in which it had the courage to step forward twenty years ago. Meantime I have given the necessary account of our pedagogic progress in educational practice and methods, since then, in some of my new works. I will go on doing this, and especially in the fifth* part of

* The fifth part of Leonard and Gertrude never appeared, for the manuscript was lost with other works left behind by Pesta-lozzi, when it was sent to Paris to Josef Schmid, in the beginning of 1840, to be published.

Leonard and Gertrude I will throw more light on this point than I have yet been able to do. But whatever historical and personal concerns I touched upon in these letters, I shall now enter on no more. I cannot well do so. I smile over much and look on it with quite different eyes than I did when I wrote it. But over much I would rather weep than smile. But I do not this either. Now I can speak neither weeping nor smiling. My conscience tells me the hour of my silence is not yet past; the wheel of my fate also is not yet turned. Smiling and weeping would alike be premature, if not with locked doors, harmful. Many of the subjects and views touched upon in this book may perhaps soon be changed. Perhaps I shall soon smile over much whereat now I should weep; and perhaps I shall shortly think very earnestly about things which I now pass with a smile. In this state I have left the book almost unaltered. Time will explain the contrast between what is said there and my present opinions about the things said, and will also explain those which appear incomprehensible and inexplicable, if it is necessary. I hardly think it will be. But if it is necessary beyond my grave, may it be in mild, not glaring colours.

PESTALOZZI.

YVERDUN, *June 1st*, 1820.

I.

MY DEAR GESSNER [4]—

You say it is time that I published my ideas on the instruction of the people.

Now I will do it; and as Lavater [5] gave his views on Eternity to Zimmermann in a series of letters, so will I give you my views, or rather, make them as clear to you as I possibly can.

I saw popular instruction like a bottomless swamp before my eyes; and waded round and round, with difficulty, in its mire, until at last I learned to know the sources of its waters, the causes of its obstructions, and the places from which there might be a possibility of diverting its foul waters.

I will now lead you about for a while in this maze of error, out of which I extricated myself, after a long time, more by accident than by sense and skill.

Ah! long enough! ever since my youth, has my heart moved on like a mighty stream, alone and lonely, towards my one sole end—to stop the sources of the misery in which I saw the people around me sunk.

It is more than thirty years since I put my hand to this work, which I am now doing. "Iselin's Ephemerides" [6] bear witness that my dreams and wishes, which I was then trying to work out, are not less comprehensive now than they were then.

But I was young; I knew neither the needs of my

9

scheme, nor the attention that its preparation required, nor
the skill that its realization called for and presupposed. My
ideal scheme included work in the fields, the factory, and the
workshop.   I had a deep but vague feeling of the value of
all three departments; I looked upon them as safe clear paths
towards the realization of my plan ; and verily, I have come
back after all the experiences of my life to nearly my early
views on the essential foundations of my plan.   Yet my
confidence in their essential truth, founded upon the apparent
certainty of my instinct was my ruin.

The truths of my opinions were truths in the air; and my
confidence in my instinct, in the foundations of my work,
was the confidence of a sleeper in the reality of his dream.
I was in all three departments, in which my experiments
should have been made, an inexperienced child.   I wanted
facility in details, that careful, persevering and accustomed
handling from which the blessed result, towards which I
strove, alone could come.   The consequence of this positive
unfitness for my task was soon felt.   The pecuniary means
to my end went quickly off in smoke, all the sooner because
I neglected to furnish myself in the beginning with a satisfactory staff of assistants in my task.   When I began to
feel keenly the need of such persons as could properly supply
that in which I was wanting, I had already lost the money
and credit which would have made the organization of this
staff possible to me.   Such a confusion in my circumstances
soon arose that the wreck of my scheme was inevitable.

My ruin was complete ; and the fight against fate was
the fight of underlying weakness against an enemy of ever-
increasing strength.   Struggles against disaster led to
nothing.   Meanwhile I had learnt in the immeasurable
struggle immeasurable truth, and had gained immeasurable
experience ; and my conviction of the truth of the principles
of my views and efforts was never greater than at the

moment when they were, to the outward eye, entirely destroyed. My heart still moved on unshaken towards the
same object, and I now found myself in misery, in a condition,
in which I perceived on the one hand the essential needs
of my work, and on the other the ways and means by which
the surrounding world of all sorts and conditions, really
thinks and acts about the object of my endeavours. So that
I perceived and comprehended the truth of these opinions,
as I never should have done in an apparently happy issue
from my premature attempts. I say it now, with inward
exaltation and gratitude towards an over-ruling Providence,
that even in my misery I learned to know the misery of
the people and its causes deeper and deeper, and as no
happier man knows them.[7] I suffered as the people suffered;
and the people showed themselves to me as they were, and
as they showed themselves to no one else. I sat long years
among them, like an owl among birds. But in the midst of
the scornful laughter, in the midst of the loudest taunts of
the men who rejected me—" You poor wretch, you are less
able than the meanest day labourer to help yourself, and do
you fancy you can help the people? "—In the midst of these
jeering taunts, which I read on all lips, the mighty stream
of my heart ceased not, alone and lonely, to struggle towards
the purpose of my life—to stop the springs of the misery in
which I saw the people around me sunk. In one way my
strength became ever greater. My misfortunes taught me
always more and more truth for my purpose. That which
deluded no one else deluded me; but that which deluded
every one else deluded me no more.

I knew the people as no one about me knew them. Their
pleasure in the prospect of profit from the newly-introduced
cotton manufacture; their increasing wealth, their bright-
ened houses, their abundant harvest, even the " Socratizing "
of some of their teachers, and the reading circles among the

under-bailiffs' sons and the barbers, deceived me not. I saw their misery; but I lost myself in the vast prospect of its scattered and isolated sources; and while my insight into their real condition became ever more wide, I did not move a step forward in the practical power of remedying the evil. Even the book that my sense of this condition forced from me, even " Leonard and Gertrude " [8] was a proof of this my inner helplessness. I stood there among my contemporaries, like a stone that tells of life, and is dead. Many men glanced at it, but understood as little of me and my aims, as I understood the details of skilled labour and knowledge that were necessary to accomplish them.

I was careless of myself, and lost myself in the whirl of powerful impulses towards outward operations of which I had not worked out the foundations deeply enough.

Had I done this, to what an inner height should I have been able to raise myself for my purpose, and how soon should I have reached my end! This I never found because I was unworthy, for I only sought it from without, and allowed my love of truth and justice to become a passion which tossed me about like an uprooted reed upon the waves of life. I myself, day by day, hindered my torn-up roots from fastening again into firm ground and finding that nourishment which they so essentially needed for my end. Vain was the hope that another might rescue this uprooted reed from the waves, and set it in the earth in which I had delayed to plant it.

Dear friend! Whoever has a drop of my blood in him now knows how low I had to sink; and you, my Gessner, before you read further, dedicate a tear to my fall.

Deep dissatisfaction devoured me now; things eternally true and right seemed to me, in my condition mere castles in the air. I clung with obstinacy to words and phrases which had lost within me their basis of eternal truth. So

I sank day by day more towards the worship of common-places and the trumpet blare of quacks, with which this modern age pretends to help the human race.

Yet, it was not that I did not feel this sinking, and struggle against it. For three years I wrote, with incredible labour, my "Inquiries into the Course of Nature in the Development of Mankind,"[9] particularly with the view of agreeing with myself as to the progress of my pet ideas, and of bringing my innate feelings into harmony with my conceptions of civil rights and of morality. But this work, too, is to me only an evidence of my inner helplessness, a mere play of my power of questioning, one-sided, without proportionate skill against myself, and void of sufficient effort towards that practical power which was so necessary for my purpose. The disproportion between my practice and my theories only increased ; and that deficiency in myself, which I was bound to supply for the accomplishment of my purpose, became greater, and I less able to supply it.

Besides, I did not reap more than I sowed. The effect of my book was like the effect of all my doings on those around me ; nobody understood it. I did not find two men who did not half give me to understand that they looked upon the whole book as a "gallimaufry."[10] And only lately, a man of importance, who rather likes me, said with "Swiss" familiarity : "But really, Pestalozzi, do you not feel yourself, that when you wrote that book, you did not exactly know what you wanted?" Yes, that was my fate, to be mis-understood and to suffer injustice. I ought to have been used to it, but I was not. I met my misfortune with inward scorn and contempt of mankind, and thereby injured my cause at those inmost foundations, which it should have had in me. I did it more harm than all those by whom I was misunderstood and despised could have done it. Yet I swerved not from my purpose ; but it was now sensibly atrophied, and lived on in an unsettled imagination and a disordered heart. I became more and more confirmed in the wish to nourish the sacred plant of human happiness on unconsecrated ground.

Gessner! In my " Inquiries " I lately defined the claims of all civil rights as mere claims of my animal nature, and, in so far as they are a real hindrance to the only thing that has any worth for human nature, looked upon them as hindrances to moral purity. But I now lowered myself, under the provocation of external force and internal passion, to expect a good issue from the tinkling cymbals of civil truth, to expect ideas of right from the men of my time, who, with few exceptions, live only to make themselves comfortable and hanker after well-spread tables.

I was grey haired, yet still a child, but a child deeply disturbed within myself. Still in all this stormy time I moved on towards the purpose of my life; but my way was more one-sided and erring than ever. I now sought a way to my end generally in the discovery of all the old sources of public ills; in passionate statements of civil rights and their foundations; in the employment of the spirit of violence, that had risen up in revolt against the individual suffering of the people. But the purer doctrine of my early days was only noise and words to the men around me:—how much more must my present view of things be foolishness to them! As usual, they steeped this kind of truth also in the mire, remained as they were, and behaved towards me as I ought to have expected, but did not expect, because I hovered in the air in the dream of my wishes, and no selfishness opened my eyes to the men about me. I was deceived, not only in every knave, but in every fool. I trusted every one who came and spoke fair words. Yet I knew the people, perhaps as no one else knew them and their bewilderment and degradation. But I cared for nothing but damming up these springs and stopping their mischief; and Helvetia's new men (*novi homines*), who did not want so little, and who knew not the people, of course found that I was not made for them. These men, who in their new place, like shipwrecked women, took every straw for a mast, by which the republic might be carried to a safe shore, despised me as a straw at which no cat would clutch. They knew it not and intended it not, but they did me good, more good than ever men had done me. They restored me to myself and left me (silently wondering at the sudden transformation of their ship's repair into ship-wreck) nothing but the word which I spoke in the first days of that overthrow, "*I will turn schoolmaster.*" For this I found confidence. I became one; and ever since I have been engaged in a mighty struggle (forced upon me in spite of myself) to fill up those internal deficiencies by which my ultimate purposes were formerly hindered.

Friend! I will openly reveal to you the whole of my being and doing since that moment. I had, during the first Direc-tory, won confidence through Legrand in my object, the cul-tivation of the people, and was on the point of bringing out an extensive plan of education in Argäu when Stanz [11] was burnt down, and Legrand at once offered me that unfortunate place for my residence. I went. I would have gone to the hindmost cavern of the mountains to come nearer my end, and now I really did come nearer it; but imagine my position —I alone—deprived of all the means of education; I alone, overseer, paymaster, handy man, and almost servant maid, in an unfinished house, surrounded by ignorance, disease, and novelty of all kinds. The number of children increased gradually to eighty, all of different ages; some full of pre-tensions, others wayside beggars; all, except a few, wholly ignorant. What a task! to form and develop these children! What a task!

I dared to attempt it, and stood in their midst pronouncing

sounds,[12] and making them imitate them. Whoever saw it
was astonished at the result. It was like a meteor that is
seen in the air, and vanishes again. No one knew its nature.
I understood it not myself. It was the result of a simple
psychological idea which I felt, but of which I was not
clearly aware.

It was exactly the pulse of the Art that I was seeking, I
seized it, a monstrous grip. A seeing man would never have
dared; I was luckily blind, or I too had not ventured. I
knew not clearly what I did, but I knew what I wanted,
that was — Death, or the carrying through of my purpose.

But the means of attaining it were absolutely nothing but
the direct result of the necessity with which I had to work
through the extreme difficulties of my situation.

I know not and can hardly understand how I came
through. In a manner I played with necessity, defied her
difficulties, which stood like mountains before me. Against
the apparent physical impossibility I opposed the force of a
will which saw and regarded nothing but what was immediately before it; but which grappled with the difficulty
at hand, as if it were alone, and life and death depended on
it.

So I worked in Stanz, until the approach of the Austrians
took the heart out of my work, and the feelings that now
oppressed me brought my physical powers to the state in
which they were when I left Stanz.[13] Up to this point I was
not yet certain of the foundations of my procedure.[14] But as
I was attempting the impossible, I found that possible which
I had not expected; and as I pushed through the pathless
thicket that no one had trodden for ages, I found footprints
in it leading to the high road, which for ages had been untrodden.

I will go a little into details. As I was obliged to give

the children instruction, alone, and without help, I learned
the art of teaching many together; and since I had no other
means but loud speaking, the idea of making the learners
draw, write, and work at the same time, was naturally developed. The confusion of the repeating crowd led me to
feel the need of keeping time, and beating time increased the
impression made by the lesson. The utter ignorance of all
made me stay long over the beginnings; and this led me
to realize the high degree of inner power to be obtained by
perfecting the first beginnings, and the result of a feeling
of completeness and perfection in the lowest stage. I
learned, as never before, the relation of the first steps in
every kind of knowledge to its complete outline; and I felt,
as never before, the immeasurable gaps, that would bear witness in every succeeding stage of knowledge, to confusion and
want of perfection on these points. The result of attending
to this perfecting of the early stages far outran my expectations. It quickly developed in the children a consciousness
of hitherto unknown power, and particularly a general sense
of beauty and order. They felt their own power, and the
tediousness of the ordinary school-tone vanished like a ghost
from my rooms. They wished,—tried,—persevered,—succeeded, and they laughed. Their tone was not that of
learners, it was the tone of unknown powers awakened
from sleep; of a heart and mind exalted with the feeling of
what these powers could and would lead them to do.

Children taught children. They tried [to put into practice]
what I told them to do, [and often came themselves on the
track of the means of its execution, from many sides. This
self-activity, which had developed itself in many ways in
the beginning of learning, worked with great force on the
birth and growth of the conviction in me, that all true, all
educative instruction must be drawn out of the children themselves, and be born within them].15 To this I was led chiefly

C

by necessity. Since I had no fellow-helpers, I put a capable child between two less capable ones; he embraced them with both arms, he told them what he knew, and they learned to repeat after him what they knew not. [They sat lovingly by each other. Joy and sympathy animated their souls, and their mutually awakened inner life led them both forward as they could only be led by this mutual self-vivification.]

Dear Friend! You have heard this crowd of collective learners and seen its courage and joy. Say yourself how you felt when you saw it. I saw your tears, and in my heart arose wrath towards men who could still say, "The improvement of the people is a dream."

No; it is no dream. I will put skill into the hand of the mother, into the hand of the child, and into the hand of the innocent; and the scorner shall be silenced and shall say no more—"It is a dream."

God, I thank Thee for my necessity! Without it I should never have spoken these words, and I should not have silenced the scorner.

I am now thoroughly convinced; it was a long time before I was; but I had children in Stanz whose powers, not deadened by the weariness of unpsychological home and school discipline, developed more quickly. It was another race. Even the paupers were different from the town paupers and the weaklings of our corn and vine lands. I saw the capacity of human nature, and its peculiarities in many ways and in most open play. Its defects were the defects of healthy nature, immeasurably different to the defects caused by bad and artificial teaching—hopeless flagging and complete crippling of the mind.

I saw in this combination of unschooled ignorance a power of seeing (*Anschauung*),[16] and a firm conception of the known and the seen of which our A B C puppets have no notion.

I learned from them—I must have been blind if I had not

learned—to know the natural relation in which real knowledge stands to book-knowledge. I learnt from them what a disadvantage this one-sided letter-knowledge and entire reliance on words (which are only sound and noise when there is nothing behind them) must be. I saw what a hindrance this may be to the real power of observation (*Anschauung*), and the firm conception of the objects that surround us.

So far I got in Stanz. I felt my experiment had decided that it was possible to found popular instruction on psychological grounds, to lay true knowledge, gained by sense-impression at its foundation, and to tear away the mask of its superficial bombast. I felt I could solve the problem to men of penetration and unprejudiced mind ; but the prejudiced crowd, like geese which, ever since they cracked the shell, have been shut up in the coop and shed, and so have lost all power of flying and swimming, I could never make wise, as I well knew.

It was reserved for Burgdorf to teach me more.[17]

But imagine,—you know me,—imagine with what feelings I left Stanz. As a shipwrecked man, after weary, restless nights, sees land at last, breathes in hope of life, and then is swung back into the boundless ocean by an unlucky wind, says a thousand times in his trembling soul, " Why can I not die? " and yet does not plunge into the abyss, but still forces his tired eyes open, looks around, and seeks the shore again, and when he sees it, strains every limb to numbness.—Even so was I.

Gessner! imagine all this ; think of my heart and my will, my work and my wreck,—my disaster, the trembling of my shattered nerves, and my bewilderment.—Such, friend, was my condition when I left Stanz and went to Bern.

Fischer got me an introduction to Zehender of Gurnigel,[18] [through whose kindness] I enjoyed some restful days at that place. I needed them. It is a wonder that I still live. But it was not my haven. It was a rock in the ocean upon which I rested in order to swim again. I shall never forget those days, Zehender, as long as I live. They saved me. But I could not live without my work. At the very moment when I looked down from Gurnigel's height upon the beautiful, boundless valley at my feet (I had never seen so wide a view before), even with that view before me I thought more of the badly taught people than of the beauty of the scene. I could not, and would not, live without my purpose.

My departure from Stanz, although I was near death, was not a consequence of my free will, but it was a consequence of military measures which rendered the continuance of my plans temporarily impossible. It renewed the old nonsense about my uselessness and utter inability to persevere in any business. Even my friends said, " Yes, for five months it is possible for him to pose as a worker, but in the sixth 'it is no go.' We might have known it before. He can do nothing thoroughly, and is at bottom no more fit for actual life than an old hero of romance. In this, too, he has but outlived himself."

They told me to my face, " It would be ridiculous to expect, because a man wrote something sensible in his thirtieth year, that he should do something reasonable in his fiftieth." They said aloud that the very most that could be said for me was :—That I brooded over a beautiful dream, and like all brooding fools might now and then have a bright idea about my dream and hobby. It was obvious that no one listened to me. Meanwhile every one agreed in the opinion that things had gone wrong in Stanz, and that every-thing always would go wrong with me. F. . . . reported a friendly conversation in support of this view. It happened in a public assembly, but I will not describe it more par-ticularly.

The first said :—" Do you see how ugly he is ? "

The other : " Yes, I am sorry for the poor fool."

The first : " And so am I ; but he cannot be helped. If ever he throws out a spark one moment, so that one might think he really is capable of something, the next moment it is again dark around him ; and when one comes near him, he has only burnt himself."

The other : " What a pity he did not burn himself to death ! He cannot be helped till he is ashes."

The first : " God knows, we must soon wish that for him."

That was the reward of my work in Stanz; a work that perhaps no mortal ever attempted on such a scale and under such circumstances, and of which the inner result brought me practically to the point at which I now stand.

They were astonished that I came down again from Gurnigel with my old will and former purpose, wishing and seeking for nothing but to take up the thread where I had dropped it, and to knot it together again in any corner, without regarding anything else.

Rengger and Stapfer rejoiced. Judge Schnell advised me to go to Burgdorf; and in a couple of days I was there, and found in Statthalter Schnell and in Doctor Grimm,[19] men who knew the shifting sand on which our old rotten schools now stand, and thought it not impossible that firm ground might yet be found under these quicksands. I am grateful to them. They gave attention to my purpose, and helped me with energy and good-will to make the path which I was seeking.

But here, too, it was not without difficulties. Luckily they looked on me at first as casually as on any other schoolmaster who runs about seeking his bread. A few rich people greeted me in a friendly way ; a few parsons courteously wished me, —[though I must say evidently without any confidence,]— God's blessing on my undertaking; a few prudent men believed that something useful might come out of it for their children.

Everybody seemed to be content enough; to be willing to wait till whatever was to peep out of it showed itself.

But the " Hintersassen " [20] schoolmaster of the brisk little town, to whose schoolroom I was sent, laid hold of the business a little closer. I believe he suspected the final end of my A B C crowing was to cram his situation, neck and crop, into my sack. The rumour once spread through the neighbouring street that the " Heidelberg " [21] was in danger. This is still the food on which the youth of the lower class of the townspeople is kept, as long as the most neglected peasantry of the villages; and you know they are kept at it till their betrothal day.

Yet the " Heidelberg " was not the only thing. Men still whispered in each other's ears in the streets that I could not even write, nor count, nor read correctly.

Now, my friend, that street gossip is not always entirely untrue; I could neither write, count, nor read perfectly. But people always shut out too much of such street truths. You have seen it in Stanz. I could teach writing without being able to write perfectly myself; and really my ignorance of all these things was essentially necessary, in order to bring me to the highest simplicity of methods of teaching, and to find means whereby the most inexperienced and ignorant man might also do the same with his children.

Meanwhile it was not to be expected of the lower classes of Burgdorf that they should accept everything beforehand, still less that they should believe in it. They did not. They decided at a meeting that they did not wish experiments made on their children with the new teaching: the burghers might try on their own. But as it happened, patrons and friends brought all the influence that was needed there for that purpose. So that at last I was admitted into the lowest school in the upper town.[22]

I considered myself happy, yet I was in the beginning

very shy. Every moment I feared they would turn me out of my schoolroom. This made me more awkward than usual; and when I think of the fire and the life with which in the first hours at Stanz I, as it were, built myself a magic temple, and then of the nervousness with which at Burgdorf I bowed myself under the yoke as a matter of business, I can hardly understand how the same man could do both.

Here was school discipline, apparently reasonable, but not free from pedantry and pretension. All this was new to me. I had never borne such a thing in my life ; but now for the sake of my purpose I bore it. I crowed my A B C daily from morn till night, and I went on without plan in the empirical way which I had had to break off in Stanz.[12] I put unweariedly rows of syllables together. I wrote whole books with these rows, and with rows of figures. I sought in all ways to bring the beginnings of spelling and counting to the greatest simplicity and into form. So that the child with the strictest psychological order might pass from the first step gradually to the second ; and then without break, upon the foundation of the perfectly understood second step, might go on quickly and safely to the third and fourth. But instead of the letters that I made the children draw with their slate pencil, I now led them to draw angles, squares, lines, and curves.

With this work the idea gradually developed of the possibility of an "A B C of Anschauung," [23] that is now important to me; and while working this out, the whole scheme of a general method of instruction in all its scope appeared, though still dimly, before my eyes. It was long before that was clear to me. To you it is still incomprehensible ; but it is certainly true. I [had for long months been working out all the beginning points of a path-breaking attempt at reducing the means of instruction to their elements, and] had done everything to bring them to the highest simplicity. Yet I knew not their connection, or at least, I was not clearly conscious of it; but I felt every hour that I was moving on, and moving steadily too.

While I was still in boy's shoes they preached to me that it is a holy thing to serve from below upwards; but I have learned now, that in order to work miracles one must, with grey hair, serve from below upwards. I shall work none, and am in no way born or made for that [24]—I shall neither reach such heights in reality nor in any way pretend to imitate them by tricks. [If I would, I could not. I know how weak my capabilities are now]; but if men at my age, who have their whole head and unshattered nerves, would or should in a cause like mine serve from below upwards they would succeed. But no; at my age such men seek, as is fair and right, their arm-chairs. This is not my condition; I must still in my old days be glad that I am allowed to serve from below upwards. I do it willingly, but in my own way. In all I do and attempt I seek the high-roads. The advantage of these is, that their straight way and open course destroy the charm of those crooked paths by which men are otherwise accustomed to reach honour and ad-miration. If I could do fully what I try to do, I only need to explain it, and the simplest man could do it afterwards. But in spite of my clear conviction that I shall bring it neither to admiration nor honour, I still regard it as the crown of my life; all the more since I have served this object for long years, and in my old age from below upwards. The advantages of it strike me more every day. While I thus took in hand all the dusty school duties, not merely superficially, and while I always went on and on from eight in the morning till seven in the evening, a few hours excepted, I naturally pounced every moment upon matters of fact that might throw light on the existence of physico-mechanical laws, according to which our minds pick up and keep outer impressions easily or with difficulty. I adapted my teaching daily more to my sense of such laws; but I was not really aware of their principles, until the Executive Councillor Glayre, to whom I had tried to explain the essence of my works last summer, said to me, " Vous voulez méchaniser l'éducation." [25] [I understood very little French. I thought by these words, he meant to say I was seeking means of bringing education and instruction into psychologically ordered sequence; and, taking the words in this sense] he really hit the nail on the head, and according to my view, put the word in my mouth, which showed me the essentials of my purpose and all the means thereto. Perhaps it would have been long before I had found it out, because I did not examine myself as I went along, but surrendered myself wholly to vague though vivid feelings, that indeed made my course certain, but did not teach me to know it. I could not do otherwise. I have read no book for thirty years. I could and can read none. I had nothing more to say to abstract ideas. I lived solely upon convictions, that were the result of countless, though, for the most part, forgotten intuitions.

So, without knowing the principles on which I was working, I began to dwell upon the nearness with which the objects I explained to the children were wont to touch their senses, and so, as I followed out the teaching from its beginning to its utmost end, I tried to investigate the early history of the child who is to be taught, back to its very beginning, and was soon convinced that the first hour of its teaching is the hour of its birth. From the moment in which his mind can receive impressions from Nature, Nature teaches him. The new life itself is nothing but the just-awakened readiness to receive these impressions; it is only the awakening of the perfect physical buds that now aspire with all their power and all their impulses towards the development of their individuality. It is only the awakening of the now perfect animal; that will and must become a man.

All instruction of man is then only the Art[26] of helping Nature to develop in her own way; and this Art rests essentially on the relation and harmony between the impressions received by the child and the exact degree of his developed powers. It is also necessary, in the impressions that are brought to the child by instruction, that there should be a sequence, so that beginning and progress should keep pace with the beginning and progress of the powers to be developed in the child. I soon saw that an inquiry into this sequence throughout the whole range of human knowledge, particularly those fundamental points from which the development of the human mind originates, must be the simple and only way ever to attain and to keep satisfactory school and instruction books, of every grade, suitable for our nature and our wants. I saw just as soon, that in making these books, the constituents of instruction must be separated according to the degree of the growing power of the child; and that in all matters of instruction,[27] it is necessary to determine, with the greatest accuracy, which of these constituents is fit for each age of the child, in order, on the one hand, not to hold him back if he is ready, and on the other, not to load him and confuse him with anything for which he is not quite ready.

This was clear to me. The child must be brought to a high degree of knowledge, both of things seen and words, before it is reasonable to teach him to spell or read. I was quite convinced, that at their earliest age, children need psychological training in gaining intelligent sense-impressions of all things. But since such training, without the help of art, is not to be thought of or expected of men, as they are, the need of picture-books struck me perforce. These should precede the A B C books, in order to make those ideas, that men express by words, clear to the children [by means of well-chosen real objects,[28] that either in reality, or in the form of well-made models and drawings, can be brought before their minds.]

A happy experiment confirmed my then unripe opinion in a striking way, [in spite of all the limitations of my means, and the error and one-sidedness in my experiments]. An anxious mother entrusted her hardly three-year-old child to my private teaching. I saw him for a time, every day for an hour; and for a time, felt the pulse of a method with him. I tried to teach him by letters, figures, and anything handy; that is, I aimed at giving him clear ideas and expressions by these means. I made him name correctly what he knew of anything—colour, limbs, place, form, and number. I was obliged to put aside that first plague of youth, the miserable letters; he would have nothing but pictures and things. He soon expressed himself clearly about the objects that lay within the limits of his knowledge. He found common illustrations in the street, the garden, and the room, and soon learned to pronounce the hardest names of plants and animals, and to compare objects quite unknown to him with those known, and to produce a clear sense-impression of them in himself. Although this experiment led to byeways, and worked for the strange and distant, to the disadvantage of the present, it threw many-sided light on the means of quickening the child to his surroundings, and showing him the charm of self-activity in the extension of his powers. But yet the experiment was not satisfactory for that which I was particularly seeking, because the boy had already three unused years behind him.[29] I am convinced that nature brings the children, even at this age, to a very definite consciousness of innumerable objects. It only needs that we should, with psychological art, unite speech with this knowledge, in order to bring it to a high

degree of clearness ; and so enable us to connect the foundations of many-sided arts and truths to that which nature herself teaches, and also to use what nature teaches as a means
of explaining all the fundamentals of art and truth that can
be connected with them.   Their power and their experience
both are great at this age ; but our unpsychological schools
are essentially only artificial stifling-machines for destroying
all the results of the power and experience that nature herself
brings to life in them.

You know it, my friend.   But for a moment picture to yourself the horror of this murder.   We leave children, up to
their fifth year, in the full enjoyment of nature ; we let every
impression of nature work upon them; they feel their power ;
they already know full well the joy of unrestrained liberty
and all its charms.   The free natural bent which the sensuous
happy wild thing takes in his development, has in them
already taken its most decided direction.   And after they
have enjoyed this happiness of sensuous life for five whole
years, we make all nature round them vanish from before
their eyes; tyrannically stop the delightful course of their
unrestrained freedom, pen them up like sheep, whole flocks
huddled together, in stinking rooms ; pitilessly chain them for
hours, days, weeks, months, years, to the contemplation of
unattractive and monotonous letters (and, contrasted with
their former condition), to a maddening course of life.

I cease describing ; else I shall come to the picture of the
greater number of schoolmasters, thousands of whom in our
days, merely on account of their unfitness for any means of
finding a respectable livelihood, have subjected themselves
to the toilsomeness of this position, which they, in accordance with their unfitness for anything better, look upon as a
way that leads little further than to keep them from starva-
tion.   How infinitely must the children suffer under these
circumstances, or, at least, be spoiled ! [30]

Friend, tell me, can the sword that severs the neck, and sends the criminal from life to death, have more effect upon his body than this change, from the beautiful guidance of nature, which they have enjoyed so long, to the mean and miserable school course, has upon the souls of children ?

Will men always be blind ? Will they never reach the first springs, from which our mental distraction, the destruction of our innocence, the ruin of our capacities, and all their consequences, flow, which lead all to unsatisfactory lives, thousands to death in hospitals, and to madness.

Dear Gessner, how happy shall I be in my grave, if I have contributed something towards making these springs known. How happy shall I be in my grave, if I can unite Nature and the Art in popular education, as closely as they are now violently separated. Ah! how my inmost soul is stirred. Nature and art are not only separated, they are insanely forced asunder by wicked men !

It is as if an evil spirit had reserved for our quarter of the world and our century an infernal gift of malicious disunion, in order to make us more weak and miserable in this philosophical age, than ever yet self-deception, pre-sumption, and self-conceit have made mankind in any part of the world, in any age.

How gladly would I forget such a world! How happy I am in this state of things, by the side of my dear little Ludwig, whose whims force me to penetrate, ever more deeply, into the spirit of beginning-books for infants. Yes, my friend, in these the fittest blow against the foolish in-struction of our time, must and shall be given. Their spirit grows ever clearer to me. They must start from the simplest elements of human knowledge, they must deeply impress the children with the most essential forms of all things, they must early and clearly develop the first consciousness of the relations of number [and measure] in them, they must give them words and sentences about the whole range of their knowledge and experience, and, above all, completely fill up the first steps of the ladder of knowledge by which nature herself leads us to all arts and crafts.

What a gap the want of these books makes. We want not only what we could gain by our own skill, we want also what we could never gain. We want above all that spirit, with whose life Nature herself surrounds us, without our help. This spirit is wanting in us also, and we do violence to ourselves, while we, through our miserable popular schools and their monotonous letter-teaching, extinguish within us the last trace of the burning style with which Nature would brand us.

But I return to my path. While I was thus on one side on *the track* of the first beginning-points of the practical means of psychologically unfolding human capacities and talents, which might be practicable and applicable for the development of children from the cradle upwards, I had on the other side, at the same time, to teach children who up to this time had been formed and brought up quite out of the sphere of such views and means. I naturally came while so doing in many ways in opposition to myself, and availed myself, and was forced to avail myself, of measures which seemed in direct opposition to my principles; [31] especially to the psychological sequence of knowledge of things and language, on the lines of which, the ideas of children should be developed. I could not do otherwise. I was obliged, as it were in the dark, to seek out the degree of capacity which I could not fathom in them. I set to work in every possible way, and found everywhere, that much further progress had intensively been made, even amidst the greatest rubbish, than seemed possible to me, considering the incomprehensible want of all knowledge of the Art. As far as men had influence I found unspeakable sleepiness; but behind this sleepiness Nature was not dead. I have now learned and can say: It is long, inconceivably long, before human error and unreason can wholly stifle our nature in a child's [mind and] heart. There is a God, who has put in our bosom a counterpoise to madness against ourselves. The life and truth of all Nature that surround us support this counterpoise, to the eternal pleasure of the Creator, who willeth not that the holiness of our nature should be lost in the time of our weakness and innocence, but that all children of men should, with certainty, advance to the knowledge of truth and right; until, forfeiting the worth of their inner nature, *through themselves, by their own fault,* and with *full consciousness of it,* they stray into the labyrinth of error and the abyss of vice. But [the majority of] the men [of this time] hardly know what God did for them, and allow no weight to the infinite influence of *Nature* on our development. On the contrary, they make a great fuss about any poor invention, crooked and stupid enough compared to her work, as if their skill did everything, and Nature nothing for the human race; and yet Nature only does us good; she alone leads us uncorrupted and unshaken to truth and wisdom. The more I followed her track, the more I sought to unite my deeds to hers and strained my powers to keep pace with her footsteps, the more infinite this step appeared to me. But the power of children to follow her is just as infinite. I found weakness nowhere, except in myself, and in the art of using what is there. I tried to drive where no driving was possible; where it was only possible to invite into a vehicle, which had its own power of going in itself; [or rather, I tried to force in, where it is only possible to bring out from within the child, that which lies in him, and is only to be stimulated within him, and cannot be put in him]. I now considered three times before I thought of anything: "The children cannot do it"—and ten times before I said: "It is impossible for them." They did what seemed to me impossible at their age. I let children of three years old spell the wildest nonsense merely because it was nonsensically hard.[32] Friend, you have heard children under four spell out the longest and hardest sentences. Would you have believed it possible if you had not seen it? Even so I taught them to read whole geographical sheets that were written in extremely abbreviated forms, and the least known words indicated only by a couple of letters, at an age when they could hardly spell the printed words. You have seen the perfect accuracy with which they read these sheets, and the unconstrained ease, with which they could learn them by heart.

I even tried to make gradually clear to a few older children complicated and, to them, wholly incomprehensible propositions in natural science. They learned the propositions thoroughly by heart, by reading and repetition, and also the questions explaining these propositions. It was at first, like all catechisms, a mere parrot-like repetition of dull uncomprehended words. But the sharp separation of single ideas, the definite arrangement in this separation, and the consciousness deeply and indelibly impressed of these dull words, glowing in the midst of their dulness with a gleam of light and elucidation, brought them gradually to a feeling of truth and insight into the subject lying before them, that bit by bit cleared itself like sunlight from densest mist.

By these tentative and erring measures, blending their course with the clearest views of my purpose, these first trials gradually developed in me clear principles about my actions; and while every day it became clearer to me that in the youngest years we must not reason with children, but must limit ourselves to the means of developing their minds,

1. By ever widening more and more the sphere of their sense-impressions.
2. By firmly, and without confusion, impressing upon them those sense-impressions that have been brought to their consciousness.
3. By giving them sufficient knowledge of language for all that Nature and the Art have brought or may, in part, bring to their consciousness.

While, as I say, these three points of view became clearer to me every day, just as firm a conviction gradually developed within me :

1. Of the need of picture books for early childhood.
2. Of the necessity of a sure and definite means of explaining these books.
3. Of the need of a guide to names, and knowledge of words founded upon these books and their explanations, with which the children should be thoroughly familiar before the time of spelling.

The advantage of a fluent and early nomenclature is invaluable to children. The firm impression of names makes the things unforgetable, as soon as they are brought to their knowledge; and the stringing together of names in an order based upon reality and truth, develops and maintains in them, a consciousness of the real relation of things to each other. The advantages of this are progressive, only we must never think, because a child does not understand anything fully, that therefore it is of no use to him. Certain it is that when, with and by A, B, C, learning, he has himself made the sound and tone of the greater part of a scientific nomenclature his own, he enjoys through it at least the advantage that a child enjoys who in his home, a great house of business, daily becomes acquainted from his cradle upwards with the names of countless objects.

The philanthropic Fischer,[33] who had a similar purpose to

D

mine, saw my course from the beginning, and said it was wrong, so far was it removed from his own manner and views. The letter that he wrote about my experiments to Steinmüller [34] is remarkable for the view he takes of this subject at this time. I will add it here with a few observations.

"In judging Pestalozzi's pedagogic undertaking, everything depends on our knowing the psychological basis on which his structure rests. This may prove secure even though the outside of the building presents some ruggedness and disproportion. Many of these deficiencies are explained by the empirical psychological course of the author and by his external circumstances, accidents, trials, and experiments. *It is almost incredible how indefatigably he makes experiments; and since he philosophizes more after these experiments than before—a few leading ideas excepted—he must certainly multiply them; but the results gain in certainty.* To bring these last into common life, that is, to adapt them to the preconceived ideas, the circumstances and claims of men, he needs liberal and sympathetic helpers to assist him to make the forms, or else a very long time to discover them gradually by himself, and through them as it were to give a body to the spirit that animates *him.* The principles on which his method rests, are the following."

(These five special points of view, which he calls the principles of my method, are only isolated views of my attempts for my purpose. As principles they are subordinate to the fundamental views which produced them in me.

But here the first view of the purpose with which I started is wanting; that is to say, I wish to remedy the deficiencies of common school instruction, particularly in lower schools, and to seek forms of instruction that have not these deficiencies.)

1. "*He wishes to raise the capacity of the mind inten-*

sively, and not merely to enrich it extensively with conceptions.

" He hopes to attain this in many ways. While he recites words, explanations, phrases, and long sentences loudly and often to the children, and lets them repeat them, he wishes thereby (according to the distinct individual aim that each step has) to form their organs and to exercise their observation and thought. For the same reason, he allows them, during the repetition exercise, to draw on their slates freely, or to draw letters with coloured chalk."

(I allowed them even then to draw, especially lines, angles, and curves, and to learn their definitions by heart. I proceeded in the measures that I had tried in teaching to write, from the principle founded upon experience ; that the children are ready at an earlier age for knowledge of proportion and the guidance of the slate pencil, than for guiding the pen, and making tiny letters.)

" For this purpose he deals out thin little leaves of transparent horn to his scholars ; upon these little tablets are engraved strokes and letters, and the pupils use them as models, so much the more easily, since they can lay them upon the figures they have drawn, and the transparency enables them to make the necessary comparison. A double occupation at the same time, is a preparation for a thousand incidents and works in life, in which observation must *share*, without *dissipating* itself. Industrial schools, for example, are founded entirely upon this readiness."

(I had in my experiments of thirty years ago found the most decisive results. I had already at that time brought children to a readiness of reckoning while spinning, that I myself could not follow without paper. All depends, however, on the psychology of the form of teaching. The child must have the handicraft, which he carries on with his learning, perfectly in his power ; and the task which he thus learns with the work must in every case be only an easy addition to that which he can do already.)

2. " *He makes his teaching depend entirely on language.*"

(This should be exactly, *He holds, after the real sense-impression of Nature, language to be the first means of gaining knowledge of our race.* I arrived at this from the principle, that the child must learn to *talk* before he can be reasonably taught to read. But I connected the art of teaching children to talk with the intuitive ideas given to them by nature, and with those given to them by art.)

"In language the results of all human progress are recorded. It is only necessary therefore to follow its course psychologically."

(The clue to this psychological pursuit must be sought in the very nature of the development of language itself. The savage first *names* his object, then *draws* it, then *combines* it very simply, after learning its qualities, variable according to time and circumstance, with words, by terminations and combinations, in order to distinguish it more nearly. I will further unfold this view, and by so doing I will try to satisfy Fischer's demand for a psychological investigation of the course of language, under the title of *Language.*)

"He will not reason with the children until he has furnished them with a stock of words and expressions, which they bring to their places, and learn to compose and decompose. Thereby he enriches their thought with simple explanations of objects of sense, and so teaches the child to describe what surrounds him, to give an account of his ideas, and so master them, since he now, for the first time, becomes clearly conscious of those already existing in him.

(My opinion on this point is: In order to make children reasonable, and put them in the way of a power of independent thought, we must guard, as much as possible, against allowing them to speak at haphazard, or to pronounce opinions about things that they only know superficially. I believe the time for learning is not the time for judgment; the time for judgment comes with the completion of learning; it comes with the ripening of reason, for the sake of which we judge and should judge. I believe every judgment that is supposed to have inner truth for the individual who expresses it, for this reason, must of itself, out of a comprehensive knowledge, fall ripe and perfect, as the perfectly ripened grain falls, unforced and free, from the husk or shell.)

" Mechanical readiness, and a certain tact in speaking, he produces by doing exercises in inflections before them."

(These inflections were limited to descriptions of well-known objects.)

"Their mental freedom gains exceedingly by this, and when they have learned, and learned to use certain forms of description by many examples, they will, in future, reduce thousands of objects to the same formula, and impress upon their definitions and descriptions the stamp of clear vision."

(I am now trying to find in number, measurement, and language, the primary and universal foundations for this purpose.)

3. "*He seeks to provide all operations of the mind with either data, or headings, or leading ideas.*"

(That is, he seeks the fundamental points in the whole compass of art and nature, the kinds of sense-impressions, the realities, which can be used, through their distinctness and their universality, as fruitful means for making knowledge and judgment easy upon many objects subordinate to and connected with them. So he gives the children *data* that will make them observe similar objects; he *gives headings* to sequences of analogous ideas, by defining which he separates for them the *whole sequence* of objects, and makes their essential characteristics clear to them.)

" The *data*, however disjointed they be when given, depend

one upon the other. There are ideas, one suggesting the other, which for that very reason inspire the desire for inquiry through the mental necessity of completion and facility in putting together separate objects."

The *headings* lead to the classification of the ideas to be upgathered ; *they* bring order into the chaotic mass, and the set-up framework causes the child to fill up the separate shelves assiduously. That is the value of headings of Geography, Natural History, Technology, etc. Above this comes the analogy which rules in the choice of subjects for thought. The *leading ideas* lie in certain problems, which in themselves are or may be the subject of whole sciences.

When these problems, analysed to their elements, are intelligibly put before the child, connected with data which he already has or can easily find, and are used as exercises for the observing powers, the child's mind will be led to work incessantly at their solution. The simple question, " What can man use as clothing out of the three kingdoms of nature ? " is an example of this process. The child will examine and prove much from this point of view, from which he anticipates he can contribute to the solution of a technical problem. In this way he builds up his knowledge. Truly the materials must in every case be given him. To the leading ideas belong also propositions which at first can be trusted to the memory only as practical maxims, but gradually receive force, application, and signification, and become more deeply impressed and confirmed.

4. " *He wishes to simplify the mechanism of teaching and learning.**

---

* It is indisputable that the human mind is not equally susceptible to impressions aimed at in education in every form in which they may be presented. The art of finding out the methods that most readily stimulate this susceptibility is the mechanism of teaching, which every teacher should seek out in free nature, and should learn from her on behalf of his art.

" Whatever he picks up from his text-books, and wishes to teach the children, should be so simple that every mother, and later every teacher, even with the least capacity for instruction, can grasp, repeat, explain, and connect together. He particularly wishes mothers to make the earliest education of their children pleasant and important by easy instruction in speech and reading, and so, as he expresses it, gradually to cancel the need of elementary schools, and to supplement them by an improved home education. He wishes in this way to prepare experiments with mothers as soon as his text-books are printed; and it is to be hoped that the Government will help by little premiums."

(I know the difficulties of this question. People all cry that mothers will not be persuaded to undertake a new work in addition to their scrubbing and rubbing, their knitting and sewing, and all their [tiresome duties, and the distractions of their life]; and I may answer as I like: "It is no work; it is play; it takes no time, rather it fills up the emptiness of a thousand moments of depression." People have no mind for it, and answer back, "*They won't do it.*" But Pope Boniface, in the year 1519, said to the good Zwingli, "It won't do; mothers will through all eternity never read the Bible with their children, never through all eternity pray daily with them morning and evening," yet he found in the year 1522 that they did it, and said, "*I never should have believed it.*" I am sure of my means [and I know and hope, at least, before I am buried],[35] that a new Pope Boniface will speak of this matter as the old one in 1522. I may indeed wait; it will come to the Pope.)

The fifth principle is connected with this, "*He would make knowledge popular.*"

(That is, he aims in all cases at that degree of insight and power of thought that all men need for an independent and wise life. Not indeed to make the sciences as such, the fallacious plaything of bread-needing poverty; but on the contrary, to free bread-needing poverty by the first principles of truth and wisdom, from the danger of being the unhappy toy of its own ignorance, as well as of the cunning of others.)

"This is to be gained through the stock of text-books, which already contain the principal elements of knowledge in well-chosen words and propositions, and, as it were, furnish the unhewn stones which later shall be easily combined to form the arch."

(I should rather have expressed myself in this way: "This should be especially aimed at through the simplification of the first steps of human instruction, and the uninterrupted progress to all that enriches the individual knowledge of every man. The text-books themselves should only be a *skilful combination of instruction* in all branches with that which *Nature* herself does for the development of men, under all circumstances and conditions. They should be nothing but a skilful preparation of the power that man needs, for the safe use of that which nature does, in all ways, for his development.)

"This shall reach further through the division and cheap sale of the text-books. Short and intelligible, they shall be issued in a series, and supplement each other, and yet be able to stand alone, and be dispersed in single numbers. For the same end he would multiply maps, geometrical figures, etc., by woodcuts, at the very lowest prices. He dedicates the profit of these works, after deducting the cost, to the improvement of his method, viz. to practically use it in an established school, institute, or orphan's home."

(This is too much to say. I am not able *to offer to the public the whole profit, merely deducting the cost of printing,* of works that are the result of my whole life, and of pecuniary sacrifices that I made with this in view. But notwithstanding all the manifold sacrifices, that I have already made for the sake of my aim, yet, if the Government, or an individual, will make it possible for me to carry on an orphan's home according to my principles, I will sacrifice my time and all my powers, with the greater part of the profit of my school books, till I die, for this end.)

"The gain for school instruction, is that the teacher with a certain minimum of skill, not only does no harm, but is able to make suitable progress."

(This is essential. I believe it is not possible for common popular instruction to advance a step, so long as formulas of instruction are not found which make the teacher, at least in the elementary stages of knowledge, merely the mechanical tool of a method, the result of which springs from the nature of the formulas and not from the skill of the man who uses it. I assert definitely, that a school-book is only good when an uninstructed schoolmaster can use it at need, [almost as well as an instructed and talented one.] It must essentially be so arranged that uninstructed men, and even mothers, may find in its clues sufficient help to bring them always one step nearer than the child, to that progressive development of skill to which they are leading him. More is not wanted; and more, at least for centuries, the mass of schoolmasters could not give. But we build castles in the air, and are proud of ideas of reason and independence which exist only on paper, and are more wanting in schoolrooms than even in tailors' and weavers' rooms. For there is no other profession that relies so entirely on mere words, and if we consider how very long we have been relying on these, then the connection of this error with the cause from which it arises startles us.)

More could be gained in the following way. If many children are taught together, the emulation aroused and the reciprocal imparting to one another of what has been gained becomes more easy among the children themselves, and the hitherto roundabout ways of enriching the memory may be avoided or shortened by other arts, *e.g.* by analogy of subjects, discipline, increased attention, loud repetition, and other exercises."

So far Fischer. His whole letter shows the noble man who honours truth even in a nightgown, and when she seems to be surrounded by real shadows. He was transported by the sight of my children in Stanz, and since the impression that this sight made upon him, has given sincere attention to all my doings.

But he died, before my experiments had reached a ripeness in which he could see more than he really saw in them. With his death a new epoch began for me.

II.

Friend, I soon wearied in Burghof as in Stanz. If you know you can never lift a stone without help, do not go on trying for a quarter of an hour without this help. I did incomparably more than I was obliged, and they believed I was obliged to do more than I did. My breast was so torn from morning to night with school affairs, that I was again in danger of the worst.

I was in this condition when Fischer's death brought me into contact with the schoolmaster Krüsi, through whom I learnt to know Tobler and Buss,[1] who a few weeks later joined me. Their union with me saved my life and preserved my undertaking from an untimely death, before it was well alive. Meanwhile the latter danger was so great that there was nothing left for me to do but to risk everything, not only financially, but, I might almost say morally. I was driven to the point at which I despaired of the fulfilment of a dream to which my life had been devoted. This produced a state of mind and mode of acting that almost bore the stamp of madness on them ; while, owing to the force of circumstances and the continuous duration of my misfortunes and undeserved sufferings, that disturbed the centre of my efforts, I sank down into the depths of inward confusion, just at the moment in which I apparently began really to approach my aim.

The help that I received from these men in the whole scope of my purpose, restored me financially and morally to myself. The impression that my condition as well as my work made upon them, and the consequences of their union with me, are so important in relation to my method, and throw so much light on the spirit of its psychological basis, that I cannot pass over the whole course of their union with me in silence.

Krüsi, whom I first learnt to know, spent his youth in various occupations, through which he had learned much and varied manual skill, which in the lower ranks so often develop the basis of the higher mental culture, and raise men, who have enjoyed it from childhood, to general and comprehensive usefulness.

When only in his twelfth or thirteenth year, his father, who had a little business, used to send him several miles with six or eight dollars to buy goods ; to this he added some messages and commissions. Afterwards he undertook weaving and day-labourer's work. In his eighteenth year he was employed, without any preparation, in school work in his native place, Gaiss. At that time, as he now says, he did not know even the names of the first grammatical distinctions. Anything more was not to be thought of, since he never had any instruction, except at an ordinary Swiss village school, which was limited to reading, writing copies, and learning the catechism by rote, etc. But he liked the intercourse with children, and he hoped that this post might be a means of gaining culture and knowledge, the want of which he felt keenly as a messenger. For since they distilled there, he was soon commissioned to buy prepared things, sal ammoniac, borax, and a hundred other things, the names of which he had never heard in his life, while at the same time he dared not forget the most insignificant commission, and was answerable for every farthing. It was borne in upon him how advantageous it must be for every child to be brought forward in reading, writing, counting, and all mental exercises, even in learning to speak, as far as he now felt he wished to have been brought for the sake of his poor calling.

In the first few weeks he had already a hundred pupils. But the task of occupying all these children properly, teaching them and keeping them in order, was beyond his power. He knew no art of school-keeping, except *setting tasks* of spelling, reading, and learning by heart; repeating lessons by turns, *warning*, and *chastising* with the rod when the tasks were not learnt. But he knew from his own youthful experience, that under this method of school-keeping the majority of children sit idle for the greater part of school time, and even fall into all kinds of foolish and naughty ways; that in this way the precious time for culture passes useless away, and the advantages of learning are not balanced by the harmful consequences that such a school-keeping must necessarily have.

Pastor Schiess, who worked energetically against the old slow course of instruction, helped him to keep school for the first eight weeks. They immediately divided the children into three classes. These divisions, and the use of new reading books that were shortly afterwards introduced into the school, made it possible to exercise several children together in spelling and reading, and thus to occupy all, more than had been possible before.

He also lent him books necessary for his own culture, and

a good copy-book, which he copied a hundred times in order to form his handwriting; and he was soon in a position to satisfy the highest demands of the parents. But this did not satisfy him. He wished not only to teach his scholars to read and write, but also to train their understanding.

The new reading book [that the pastor introduced into his parish] contained religious instruction in proverbs and Bible stories; passages of nature-teaching and natural history, geography, politics, and so on. At every reading lesson, Krüsi saw that his pastor asked the children questions on every paragraph, to see if they understood what they had read. Krüsi tried to do likewise, and made most of his scholars perfectly conversant with the contents of the reading books. But he only succeeded in doing this, because, like the good Hubner,[2] he fitted his questions to the answers already standing in the books; and asked for and expected no answers, except exactly those which stood in the book, before the questions that should have preceded them were discovered. He was especially successful, because he did not introduce into this catechism any kind of real exercise for the understanding whatsoever. We must here notice that the original method of instruction that we call catechizing, was far from being a real exercise of the intellect. It was a simple verbal analysis of confused sentences lying before the child, and has this merit, in so far as it is a preparatory exercise for the gradual clearing up of ideas, that it presents separate words and sentences clearly, one by one, to the sense-impression of the child. "Socratizing" is now for the first time blended with this catechizing; which was originally confined to religious matters.

The pastor put Krüsi's thus catechized children as an example before his older pupils. But afterwards Krüsi, [according to the fashion of the time] tried to combine the

[limited verbal analysis that we call] catechizing, with Socratizing.   This latter implies a higher treatment of the subject ;
but the combination, by its very nature, leads no further
than the squaring of the circle, that a wood cutter with
the axe in his hand tries upon a wooden board; it will not
do.[3] The uncultured superficial man cannot fathom the
depths out of which Socrates drew spirit and truth ; therefore it is natural that it should not succeed. He wanted
a foundation for his questions, and the children needed a
background for their answers.   Further, they had no language
for that which they knew, and no books that could put a
definite answer in their mouths for questions understood,
or not understood.

Meanwhile, Krüsi did not feel clearly yet the difference
between these similar methods. He knew not yet that catechism proper, and particularly the catechism about abstract
ideas, excepting the advantage of separating words and
subjects into analytical forms, is nothing in itself but a
parrot-like repetition of unintelligible sounds. Socratizing
is essentially impossible for children, since they want both a
background of preliminary knowledge and the outward means
of expression—language.   He was unjust to himself about
this failure; he believed the cause of failure lay entirely in
himself, and thought any good schoolmaster would be able
to draw right and clear answers from children by questions,
about all sorts of religious and moral ideas.

He had fallen upon the fashionable period of Socratizing,
or rather upon an epoch in which this sublime art was
[generally absorbed by an inferior art, and] spoiled and degraded by a combination of monkish and teachers' formulas
of catechism. At that period they dreamt of drawing out
the intellect in this way, and out of veritable nothing to call
forth wonders ; but I think they are now waking from that
dream.

Krüsi, however, was still fast asleep; he was locked in it, else I should wonder if even the Appenzeller had not observed, when half awake, that the hawk and the eagle could take no eggs from the nest if none had been laid. He was determined to learn an art that seemed so essential to his calling. And as he found in the departure of the emigrating Appenzellers an opportunity of coming to Fischer, his hopes were renewed on this subject. Fischer did everything to make him a cultivated teacher, according to his views. But in my opinion, he has let the attempt to raise him into the clouds of a superficial art of catechizing, take precedence of the work, that should make the foundations of things, about which he should catechize, clearer to him.

Krüsi honours his memory, and speaks only with affection and gratitude of his benefactor and friend. But love of truth, which bound me also to Fischer's heart, demands that I leave no view and no circumstance of this subject in doubt, that, more or less contributed to develop views and opinions in me and my helpers, that now unite us on this subject. Therefore I cannot conceal that, while Krüsi admired the ease with which Fischer held a great number of questions in readiness about a crowd of subjects, and hoped with time and industry to gather together a sufficient number of questions for the elucidation of all the principal subjects of human knowledge,[4] he could ever less and less conceal it from himself, that if a teachers' seminary be a thing that must raise every village schoolmaster to this height in the art of questioning, such a seminary might still be a doubtful advantage.

The more he worked with Fischer, the greater seemed the mountain that stood before him, and the less he felt in himself the power that he saw was necessary to climb its summit. Since, however, he heard me talk with Fischer of education and the culture of the people, on the first days of his visit, and heard me distinctly declare against the Socra-

tizing of our candidates, with the expression, that I was
wholly against making the judgment of children upon any
subject, *apparently ripe before the time*, but rather would
hold it back as long as possible, until they really had seen
with their own eyes, the object on which they should express
themselves, from all sides, and under several conditions, and
had become quite familiar with words, by which they could
describe its essential characteristics. Krüsi felt that he
decidedly wanted this himself, and that he needed just this
training that I intended to give my children.

While Fischer, on his side, did everything to lead him
into several departments of knowledge, in order to prepare
him for giving instruction, Krüsi felt daily more and more
that his way was not among books, so long as he was wanting
in the fundamental knowledge of things and of words, which
these books presupposed more or less. Fortunately he became
more confirmed in this self-knowledge, by seeing before his
eyes, the effect produced on the children by being taken back
to the beginning points of human knowledge, and by my
patient dwelling upon these points. This changed his whole
view of instruction, and all the fundamental ideas he had
formed thereon. He now saw that in all that I did, I tried
more to *develop the inner capacity* of the child, than to
produce isolated results by my actions; and he was convinced,
through the effect of this principle in the whole range of my
method of development, that in this way the foundations of
intelligence and further progress were laid in the children
as could never be attained in any other way.

Meanwhile Fischer's plan of founding a schoolmaster's
seminary was hindered. He was elected again into the
Bureau of Ministers of Education. He promised himself to
wait for better times for his seminary, and meanwhile to
direct the schools in Burgdorf even in his absence. They
should be remodelled, and they needed it; but, owing to his

absence and the diverting of all his time and strength, he had not even been able to begin; and certainly would not have been able in his absence, and in the midst of varied occupations, to set it working. Krüsi's condition was aggravated by Fischer's absence. He felt less and less capable of what Fischer expected of him, without his personal presence and sympathy. Soon after Fischer's departure, he expressed to him, and to me, his wish to join himself and his children to my school. But though I sorely needed help, I rejected it then, because I would not annoy Fischer, who showed continual zeal for his seminary, and who depended upon Krüsi. But he was ill soon after, and Krüsi told him of the need of this union, in the last hours that he spoke with him. An affectionate nod of the head was the dying man's answer. His memory will be always dear to me. He worked towards a like purpose to mine, energetically and nobly. Had he lived and been able to wait for the ripening of my experiment, we should certainly have entirely agreed.

After Fischer's death I myself proposed to join Krüsi's school to mine, and we now both saw our work much lightened; but the difficulties of my plan much increased. I had already, from Burgdorf, children unequal in age, cultivation and manners. The arrival of children from the little cantons increased the difficulties, for beside similar inequalities, they brought into my schoolroom a natural independence of thought, feeling, and speech, that, combined with insinuations against my method, and the want of a firm organization in my teaching, which might still be looked on as a mere experiment, made every day more depressing. In my condition I needed free play for my experiments, and yet at every moment, private people sent particular orders as to how I should set to work to teach the children who were sent to me. In one place, where they had been accustomed for ages, to be content with very little in the way of in-

E

struction and teaching, they now demanded from me, that a
method of teaching, embracing all the elements of human
knowledge, and one that was compiled for the early use of
little children, should also have a great, universal, and absolute effect upon children, who up to their twelfth or four-
teenth year, had remained in the most thoughtless mountain
freedom, and had therefore become distrustful of all teaching.   It was certainly not such a method; and they said,
as it had not this effect, it was no use.   They confused it
with an ordinary modification of the method of teaching A, B,
C, and writing.   My aim of seeking firm and sure foundations
in all branches of human art and human knowledge; my
efforts to strengthen the capacities of children simply and
generally for every art; and my calm and apparently indif-
ferent way of waiting for the results of principles that should
gradually develop out of themselves—these were castles in
the air.   They anticipated nothing from, and saw nothing
in them; on the contrary, where I built up capacity, they
found emptiness.   They said: "The children do not learn
to read," just because I taught them reading properly; they
said: "They are not learning to write," because I taught
writing properly, and at last: " They do not learn to be good,"
just because I did all I could, to remove out of the way the
first hindrances to goodness, that were in the school, and
especially opposed the idea, that the parrot-like learning by
heart of the "Heidelberg," can be the only method of teaching,
by which the Saviour of the world sought to raise the human
race to reverence God and to worship Him *in Spirit and in
Truth.*   It is true, I have said fearlessly, God is not a God
to whom stupidity and error, hypocrisy and lip-service are
pleasing.[5]   I have said fearlessly: Take care to teach children
to think, feel, and act rightly, to quicken and make use of
the blessings of faith and love in themselves, before we drill
the subjects of positive theology and their never-ending

controversies into their memories, as a *means of cultivating their intellect,* and a *spiritual exercise.* This cannot be opposed to God and religion. But I cannot be offended at being misunderstood; they meant well; and I perfectly comprehend that, owing to the quackery of our educational methods, my rough attempts at a new way must disappoint people, who, like many others, would rather see one fish in their pond, than a lake full of carp the other side of the mountains.

Meantime I took my own way, and Krüsi stood more and more firmly by me.

The principal points of which he was quickly convinced, [not however as ripe educational truths, but only as preliminary views that gradually unfolded themselves as clearly developed principles of education,] are especially these:

1. That through a well-arranged nomenclature, indelibly impressed, a general foundation for all kinds of knowledge can be laid, by which children and teacher, together, as well as separately, may rise gradually, but with safe steps, to clear ideas in all branches of knowledge.

2. That by exercises in lines, angles, and curves, which I began to use at this time, a readiness in gaining sense-impressions of all things is produced in the children, as well as skill of hand, of which the effect will be to make everything, that comes within the sphere of their observation, gradually clear and plain.

3. That by exercising children beginning to count, with real objects, or at least with dots representing them, we lay the foundations of the whole of the science of arithmetic, and secure their future progress from error and confusion.

4. The descriptions that the children learnt by heart of

going, seeing, standing, lying, etc., showed him the connection of the first principles, with the end that I was aiming at through them, the gradual clearing up of all ideas. He soon felt, that while we make children describe *things that are so plain to them that no experiment can make them clearer*, they are checked in the presumption of wishing to describe that which they do not know, and gain the power of describing what they do know, and what comes within the sphere of their observation, with brevity, clearness, and understanding.

5. A few words that I spoke about the influence of my methods in counteracting prejudice, made the deepest impression upon him. I said: Truth that springs from sense-impression may make tiresome talk and tedious arguments superfluous (these have almost as much effect against error and prejudice as bell-ringing against a storm), because truth so acquired generates a power in the man that makes his soul proof against prejudice and error; and even when through the continual chatter of our race they come to his ears, they become so isolated in him, that they cannot have the same effect, as upon the commonplace men of our time, on whom truth and error alike, without sense-impression, with mere cabalistic words, are thrown, as through a magic lantern, upon the imagination.

These expressions convinced him that it might be possible to do more against error and prejudice by the still silence of my method, than has yet been done through the endless talk that we have permitted against it, or rather have been guilty of.

6. The plant-collecting that we pursued last summer, and the conversations to which it gave rise, particularly

developed in him the conviction that the whole circle of knowledge generated through our senses rests upon attention to *Nature* and on *industry* in *collecting* and *holding firm* everything that she brings to our consciousness.

All these views, joined with his growing need of bringing all means and subjects of instruction into harmony with each other, convinced him of the possibility of founding a method of instruction, in which the principles of all action and knowledge should be so united, that a teacher need only learn *how to use them,* in order, by their help, to raise himself and the children to any standard that can be aimed at by teaching.[6] By this plan, not *erudition,* but only *healthy human understanding* and *practice in the method* was wanted, to lay solid foundations of all knowledge in the children, and to raise a satisfactory inner self-activity in both parents and teachers, by simply using these means of gaining knowledge.

As has been said, he was six years village-schoolmaster, over a very large number of children of all ages; but with all the pains he took, he had never so developed the capacities of children, and had never seen the firmness, security, comprehension and freedom reached, to which we had risen.

He sought the causes, and found many.

He saw firstly, that the principle of beginning with the easiest and making this complete before going further, then gradually adding, little by little, to that already perfectly learnt, does not actually, in the first moments of learning, produce a feeling and a self-consciousness of power, but it keeps alive in the children, this high witness of their unweakened natural power.

"We must," said he, "never drive the children, but only lead them by this method." Before, when he began to teach, he used to say : " Consider that. Do you not remember ? "

It was inevitable for instance, when he asked, in arithmetic, How many times is seven contained in sixty-three? The child had no real background for his answer, and must, with great trouble, dig it out of his memory. Now, by the plan of putting nine times seven objects before his eyes, and letting him count them as nine sevens standing together, he has not to think any more about this question; he knows from what he has already learnt, although he is asked for the first time, that seven is contained nine times in sixty-three. So is it in other departments of the method.

For example. If he wanted them to write nouns with capital letters, they always forgot the rule; but when he took a few pages of the methodical dictionary as a simple exercise in reading with them, they began of their own accord to set down these sequences of nouns that were known to them alphabetically. This experiment presupposed an intelligent consciousness of the difference between these kinds of words and others. It is perfectly true that the method is incomplete [for the child] on any point where it needs in any way a spur to the thought; it is incomplete wherever a distinct exercise does not come by itself, and without a strain, from that which the child already knows.

He remarked further, that the words and pictures that I laid before the children singly at the reading lesson, had quite a different effect upon the mind than the collective phrases that were served up in ordinary instruction. And while he now fixed his eye upon these phrases he found them of such a quality that the children could have no sensible image of the nature of the separate words; and when put together looked, not at simple well-known parts, but at a confusion of incomprehensible combinations of unknown objects, with which we lead them, against their nature, above their strength, and with many delusions, to get hold of sequences of thought which are not only wholly strange to them, but need an art of speaking, the beginning of which they have not even tried to learn. Krüsi saw that I threw away the rubbish of our school wisdom, and, like Nature with the savage, always put a picture before the eye, and then sought for a word for the picture. He saw that this simplicity of procedure created in them no judgment and no inference, while it was put before them, not as a dogma, nor in any way connected either with truth or error, but only as material for observation, and as a background for future criticism and inference, and as a guide—on whose track they might go further by themselves, by uniting their early and future experiences.

As he learnt more, and saw deeper into the spirit of the method of reducing all branches of knowledge to the first beginning-points, and the gradual joining on of a little addition to the first step, in every branch, and found that the consequence of that is a steady progress to new and further additions, he became daily more ready to work with me in the spirit of these principles; and he helped me to bring out a spelling book and an arithmetic book, in which these principles are essentially followed.

In the first days of his union with me he wished to go to Basle, in order to tell Tobler, to whom he was much attached, of Fischer's death, and about his present situation. I took this opportunity of saying to him that I was indispensably in need of help in my writing work, and that I should be very glad if it were possible for Tobler to join me. I already knew him from his correspondence with Fischer. I told him, at the same time, that I needed just as much for my purpose, a man who could draw and sing. He went to Basle, talked with Tobler, who decided almost directly to accede to my wish, and came in a few weeks to Burgdorf; and since Krüsi told him that I also wanted a draughtsman, he fell in with Buss, who undertook the task directly. Both have been here eight months; and I think it would interest you to read a precise account of their experience on this subject. Tobler was five years tutor in an important house in Basle.

His opinion of the nature of my undertaking, comparing it with his own course in his own words is the following :—

"After the efforts of six years, I found the results of my instruction did not correspond to my expectations. The intensive powers of my children did not increase in proportion to my efforts; they did not even increase as they should have done according to the degree of their real knowledge. They did not seem to perceive the inner connection of the isolated bits of information I gave them, nor to give them the strict long-continued reflection that they needed. I used the best instruction-books of our time. But these were partly expressed in words that the children could hardly understand, and partly so filled with ideas that went beyond their experience, and were so opposed to their own way of looking at things, at their age, that it demanded infinite time and trouble to explain the incomprehensible. These explanations were themselves a continual worry, which had no more effect on their real inner development, than a single beam of light in a dark room, or in a thick fog. This was more the case since many of these books, with their pictures and representations, descended to the deepest depths of human knowledge, or ascended above the clouds, right up to the heaven of eternal glory, before they allowed the children to set foot on the firm ground, on which men must stand before they learn to fly, or grow wings wherewith to rise.

"The gloomy consciousness of all this impelled me to try to entertain my younger pupils with pictures of objects; but to raise my elder ones to clear ideas by Socratizing. The first result was, that the little ones made themselves masters of much knowledge that other children of their age do not possess. I wished to combine this kind of instruction with the formulas of teaching that I found in the best books; but all the books that I wanted to use, were written in a manner that presupposed all which must first be given to the children—namely *Language*. Therefore my Socratizing with the elder scholars had the result, that all word-explanations are certain to have, that are not based upon a knowledge of things, and are expressed in a language which conveys no clear ideas to the children. That which they grasped to-day, vanished from their minds, in an incomprehensible manner, in a few days; and the more pains I took to make things clear to them, the more they seemed to lose the power of seeking it themselves, out of the mist in which Nature had placed it.

"So, on the whole, I felt insurmountable hindrances to my progress in my purpose. My conversations with teachers and educators in society strengthened my conviction, that in spite of the immense educational libraries that our age produces, they were in the same perplexity in their daily work with their pupils. I felt that these difficulties were doubled, and must weigh ten times heavier upon the under teachers, if a miserable kind of dabbling work did not make them wholly incapable of such a feeling. I lived in ardent, though misty consciousness of the gaps which I saw in the whole compass of education, and I tried by all means in my power to fill them up; and undertook to collect, partly from experience, partly from educational books, all means and advantages by which it might be possible to obviate the educational difficulties that struck me in all children of all ages. But I soon felt my life would not be long enough to reach this end. I had already written whole books on this subject, when Fischer drew my attention in several letters, to Pestalozzi's method, and made me suspect that perhaps, in other ways than mine, he might reach the end I sought. I thought: My systematic scientific course perhaps creates the difficulties that do not stand in his way; and the art of our time may itself produce the gaps that he need not fill up, because he neither knows nor uses this art. Many of his means, *e.g.* drawing on slates,[7] etc., seemed to me so simple, that I could not understand why I had not thought of them long ago. It struck me, that what already lay near to hand was used by him. This principle of his method particularly attracted me —educating mothers for that to which they are so remarkably designed by nature;—because all my experiments were founded upon it.

"These opinions were confirmed by Krüsi's arrival in Basle, who practically showed Pestalozzi's methods of teaching reading and arithmetic in the Girl's Institute. "Pastor Fäsch and Von Brunn, who had organized the instruction and part of the direction of this Institute according to the first indications of Pestalozzi's method, which as yet we hardly knew, saw at once the firm impression that the drill in simultaneous reading and spelling made upon the children. The few materials that Krüsi brought with him for teaching writing and arithmetic after this fashion, as well as a few copies of a dictionary that Pestalozzi had designed as the first reading book for children, showed us that these methods had a deep psychological basis. All this made me quickly decide to accede to Pestalozzi's wish and join him.

"I came to Burgdorf, and found my expectations fulfilled at the first glance at this growing undertaking. The remarkable and general self-expressing capacity of his children, as well as the simplicity and multiplicity of means of development by which this capacity was created, filled me with astonishment. His complete disregard of all former school routine, the simplicity of the pictures he impressed, the sharp separation of the inner parts of his subject of instruction into portions that must be learnt progressively

at odd times, his rejection of everything involved or confused, his silent influence upon all the inherent powers,
his firm hold upon words whenever they were needed, and particularly the force with which his few means of instruction
seemed to spring, like a new creation, out of the elements of
art and human nature—all this stretched my attention to
the utmost.

"Certainly there seemed to me a few very unpsychological
things in his experiment, *e.g.* the repetition of difficult, confused propositions, of which the first impression must be
quite vague to the child. But as I saw with what power he
prepared for the gradual clearing of ideas, and how, as he
told me, Nature herself wraps all sense-impressions at first in
confused mistiness, but gradually clears them up, I found I
had nothing more to say; and certainly less, as I saw that
he set little value on the individual portions of his undertaking, but tried much, only to reject it. By many of these
experiments he was only seeking to raise the inner capacity
of the children, and to find the explanation of the grounds and
principles which occasioned the use of these various methods.
I did not let myself be misled, when a few of his means
came upon me, in the trembling weakness of isolated first
experiments; the less so, as I soon convinced myself that
progressive advance lay in their very nature. Certainly
I saw this in arithmetic, drawing, and in the fundamental
methods of language-teaching.

"Now it became clearer to me every day, that his special
methods, through the connection of the whole with *each*,
depended especially on the susceptibility of the children to
each ; and so I saw, that these methods grew ripe through his
daily work, before they were spoken of as principles, which
must necessarily forward the end he was seeking. In his
attempts and experiments he relied upon none of these
means, until *he held* it almost physically impossible to

simplify their essence any further, or to penetrate deeper to their foundations. These steps towards simplifying the whole, and completing the single parts, confirmed the conviction that I before held vaguely, that all means which seek the development of the human mind through a complicated terminology, carry the hindrance to their result in themselves; and that all means of education and development must be reduced to extreme simplicity of their inner being, as well as to an organization of language teaching, psychological and harmonious, if we would help Nature in that self-activity, that she shows in the development of our race. So gradually his object in breaking up the study of language became clear to me, and also why he reduced arithmetic to the principle always to be kept in mind, that all arithmetic is only a short method of counting, and counting only a short method, instead of the tiresome expression one, and one, and one, etc. makes so much; and why he built all power of doing,—even the power of clear representation of all real objects,—upon the early development of the ability to draw lines, angles, rectangles, and curves.

"It followed of course that my conviction of the advantages of the method should be daily strengthened, as I daily saw the effect produced on measurement, arithmetic, writing, and drawing, by the power universally awakened and used according to these principles. I raised myself daily more to the conviction, that it might be possible to reach the end which I mentioned above, as having animated my own actions, namely, to educate mothers for that to which they are eminently designed by nature; and through it, even the lowest material of ordinary school-instruction might be founded upon the results of companionable motherly instruction. I saw a universal psychological method formed, by which every father and mother who found the motive in themselves, might be put in a position to instruct their own children, and thereby to obviate the imaginary necessity of cultivating teachers by costly seminaries and educational libraries for a long period.

"In a word, through the impression of the whole, and through the constant similarity of my experiences, I am restored to the faith that I cherished so warmly in the beginning of my pedagogic course, but which I nearly lost as I went on under the burden of such art and help as is provided by the age—the *faith*, namely, *in the possibility of improving the human race.*"

III.

You have now read Tobler's and Krüsi's opinion of my object. I will now send that of Buss. You know my opinion of the latent capacities of the lower classes. What a proof Buss is of this! How this man has developed in six months! Show Wieland his attempt at an A, B, C, of Anschauung.[1] I know how interested he is in all that can throw light on the course of development of the human race; he will certainly, in this attempt, find a proof of how many apparently wasted and neglected powers can be used and increased by gentle help and stimulus.

Dear friend,—The world is full of useful men, but empty of people who can put these useful men into their places. In our time every one limits his idea of human usefulness within his own skin [or at most extends it to men who lie as near as his shirt].

Dear friend,—Seriously imagine these three men and what I do with them. I wish you knew them and their way of life more exactly. Buss tells you at my request, something about it himself.

Tobler's first education was sheer neglect. In his two-and-twentieth year he found himself, as by a miracle, thrown into the midst of scientific systems, and particularly in the department of education. He thought to master them ; but now he sees they mastered him, and caused him, in spite of a presentiment of the insufficiency of his own education, to trustfully follow the way of books, without following Nature herself by the way of sense-impression, of which he dimly felt the need. He sees the danger in which he stood, of losing himself in a sea of thousands upon thousands of details separately rational, without at that time finding principles of education and school-culture whose result would be, not rational words and rational books, but [through the cultivated power of reason], rational men. He lamented that in his two-and-twentieth year, when book-study had not yet begun to lessen his native capacity, he had not already found the path that he now trod in his thirtieth year.

He felt deeply how this intervening epoch had injured him ; and it does his heart and the method equal honour that he says himself, that ignorant and uninstructed men could find the beginning points, more easily and certainly than he, and could then go on. Meanwhile he is true to his conviction. His talents make his progress sure. When he has worked through the difficulties of the simple beginnings, these, and former knowledge which he combines with them, will make it easy for him to connect the method with the higher points of school-instruction, to which we have not yet come.

You know Krüsi, and have seen the power he shows in his vocation. It is extraordinary. Whoever sees him working is astonished. He possesses an independence in his vocation, that is only displeasing to the man who has none himself; and yet, before he knew the method he was, except in mechanical school-teacher's routine, far behind Buss in all branches. He now says himself, without knowledge of the method, all his efforts towards independence would not have enabled him to stand on his own feet, but he should have remained always dependent upon others' guidance; and that is entirely opposed to his Appenzel spirit. He has given up a post of 500 florins, and has remained in the most straitened circumstances of his present situation, just because he felt and saw that here he now might indeed become a schoolmaster, but there he could be nothing else, and even that not satisfactorily. You will not wonder how he came to this decision; his simplicity led him to it; he entirely lost himself in the method. The result is natural; as Tobler truly said, "it was easy enough for him, because he had no art, and he gained it precisely because he knew nothing, but had ability."

Friend, have I not reason to be proud of the first-fruits of my method? Shall men always, as you said to me two years ago, have no mind for the simple psychological ideas on which it is founded? May all its fruits be like these three firstlings. Read Buss's opinion too, and then hear me again.

"My father," said Buss, "held an office in a Theological College at Tübingen, and had free lodging there. He sent me from my third to my thirteenth year to the Latin school, where I learnt whatever was taught at that age. At that time I lived mostly, when out of school, with students, who were pleased to play with a very lively boy. In my eighth year one of them taught me piano-playing, but as he left Tübingen in half a year my lessons were broken off, and I was left to teach myself. Steady perseverance and practice brought me so forward, that I was able in my twelfth year to give lessons in this subject to a lady and a boy, with the best results.

"In my eleventh year, I enjoyed also instruction in drawing, and continued perseveringly the study of Greek and Hebrew, Logic and Rhetoric. The aim of my parents was to devote me to study, and for this end to send me either to the newly built Academy of Arts and Sciences at Stuttgart, or to the direction of the professors of the University at Tübingen.

"Up till now, men of all ranks were admitted into the Academy, some paying, some free. My parents' means did not allow them to spend the least sum upon me. For this reason a petition was sent for free admission to the Academy, but it was returned with a negative answer, signed by *Carl* himself.[2] This, with, as far as I remember, the simultaneous notice of the closing of studies against the sons of all the *middle* and *lower* classes, had a great effect upon me. I turned my attention entirely to drawing, but was again interrupted within the half-year, for my teacher, on account of bad conduct, was obliged to leave the town, and so I was left without means or prospects of being able to help myself, and soon found it necessary to bind myself apprentice to a bookbinder.

"My frame of mind had sunk almost to indifference. I took up this trade as I should have taken any other in order to extinguish all remembrance of my youthful dreams, by constant manual labour. This I could not do. I worked, but I was unspeakably discontented, and nourished hasty feelings against the injustice of a power that against *precedent* shut me out, merely because I belonged to the lower classes, from any means of culture and from my hopes and prospects, to reach which I had spent a great part of my youth. Yet I nourished the hope of earning, through my trade, the means of giving up my unsatisfactory handicraft, and of somehow retrieving what I had lost.

"I travelled; but the world was too narrow for me. I became melancholy, sick, had to go home again, tried anew to renounce my calling, and hoped to earn my necessary subsistence in Switzerland, by means of the little I knew of music.

" I went to Basle, and hoped to find some opportunity of giving lessons. But my former position produced a certain shyness, that prevented me from taking the first steps towards earning money. I had not the heart to say anything of all that must be said, in order to obtain what I wanted, from people as they are. A friend, who accidentally met me in this embarrassment, reconciled me for the moment to my bookbinding. I went into a workshop again, but also dreamed again, from the first day I sat down in it, of the possibility of finding something else with time and opportunity, although I was almost convinced that I was too far behind in music and drawing, to enable me to procure a secure independence by their means. In order to gain time to improve myself, I soon changed from my first place, and gained two hours a day for myself, and found acquaintances who made my work easier.

" Among others I learned to know Tobler, who soon observed the trouble that was gnawing me, and wished to remove me from my position. He thought of me directly, when Krüsi told him that Pestalozzi's newly organized method of instruction required a man, who understood music and drawing.

" I knew I was backward in general culture and in drawing, and my hope of finding opportunity of advancing in both made me quickly decide to go to Burgdorf, although I was warned by several people against having any connection with Pestalozzi, because he was half an idiot, and did not know his own mind.* This tale is still repeated, with variations; how once he came into Basle with straw-bound shoes, because he had given his buckles to a beggar

---

* I naturally feel that the public expression of this part of my opinion is unseemly. But Pestalozzi wished it, and demanded an unconstrained candid statement of the impression that he and everything else had made upon me.

outside the gate. I had read 'Leonard and Gertrude,' and believed in the buckles, but that he was a fool I did not believe.

"In short, I wished to try. I came to Burgdorf. His first appearance hardly surprised me. He came down from an upper room with ungartered stockings, very dirty, and looking thoroughly put out, with Ziemssen, who had just come to visit him. I cannot describe my feeling at that moment; it almost approached pity, mixed with astonishment.

"Pestalozzi!—and what did I see! His benevolence, his joy over me, a stranger, his freedom from presumption, his simplicity, and the disorder in which he stood before me, all carried me away in a moment. No man had ever so touched my heart, no man had ever so won my trust.

"The next morning I went into his school, and saw really nothing at first but apparent disorder, and, to me, unpleasant confusion. But from the warmth with which Ziemssen had spoken the day before of Pestalozzi's plans, my attention was ready to be roused beforehand, so that I soon got over this impression, and it was not long before I was struck by some advantages of this method of teaching. I thought at first that dwelling too long upon a point strained the children too much; but when I saw the perfection to which he brought his children in the beginning-points of their exercises, the flitting-around and springing-about permitted by the course of instruction given in my youth, appeared for the first time at a disadvantage. It made me think that if I had been made to dwell as long and as steadily on the beginnings, *I should have been in a position to help myself in progressing towards the higher steps*, and so to conquer all the evils of life and the melancholy in which I was now plunged.

"This reflection agreed with Pestalozzi's principle *of enabling men by his method to help themselves, since, as he says, on God's earth no one helps them, or can help them.* I shuddered when I read this passage in ' Leonard and Gertrude' for the first time. But it is the experience of my life, that no one on God's earth will or can help him who cannot help himself. It was now evident to me that the gaps, which I could not fill up to attain my end, had their origin in [3] the weakness and superficiality of the instruction I had received in the branch of art in which I had now to work, without knowing anything of the principles on which that art was founded.

" I certainly now threw all my energy into the department in which Pestalozzi wanted my help, but for a long time I could not understand a single one of his opinions on drawing, and at first knew not what he wanted when he said :—

" ' Lines, angles, and curves are the foundations of the art of drawing.' In order to explain himself to me, he said, ' Here, too, the human being must be raised from dim sense-impressions to clear ideas.' But I could not understand how that could be done by drawing. He said, ' This must be obtained by the division of squares and curves into parts, and by analysing their parts to units, that can be seen and compared.' I tried to find this analysis and simplification, but I could not find the beginning-point of simplicity, and with all my trouble found myself in a sea of single figures, that were certainly simple in themselves, but did not make Pestalozzi's laws of simplicity clear. He could, unfortunately, neither write nor draw, though he had brought his children, by some incomprehensible way, far on in both. In short, for months I did not understand him, and for months did not know what to make of the lines that he gave me as a pattern, until at last I felt, either I ought to know less than I did, or at least must throw away my knowledge, and stand upon the simple points, which I saw gave him his power, that I could not follow. It was hard. At last my ripened insight com-

pelled me, seeing how far his children were brought by persevering upon his beginning-point, to go down to these points.
Then was my attempt at an A B C of Anschauung complete
in a couple of days.

There it was, and as yet I knew not what it was; but the
first recognition of its existence had the greatest effect upon
me. I knew not before that this art consisted of lines only.

Now every thing that I saw suddenly stood between
lines that defined its outline. In my representations I had
never separated the outlines from the object. Now, in my
imagination, they freed themselves from it, and fell into
measurable forms, from which every deviation was sharply
distinct to me. But as at first I saw only *objects*, now I saw
only *lines*, and believed these must be used with the children
absolutely, and to the utmost extent before giving them real
objects to imitate, or even examine. But Pestalozzi thought
of these rules of drawing in connection with his whole purpose, and in connection with Nature, which allows no part
of the Art long to stand separate in the human mind. With
this intention he had put a double series of figures before the
children from the cradle upwards,—some in the book for early
childhood, some in preparation for definite forms. With the
first he wished to help Nature, and develop knowledge of
words and things as early as possible in the children, by
means of a series of representations of Nature. With the
second he wished to combine the rules of art with the sense-
impression of art, and to support the consciousness of pure
form, and of objects which fit into it, in the minds of the
children by means of juxtaposition; and, lastly, to secure
thereby a gradual psychological progress in art, so that they
can use every line that they can draw perfectly, for objects,
the complete drawing of which is only a repetition of the
measure-form, that is already familiar to them.

" I feared to weaken the power of sense-impression in the

children by laying down figures, but Pestalozzi wanted no unnatural power. He said once, 'Nature gives the child no lines, she only gives things, and lines must be given him, only in order that he may perceive things rightly. The things must not be taken from him in order that he may see only lines.' And another time he became so angry about the danger of rejecting Nature for the sake of lines, that he exclaimed, 'God forbid that I should overwhelm the human mind and harden it against natural sense-impression, for the sake of these lines and of the Art, as idolatrous priests have overwhelmed it with superstitious teaching, and hardened it against natural sense-impressions.

" Lastly, I observed and found in the plans of both books full agreement with the course of Nature, and only so much art, as is necessary to make Nature have that effect upon the human mind, which is essentially wanted for the development of its talents.

" Before this I had been in a dilemma. Pestalozzi said to me, the children must be taught to read these outlines like words, and to name the separate parts of curves and angles with letters, so that their combination can be as clearly expressed upon paper, as any word by the combination of letters. These lines and curves should be an A B C of Anschauung, and thereby become the foundation of an art-language, by which all varieties of forms should not only be most clearly known, but distinctly expressed in words. He did not rest till I understood. I saw how much trouble I gave him; I was sorry; but it was of no use; no A B C of Anschauung would have been found without his patience.

" At last it was found. I began with the letter A ; that was what he wanted, and one followed another, so that I had no more trouble. The thing already existed in the finished drawing, but the difficulty was that I could not express what I really knew, nor understand the expressions of others.

" It is, however, one of the essential results of the method, that this evil will be remedied. The art of speaking will be firmly connected with the knowledge given us by Nature and Art, and the children will learn to express themselves about every step of knowledge.

" It was commonly remarked among us teachers, that we could not clearly and fully express ourselves about matters that we thoroughly knew. It was difficult even to Pestalozzi always to find words [for stating his views of the aims of education] that would clearly express his meaning.

" It was owing to this want of [definite] speech, that I fumbled about so long in doubt about my department, and did not and could not see Pestalozzi's principles.

" After I had overcome this difficulty, I recognised the advantages of the method every day, and particularly saw how the A B C of Anschauung through the definite language which it gives the children about objects and art, even in that degree, must form in them a far more exact feeling of rightness and proportion. I felt especially how men [4] who have been taught to speak with art and care about their surroundings, become able, merely through knowing rightly the names of objects, to distinguish them more clearly and be more conscious of their characteristics, than can be possible to those who have not been so taught. Experience confirmed my expectation. Children criticised these different parts more justly than men accustomed to measurement and drawing from their youth. Their progress in this art was so rapid that it could not be compared with the ordinary progress of children.

" And though I only saw the whole method, through the medium of my department, and its limited effect, yet from the energy and care with which I worked within this limit, I learnt gradually, step by step, not only to guess its effect upon other branches, but to see and understand it. So I came

to see, by the limited clue given by my lessons in drawing, how it might be possible,[5] by the psychology of language,
by the gradual progress of lessons from sound to word, from
word to speech, to attain to the formation of clear ideas, as
well as by the progress from lines to angles, from angles to
figures, and from figures to objects. I understood the same
course in arithmetic. Till now I had looked upon each number without any definite consciousness of its proper value or
contents, merely as an independent entity, just as formerly I
regarded the objects of art, without any discriminating consciousness of their definite outlines or proportions, *i.e.* of their
contents. Now I was sensibly conscious of the definite contents of any number, and I recognised the progress made by
children who enjoyed this teaching, and saw at the same time,
how essential it is for every branch of knowledge, that simultaneous instruction should be given in number, form, and
language. As I had recognised the stoppage in my branch
owing to want of language, so now I recognised the deficiencies owing to the want of arithmetic. For example,
I saw that the child cannot represent the separate parts of
any form without being able to count them, just as until he
distinctly knows that the number 4 is composed of four units,
he cannot understand how the single number can be divided
into four parts. Thus, from the clearness to which my
work now brought me daily, as much *as through myself*,
the conviction developed that the method, by its influence
upon the human mind generally, produces in children the
power of *helping themselves* further on in every branch, and
is essentially a fly-wheel, that needs only to be set going, in
order to go on by itself. But I was not the only one to find
this out. Hundreds of men came, saw, and said, 'This cannot fail.' Peasant men and women said, 'I can do that
with my child at home.' And they were right.

"The whole method is play for any one, as soon as he grasps

the clue of the beginnings. This secures him from wandering in byways, which alone make the Art difficult to the human race, because they lead away from Nature herself, and from the firm ground upon which alone it is possible to rest its foundations. She requires nothing of us that is not easy, if we seek it in the right way and from her hands only.[6]

"I have but this to add. Knowledge of the method has in great measure restored the cheerfulness and strength of my youth, and animated my hopes for myself and the human race, that I had long before this time regarded as dreams, and which I threw away, in spite of the yearnings of my heart."

IV.

Friend, you have now learned to know the men who are still working with me; but I did not have them when I first came here. I did not look for them at first. After I left Stanz I was so tired and shaken, that even the ideals of my old plans for popular education began to wither up in me, and I limited my purpose at that time, only to improvements of detail in the existing miserable condition of schools. It is owing simply to my needs and the circumstance that I could not even do this, and that I was forced back into the only track by which the spirit of my old purpose was attainable. Meanwhile, I worked several months within the limits to which my own diffidence had confined me. It was a strange state of things. Ignorant and unpractical as I was, but with my power of comprehension and of simplifying, I was at the same time the lowest hedge-schoolmaster and also reformer of instruction—and this in an age, in which, since the epochs of Rousseau and Basedow,[1] half the world had been set in motion for this purpose. I really knew nothing of what they wanted and were doing. I saw only this much—the higher points of instruction, or rather the higher instruction itself, here and there brought to a pitch of perfection, the splendour of which dazzled my ignorance, as sunlight dazzles a bat. I found the middle stages of instruction raised far above the sphere of my knowledge; and I saw even the lowest, worked here and there with an ant-like industry and fidelity, the use and result of which I could in no way mistake.

When, then, I looked upon the whole of instruction, or rather on instruction as a whole, and in connection with the real true position of the mass of individuals who need to be instructed, the little that I could do, in spite of my ignorance, seemed to me infinitely more than that which I saw the people really received. The more I looked upon the people, the more I found that what seems to flow to them like a mighty stream from books, when one observes it in village or schoolroom, vanishes in a mist, whose moist darkness leaves the people neither wet nor dry, and gives them the advantages of neither day nor night. I could not hide from myself that school-instruction, at least as I saw it actually practised, was for the great majority, and for the lowest classes, of no use at all.

As far as I knew it, it seemed to me like a great house, of which the upper story was bright with the highest and best art, but inhabited by few men. In the middle many more dwelt, but there were no steps by which, *in a human way,* they could mount to the upper story; and if a few showed a desire to clamber up to the higher story, animal-fashion, whenever they were seen, sometimes a finger, here and there an arm or a leg, by which they were trying to climb, was cut off. Lastly, below, lived a countless herd of men, who had an equal right with the highest to sunshine and healthy air, but they were not only left in nauseous darkness, in starless dens, but by binding and blinding the eyes, they were made unable even to look up to the upper storeys.[2]

Friend, this view of things led me naturally to the conviction that it is essential and urgent, not merely to plaster over the school-evils, which enervate the great majority of the men of Europe, but to heal them at the root,—that consequently half-measures in this matter will easily turn into second doses of poison, which not only cannot stop the effects of the first, but must surely double them. I certainly did not want that. Meanwhile, the consciousness began daily to develop in me that it must be absolutely impossible to remedy school-evils as a whole, if one cannot succeed in reducing the mechanical formulas of instruction to those eternal laws, according to which the human mind rises from mere sense-impressions to clear ideas.

This consciousness, which, as I said, was daily confirmed, led me also at the same time to a point of view, which commanded the whole field of education. Then, though in my innermost state of mind I resembled a mouse in her hole, frightened by a cat, and hardly daring to peep out, yet I was forced to see that the faint-hearted half-measures, adopted in my discouragement, could not only do nothing satisfactory for the needs of schools as a whole, but, in circumstances that might easily arise, might here and there even have the effect of making the poor children take a second dose of that opium, which they were accustomed to swallow within the school walls.

But without fearing so much from the lifeless inanity of my solitary school-keeping, it displeased me more every day. I seemed in my endeavours like a seafarer, who, having lost his harpoon, tries to catch a whale with a hook. Of course it cannot be done. He must, if he wants to reach shore safe and sound, either take a harpoon in his hand, or let the whale go. As soon as I began to comprehend what was wanted to satisfy the urgent needs of my purpose, and to make the principles of instruction agree with the course of nature, I was in a like case. The claims of Nature upon my work were no longer isolated. They stood together as a connected whole before my eyes; and if, like the whale-fisher, I would reach home safe and sound, I must either give up the thought of doing anything, even the least, in my profession, or respect the unity of Nature, whithersoever it might lead me. I did the last. I trusted myself once and for ever blindly to her guidance, and, after I had been knocking about a will-less hedge-schoolmaster, driving the empty A B C wheelbarrow, I threw myself suddenly into an undertaking that included the founding of an orphan's home, a teacher's seminary, and a boarding-school, and which needed in the first year, an advance of money, even the tenth part of which I could not anticipate getting into my hands.

But it succeeded. Friend, it succeeds and it must succeed. Deep experience has taught me that the human heart, even the misled government heart that [under certain circumstances] is the hardest of all human hearts, cannot resist any great and pure effort of devotion to humanity, if its fertile bud has once fully blossomed before its eyes, nor let it pine and sink helpless away. And, Gessner, a few of my early experiments have borne ripe fruit.[3]

Friend, man is good, and desires what is good; at the same time he desires his own welfare with it. If he is bad, certainly the way is blocked up *along which he would be good.* Oh! this blocking up is a terrible thing; and it is so common, and man is therefore so seldom good. Yet I believe everywhere and always in the human heart. In this faith I now go on in my untrodden way, as if it were on a paved Roman road.

But I wished to lead you into the confusion of ideas, through which I had to work, to gain light for myself upon the mechanical formulas of instruction, and their subordination to the eternal laws of human nature.

Friend, for this purpose I will copy for you a few passages
from the Report on my experiments, which I made to a few
friends of my Institute, six months ago.[4] They will throw
much light on the progress of my ideas.

"Man," I said, in this Account, "becomes man only through
the Art; * but however far this guide created by ourselves
goes, it must always be united with the simple course of
Nature. Whatever it does, and however boldly it may lift
us above the condition, and even the privileges of our animal
nature, yet it cannot add a hair's breadth to the spirit of that
form, through which our race is raised from confused sense-
impressions to clear ideas. And it ought not. It fulfils its
end—our ennobling—essentially in this only, that it develops
us in this and in no other form; and so soon as it tries another
way, throws us back into that inhuman state, out of which it
is destined by the Creator of our nature, to raise us. The
soul of Nature from which springs the form of development
which our race requires, is in itself unshaken and eternal.
It is, and must be, the eternal and unshaken foundation of
the Art. It also appears to the eye of every one who sees
beneath the surface, in its highest splendour, only like a
magnificent house, that by imperceptible additions of single
tiny bits, has been raised upon a great everlasting rock. So
long as it is inherently bound up with the rock, it rests
unshakenly upon it, but falls suddenly asunder into the tiny
bits of which it was composed, if the bond between it and
the rock is broken in the least degree. So immense is the
result of the Art in itself as a whole, so little and imperceptible is, in every case, the single thing that the Art adds to
the course of Nature, or rather, builds on her foundations.
Its means for the development of our faculties are limited
essentially to this :—what Nature puts before us scattered
over a wide area, and in confusion, the Art puts together in

* The Art, *i.e.* The art of Instruction or Education.

narrower bounds, and in regular sequence, and brings nearer to our five senses, by associations which facilitate and strengthen our susceptibility to all impressions, and so raise our senses to present to us the objects of the world, daily in greater numbers, for a longer time, and in a more precise way. But the power of the Art depends on the harmony of its results and work, with the essential workings of Nature. Its whole action is one and the same with that of Nature.

" Man ! imitate this action of high Nature, who out of the seed of the largest tree first produces a scarcely perceptible shoot, then, just as imperceptibly, daily and hourly, by gradual stages, unfolds first the beginnings of the stem, then the bough, then the branch, then the extreme twig on which hangs the perishable leaf. Consider carefully this action of great Nature,—how she tends and perfects every single part as it is formed, and joins on every new part to the permanent growth of the old.

" Consider carefully how the bright blossom is unfolded from the deeply hidden bud. Consider how the bloom of its first day's splendour is soon lost, while the fruit, at first weak but perfectly formed, adds something important every day to all that it is already. So quietly growing for long months, it hangs on the twig that nourishes it, until fully ripe and perfect in all its parts, it falls from the tree.

" Consider how mother Nature, with the uprising shoot, also develops the germ of the root, and buries the noblest part of the tree deep in the bosom of the earth; again, how she forms the immovable stem from the very heart of the root, and the boughs from the very heart of the stem, and the branches from the very heart of the boughs. How to all, even the weakest, outermost twig she gives enough, but to none useless, disproportionate, superfluous strength."

The mechanism of physical [human] nature is essentially subject to the same laws as those by which physical Nature generally unfolds her powers. According to these laws, all instruction should engraft the most essential parts of its subject of knowledge firmly into the very being of the human mind; then join on the less essential gradually, but uninterruptedly, to the most essential, and maintain all the parts of the subject, even to the outermost, in one living proportionate whole. I now sought for laws to which the development of the human mind must, by its very nature, be subject. I knew they must be the same as those of physical Nature, and trusted to find in them a safe clue to a universal psychological method of instruction. "Man," said I to myself, while dreamily seeking this clue, " as you recognise in every physical ripening of the complete fruit the result of perfection in all its parts, so consider no human judgment ripe that does not appear to you to be the result of a complete sense-impression of all the parts of the object to be judged; but on the contrary, look upon every judgment that seems ripe before a complete observation (*Ansch.*) has been made, as nothing but a worm-eaten, and *therefore apparently* ripe fruit, fallen untimely from the tree.

1. Learn therefore to classify observations and complete the simple before proceeding to the complex. Try to make in every art, graduated steps of knowledge, in which every new idea is only a small, almost imperceptible, addition to that which has been known before, deeply impressed and not to be forgotten.

2. Again, bring all things, essentially related to each other, to that connection in your mind which they have in Nature. Subordinate all unessential things to essential in your idea. Especially subordinate the impression given by the Art to that given by Nature and reality ; and give to nothing a greater weight in your idea, than it has in relation to your race in Nature.

3. Strengthen and make clear the impressions of important objects by bringing them nearer to you by the Art, and letting them affect you through different senses. Learn for this purpose the first law of physical mechanism, which makes the relative power of all influences of physical Nature depend on the physical nearness or distance of the object in contact with the senses. Never forget this physical nearness or distance has an immense effect in determining your positive opinions, conduct, duties and even virtue.[5]

4. Regard all the effects of natural law as absolutely necessary, and recognise in this necessity the result of her power, by which Nature unites together the apparently heterogeneous elements of her materials, for the achievement of her end. Let the Art with which you work through instruction, upon your race, and the results you aim at, be founded upon natural law, so that all your actions may be means to this principal end, although apparently heterogeneous.

5. But the richness of its charm, and the variety of its free play cause physical necessity, or natural law, to bear the impress of freedom and independence.

Let the results of your art and your instruction, while you try to found them upon natural law, by the richness of their charm and the variety of their free play, bear the impression of freedom and independence.

All these laws, to which the development of human nature is subject, converge towards one centre. They converge towards the centre of our whole being, and we ourselves are this centre.

Friend, all that I am, all I wish, all I might be, comes out of myself. Should not my knowledge also come out of myself?

V.

In these several propositions I have given you threads, from which I believe a general and psychological method of instruction may be woven.

They do not content me ; I feel I am not in a position to state the essential laws of Nature on which these propositions rest, in all their simplicity and completeness.   So far as I see they have, collectively, a threefold source.

The *first* source is Nature herself, by whose power our mind rises from misty sense-impressions to clear ideas. From this source flow the following principles, which must be recognised as foundations of the laws, whose nature I am seeking.

1. All things which affect my senses, are means of helping me to form correct opinions, only so far as their phenomena present to my senses their immutable, unchangeable, essential [1] nature, as distinguished from their variable appearance or their external qualities.   They are, on the other hand, sources of error and deception so far as their phenomena present to my senses their accidental qualities, rather than their essential characteristics.

2. To every sense-impression, perfectly and indelibly impressed on the human mind, a whole train of sense-impressions, more or less closely associated, may be added easily, as it were involuntarily.

3. Now if the essential nature, rather than the accidental qualities, of a thing is impressed with a force disproportionately strong upon your mind, the organism [2] of your nature leads you, of itself, in relation to this subject, daily from truth to truth.   If, on the contrary, the variable quality rather than its essential nature is impressed with disproportionately stronger

force upon your mind, the organism[2] of your nature leads you, on this subject, daily from error to error.

4. By putting together objects, whose essential nature is the same, your insight into their inner truth becomes essentially and universally wider, sharper, and surer. The one-sided, biassed impression made by the qualities of individual objects, as opposed to the impression that their nature should make upon you, becomes weakened. Your mind is protected against being swallowed up by the isolated force of single, separate impressions of qualities, and you are saved from the danger of thoughtlessly confusing the external qualities, with the essential nature of things, and from fantastically filling your head with incidental matters to the detriment of clearer insight. It follows, the more a man makes essential, comprehensive, and general views of things his own, the less can limited, one-sided views lead him astray about the nature of his object. Again, the less he is exercised in comprehensive sense-impressions of Nature, the easier can single views of an object, under varying conditions, confuse in him the essential view, and even blot it out.

5. The most complex sense-impressions rest upon simple elements. When you are perfectly clear about these, the most complex will become simple.

6. The more senses you have questioned about the nature or appearance of a thing, the more accurate will be your knowledge of it.

These seem to me the principles of the physical mechanism, which are themselves derived from the very nature of our minds. With these are connected the general laws of this mechanism itself, of which I now only say, "Perfection is the great law of Nature; all imperfection is untrue."

G

The *second* source of these physico-mechanical laws is the power of sense-impression intimately interwoven with the sensibility of my nature.

This wavers in all its actions, between the desire of seeing, and knowing everything, and that of enjoying everything, which lulls the impulse towards knowing and learning. As a mere physical power, the laziness of my race is stimulated by curiosity, while curiosity is lulled again by laziness. But neither the stimulus of the one nor the sedative of the other has, in itself, more than physical value. But curiosity has great value as a sense-foundation for my power of inquiry, and inertia is valuable as a sense-foundation for cool judgment. We attain all our knowledge through the infinite charm that the tree of knowledge has for the sensibility of our nature, while, owing to the principle of inertia, that checks our easy superficial flitting about from one sense-impression to another, in many ways a man ripens to truth before he expresses it.

But our truth-amphibia know nothing of this ripening. They croak truth before they have an inkling of it, let alone know it. They cannot do otherwise. They have not the power of quadrupeds to stand firm on the ground; the fins of fishes to swim over gulfs; the wings of birds to soar above the clouds. They know as little of *unconscious* sense-impressions of objects as Eve, and when, like Eve, they swallow the unripe fruit of truth, they share her fate.

The *third* source of these physico-mechanical laws lies in the relation of my outer condition to my power of perception.

Man is bound to his nest, and if he hangs it upon a hundred threads and describes a hundred circles round it, what does he more than the spider, who hangs her nest upon a hundred threads and describes a hundred circles round it? And what is the difference between a somewhat larger or smaller spider? The essence of their doing is: they sit in the centre of the circle they describe; but man chooses not the centre in which he spins, and weaves; he learns all the realities of the world in their mere physical aspects, absolutely in proportion as the objects of the world that reach his sense-impressions approach the centre in which he spins and weaves [for the most part, without his help].

VI.

Friend! You see at least the pains I take to make the theory of my doings clear to you. Let this painstaking be a kind of excuse when you feel how little I have succeeded. Since my twentieth year, I have been incapable of philosophic thought, in the true sense of the word. Happily for the practical working out of my plan, I wanted none of that philosophy that seems to me so tiresome. I lived at the highest nerve-tension on every point in the circle wherein I worked. I knew what I wanted, took no thought for the morrow, and felt at the moment what was really necessary for the subject that particularly interested me. And if my imagination drove me to-day a hundred steps farther than I found firm ground, to-morrow, I retraced these hundred steps. This happened thousands of times. Thousands and thousands of times I believed I was approaching my goal, and suddenly found this apparent end to be only a new mountain against which I stumbled. So I went on, particularly when the principles and laws of physical mechanism began to become clearer to me, I thought directly it needed no more than simply to use them in the branches of instruction, which the experience of ages has put into the hands of the human race, for the development of the faculties, and these I looked upon as the elements of all art and knowledge, *i.e.* reading, writing, arithmetic, etc.

But as I tried to do this, increasing experience gradually

developed the conviction that these branches of instruction cannot be regarded as the elements of all art and of all knowledge. On the contrary, they must be subordinate to far more general views of the subject. But the consciousness of this truth, so important for instruction, which was developed by working in these branches, appeared to me, for a long time, in isolated glimpses only; and then only in connection with the special branch with which each separate experience was connected.

Thus I found, in teaching to read, the necessity of its subordination to the power of talking; and in the endeavour to find a means of teaching children to talk, I came on the principle of joining this art to the sequences by which Nature rises from sound to word, and from word, gradually to language.

Again, I found in the effort to teach writing, the need of subordinating this art to that of drawing, and in the efforts to teach drawing the combination with, and subordination of, this art to that of measurement. Also teaching spelling developed in me the want of a book for early childhood, through which I trusted to raise the actual knowledge of three and four year old children, above the knowledge of seven and eight year old school-children. These experiences that I learned practically, led me indeed to isolated helps in instruction, but at the same time made me feel that I did not yet know the true scope and inner depth of my subject.

I long sought for a common psychological origin for all these means of instruction, because I was convinced, that only through this, it might be possible to discover the *form,*[1] in which the *cultivation* of mankind is determined through the *very laws of Nature* itself. It is evident this form is founded in the general organization of the mind, by means of which our understanding binds together in receptivity, the impressions received by the sensibility of our Nature, into a whole, that is into an idea, and gradually unfolds this idea (or conception—*Begriff*) clearly.

"Every line, every measure, every word," said I to myself "is a result of understanding generated from ripened sense-impressions and must be regarded as a means towards the progressive clearing up of our ideas." Also, all instruction is essentially nothing but this. Its principles must therefore be derived from the immutable prototype of human mental development.

Everything depends on the exact knowledge of this prototype. I therefore, once more began to keep my eye on these beginning-points, from which it must be derived.

"The world," said I in this reverie, "lies before our eyes like a sea of confused sense-impressions, flowing one into the other. If our development, through Nature only, is not sufficiently rapid and unimpeded, the business of instruction is to remove the confusion of these sense-impressions; to separate the objects one from another; to put together in imagination those that resemble or are related to each other, and in this way to make all clear to us, and by perfect clearness in these, to raise in us distinct ideas. It does this when it presents these confused and blurred sense-impressions to us *one by one*; then places these separate sense-impressions in different changing positions before our eyes; and lastly, brings them into connection with the whole cycle of our previous knowledge.

So our knowledge grows from confusion to definiteness; from definiteness to plainness; and from plainness to perfect clearness.

But Nature, in her progress towards this development, is constant to the great law, that makes the clearness of my knowledge depend on the nearness or distance of the object in touch with my senses. All that surrounds you reaches your senses, *ceteris paribus,* confused and difficult to make

clear to yourself in proportion to its distance from your
senses; on the contrary, everything that reaches your senses
is distinct and easy for you to make clear and plain, in proportion as it approaches your five senses.

You are, as a physical living being, nothing but your five
senses; consequently the clearness or mistiness of your ideas
must absolutely and essentially rest upon the nearness or
distance with which all external objects touch these five
senses, that is, yourself, the centre, because your ideas converge in you.

You, yourself, are the centre of all your sense-impressions, you are also yourself an object for your sense-impressions. It is easier to make all that is within you clear and
plain than all that is without you. All that you feel of yourself is in itself a *definite* sense-impression; only that which
is without can be a confused sense-impression for you. It
follows that the course of your knowledge, in so far as it
touches yourself, is a step shorter than when it comes from
something outside yourself.

All that you know of yourself, you know clearly; all that
you yourself know is in you, and in itself clear through you.
It follows that this road to clear ideas is easier and safer in
this direction than in any other; and among all that is clear
nothing can be clearer than this principle—man's knowledge
of truth comes from his knowledge of himself.

Friend! Living but vague ideas of the elements of
instruction whirled about in my mind for a long time in
this way. So I depicted them in my Report without at that
time being able to discover the unbroken connection between them and the laws of physical mechanism; [2] and
without being able to define, with certainty, the beginning-
points from which the sequences of our views of the Art
should proceed, or rather the form by which it might be
possible to *determine the improvement* of mankind through

his own essential nature. At last, suddenly, like a *Deus ex machinâ*, came the thought—the means of making clear all knowledge gained by sense-impression comes from *number*, *form* and *language*. It suddenly seemed to throw a new light on what I was trying to do.

Now after my long struggle, or rather my wandering reverie, I aimed wholly and simply at finding out how a cultivated man behaves, and must behave, when he wishes to distinguish any object which appears misty and confused to his eyes, and gradually to make it clear to himself.

In this case he will observe three things:—

    1. How many, and what kinds of objects are before him.

    2. Their appearance, form or outline.

    3. Their names; how he may represent each of them by a sound or word.

The result of this action in such a man manifestly presupposes the following ready-formed powers.

    1. The power of recognising unlike objects, according to the outline, and of representing to oneself what is contained within it.

    2. That of stating the number of these objects, and representing them to himself as one or many.

    3. That of representing objects, their number and form, by speech, and making them unforgetable.

I also thought *number, form* and *language* are, together, the elementary means of instruction, because the whole sum of the external properties of any object is comprised in its outline and its number, and is brought home to my consciousness through language. It must then be an immutable law of the Art to start from and work within this threefold principle.

    1. To teach children to look upon every object that is brought before them as a unit, that is, as separated from those with which it seems connected.

2. To teach them the form of every object, that is, its *size* and *proportions*.

3. As soon as possible to make them acquainted with all the words and names descriptive of objects known to them.

And as the instruction of children should proceed from these three elementary points, it is evident that the first efforts of the Art should be directed to the primary faculties of counting, measuring, and speaking, which lie at the basis of all accurate knowledge of objects of sense. We should cultivate them with the strictest psychological Art, endeavour to strengthen and make them strong, and to bring them, as a means of development and culture, to the highest pitch of simplicity, consistency, and harmony.

The only difficulty which struck me in the recognition of these elementary points was: Why are *all* qualities of things we know through our five senses, not just as much elementary points of knowledge as number, form, names? But I soon found that all possible objects have absolutely number, form, and names; but the other characteristics, known through our five senses, are not common to all objects. I found, then, such an essential and definite distinction between the number, form, and names of things and their other qualities, that I could not regard other qualities as elementary points of knowledge. Again, I found all other qualities can be included under these elementary points; that consequently, in instructing children, all other qualities of objects must be immediately connected with form, number, and names. I saw now that through knowing the unity, form, and name of any object, my knowledge of it becomes *precise*; by gradually learning its other qualities my knowledge of it becomes *clear*; through my consciousness of all its characteristics, my knowledge of it becomes *distinct*.

Then I found, further, that all our knowledge flows from three elementary powers.

1. From the power of making sounds, the origin of language.

2. From the *indefinite, simple sensuous-power of form-ing images*, out of which arises the consciousness of all forms.

3. From the *definite*, no longer merely *sensuous-power of imagination*, from which must be derived consciousness of unity, and with it the power of calculation and arithmetic.

I thought, then, that the art of educating our race must be joined to the first and simplest results of these three primary powers—sound, form, and number; and that instruction in separate parts can never have a satisfactory effect upon our nature as a whole, if these three simple results of our primary powers are not recognised as the common starting-point of all instruction, determined by Nature herself. In consequence of this recognition, they must be fitted into forms which flow universally and harmoniously from the results of these three elementary powers, and which tend, essentially and surely, to make all instruction a steady, unbroken development of these three elementary powers, used together and considered equally important. In this way only, is it possible to lead us in all three branches, from vague to precise sense-impressions, from precise sense-impressions to clear images, and from clear images to distinct ideas.

Here at last, I find the Art in general and essential harmony with Nature, or rather, with the prototype by which Nature makes clear to us the objects of the world, in their essence, and utmost simplicity. The problem is solved: *How to find a common **basis** of all methods and arts of instruction, and with it a form by which the development of our race might be decided through the essence of our own very* *nature.* The difficulties are removed of applying *mechanical laws*, which I recognised as the foundation of all human instruction, to the *form of instruction* which the experience of ages has put into the hands of mankind for the development of the race; that is, to apply them to reading, writing, arithmetic, and so on.

VII.

The first elementary means of instruction is, then,

Sound.

This leads to the following special means of instruction :—

    I. *Sound teaching*,[1] or training the organs of speech.

    II. *Word teaching*, or teaching about single objects.

    III. *Language teaching*, or the means whereby we are led to express ourselves accurately about well known objects, and about all we know of them.

I. Sound Teaching

Is divided into teaching sounds spoken, and sounds sung.

Of Sounds Spoken.

In regard to these, we cannot leave it to chance whether they be brought to the child's ear sooner or later, combined or separately. It is important that they reach his consciousness in their whole compass as early as possible.

This consciousness should be perfect in him before his power of speech is formed; and the power of repeating them easily should be complete before the forms of letters are put before his eyes, or the first reading lessons begun.

The Spelling Book[2] must therefore contain all the sounds of which speech consists, and these should, in every family, be brought to the ear of the child in the cradle, be deeply impressed and made unforgetable by constant repetition,[3] even before he is able to utter a single one.

No one can imagine, for it is not seen, how the utterance of these simple sounds, *ba ba ba, da da da, ma ma ma, la la la,* etc., may rouse the observation of infants and please them ; nor what can be gained for the general power of learning in children, by the early knowledge of these sounds.

* In consequence of this principle of the importance of consciousness of sounds and tones before the child can imitate them, and of the conviction that the kind of objects and pictures that lie before the eyes of the infant can be as little a matter of indifference, as the sounds that are brought to his ears, I have prepared a book for mothers, in which I have, not only represented by illuminated woodcuts the beginnings of number and form, but also the other most essential characteristics in objects, which our five senses make evident to us. Through a knowledge of many names, thus strengthened and enlivened by all sorts of observation, I prepare for and make his future reading easy, just as, by making impressions of sounds precede letters, I prepare for, and make this work easy for the child, at this same age. By means of this book I make these sounds at home in his head, if I may so express myself, before he can utter a syllable.

I will accompany these tables of sense-impression for earlier childhood, with a book of methods, in which every word that the child should use about the object represented, is expressed so exactly that even the most unpractised mother can work sufficiently for my purpose, because she need not add a word to what I say.

Thus, by means of the book prepared for mothers, and by constantly hearing the sounds in the Spelling Book, the

* These attempts were afterwards found to be superfluous, owing to a deeper knowledge of the psychological course of development and the gradation in the foundation of our knowledge, and were no longer used. This whole statement must be regarded as only a vague aspiration towards methods of education, about the nature of which I was far from clear.—*Pestalozzi.*

child, as soon as his organs of speech are formed, must be accustomed to imitate a few of the sounds of the Spelling Book, several times a day, with just the same playful ease, with which he imitates purposeless sounds.

This book differs from all preceding books in this:—Its form of teaching proceeds generally from the vowels, which can be apprehended by the pupil himself. Adding consonants one by one, before and after the syllables, evidently makes the art of reading and pronouncing more easy.

This was our way. After every vowel we added on one consonant after another, from *b* to *z*, and so first formed the simple easy syllables, *ad ab af*, etc., then put those consonants before these simple syllables which actually accompany them in ordinary speech.

For example—

$$ab, \ b, \ g, \ sh, \ st, \qquad \begin{array}{l} b, \ \ ab, \\ g, \ \ ab, \\ sh, \ ab, \\ st, \ \ ab, \ etc. \end{array}$$

So we formed first easy syllables, by simply adding consonants to all the vowels, and afterwards more difficult words, by the addition of more syllables. This ensures a constant repetition of simple sounds, and an orderly putting together of syllables resembling each other, from having a common basis. This gives an unforgetable impression of their sound, and makes learning to read very easy.

The special advantages of this book are—

1. The children are kept so long at exercises in spelling syllables, that their faculties are sufficiently formed in this direction.

2. That by the use of similar sounds, the repetition of the same form is made pleasant to the children, and in this way, the object of making an indelible impression is more easily attained.

3. That it helps the children very quickly to pronounce at a glance any new word that is formed, by adding single consonants to others that are well known, without being obliged to spell it; and afterwards to be able to learn to spell these compound words by heart. This makes writing them correctly afterwards very easy.

In the short directions for using this book given in the preface, mothers are asked to pronounce to the children before they can speak, these sequences of sounds several times every day, and in different ways, in order to rouse their observation, and to accustom them to these sounds. This pronouncing must be carried on with redoubled zeal, and be begun again from the beginning, as soon as the children begin to talk, in order to induce them to imitate, and thereby teach them to talk quickly.

In order to make the knowledge of letters, which must precede spelling, easy to the children, I have added large printed letters to the book, so that the children can better observe the differences between them.

These letters are, each one separately, glued upon stiff paper, and given to the child one by one, We begin with the different vowels, painted red, which they must know perfectly, and be able to pronounce, before we can go farther. Afterwards they are shown the consonants one by one, but always in connection with a vowel, because they cannot be pronounced alone.

As soon as the children, partly by means of these special exercises, partly by means of real spelling (of which I will speak directly) have begun to be tolerably acquainted with the letters, we can change them for the threefold letters, also accompanying this book, on which, over the German printed letters (that may now be smaller) stand German, written letters, and under them Roman letters. Then let the child spell every syllable with the middle form already known to him, and repeat it in the other two; so without losing time he learns to read the threefold alphabet.

The fundamental rule of spelling is that all syllables are only additions, by means of consonants, to the original sound of a vowel; and that the vowel is always the foundation of the syllable. This vowel also will be first laid down, or put on the hanging board (which should have a groove on its upper and lower edge for the letters to stand in, and in which they can easily be shifted about). This vowel will, according to the guide, gradually have consonants added before and after *a—ab—b ab—g ab*, and so on. Then every syllable should be pronounced by the teacher and repeated by the children, until they cannot forget it. Then the letters are repeated in and out of their order (the first, the third, and so on), then syllables, which are hidden from them, are spelt by heart.

It is particularly necessary, in the first paragraphs of the book, to proceed very slowly, and never to go on to anything new, until the old is indelibly impressed upon the children because this is the foundation of all instruction in reading; all that follows is built upon it by small and gradual additions.

When the children have reached a certain readiness in spelling in this manner, we can change it for other methods. For example, we can put the letters of a word one after the other until it is complete, and let each of the letters be spoken alone and together with the next, *e.g., G—Ga—Gar—Gard—Garde—Garden—Gardene—Gardener.* Then, by taking away the letters one by one, go back in the same way, and repeat these again and again, until the children can spell the word perfectly by heart. We can, in this way, spell the word backwards.

At last the word is divided into syllables, and each is pronounced in and out of its order according to its number. One special advantage for school instruction is that the children may be accustomed *from the beginning* to pronounce, all together, and at the same moment, every sound that is given them, or that which they are called upon to pronounce by the number of the letter or syllable, so that sounds uttered by all are heard as one sound. This makes the art of teaching quite mechanical, and works with incredible force upon the children's senses.

When these spelling exercises on the board are quite finished, the book can be put into the child's hands as his first reading book and used till he can read perfectly easily in it.

So much for teaching sounds spoken. I shall now say a word about teaching singing sounds. But since song proper cannot be regarded as a means of rising from vague sense impressions to clear ideas, but rather as a faculty that must be developed at another time, and for another purpose, I will put off treating it till I take a bird's-eye view of education. I shall only say here, that, according to the general principle, the teaching of singing should begin with the simplest; complete this, and only gradually proceed from one complete step to the beginning of a new exercise; and it should never tend through an unfounded belief in the stability of the foundation, to check or confuse the faculties.[4]

II.

The second special means of instruction flowing from the power of making sounds, or the elementary method of sound, is

WORD OR RATHER NAME-TEACHING.

I have already said, the child must receive his first guidance in this direction, from the *Mother's Book.*[5] This is so arranged, that the most important objects of the world, especially those which, like *race*, and *kind*, include a whole series of objects, should be all spoken about, and mothers made able to make the child quite familiar with their right names, so that the children are prepared, from the earliest age, for *name-teaching;* that is, for the second special method of instruction, founded upon the power of making sounds.

This name-teaching consists of lists of names of the most important objects in all divisions of the kingdom of nature, history, geography, human callings and relations. These lists of words are given to the child simply as exercises in reading, immediately after the completion of his Spelling Book; and experience has shown me, that it is possible to bring the children to learn these lists of names perfectly by heart, in the time which is given to complete their power of reading. The gain to the children at this time, of so wide and complete a knowledge of so many and such comprehensive lists of names, is immense for making later instruction easier, [and is only to be regarded as the chaotic collection of materials for a house that will be built later.]

III.

The third special means of instruction, based on the power of making sounds, is

LANGUAGE-TEACHING PROPER.

And here I arrive at the point at which the special form begins to disclose itself, according to which the Art, by using the special characteristic of our race, language, can keep pace with the course of Nature, in our development. But what do I say? The form discloses itself, by which man, according to the will of the Creator, should take the instruction of our race out of the hands of blind and senseless Nature, and put it into the guidance of those better powers, which he has developed in himself for ages. The form discloses itself, independent, like the human race, by which man can give a precise and comprehensive direction to, and hasten the development of, these faculties, for whose development Nature has given him powers and means, but no guidance. This she can never give, because he is man. The form unfolds itself by which man can do all this, without destroying the loftiness and simplicity of the course of physical nature, or the harmony our physical development always has, or robbing ourselves, by a single fraction of a hair, of that uniform care that mother Nature confers upon our physical development.

All this must be aimed at through the perfect art of language-teaching, and the highest psychology, in order to bring the mechanism of nature's march from confused sense-impressions to clear ideas, to the greatest perfection. This I am far from being able to do, and I feel verily like the voice of one crying in the wilderness.

But the Egyptian who first bound the bent shovel to the horns of the ox, and so taught it the work of the digger, led the way to the discovery of the plough, though he did not bring it to perfection.

Let my merit be only the bending the shovel, and binding it to a new horn. But why do I speak in parables? I will say what I want to say straight out, without beating about the bush.

I would take school instruction out of the hands of the old order of decrepit, stammering, journeymen-teachers, as well as from the new weak ones, who are generally no better for popular instruction, and entrust it to the undivided powers of Nature herself, to the light that God kindles and ever keeps alive in the hearts of fathers and mothers, to the interest of parents who desire that their children should grow up in favour with God and man.

H

But in order to define the form, or rather, the different methods of teaching language by which we can attain to this purpose, that is, by which we must be led, in order to be able to express ourselves clearly about objects that are becoming known to us, and all that we can learn about them, we must ask ourselves:—

1. What is the end of language for man?
2. What are the means, or rather, what is the course of progress by which nature leads us to this end, by the gradual development of the art of speaking?

1. The final end of language is obviously to lead our race from vague sense-impressions to clear ideas.
2. The means, by which it leads us gradually towards this end, unquestionably follow in this order:—
   a. We recognize every object as a whole, or generally; name it as a unit—*i.e.* as one object.
   b. We gradually become acquainted with its characteristics and learn to name them.
   c. We acquire, through language, the power of defining the qualities of things by verbs and adverbs, and to make the changes, caused by change of condition, clear to ourselves, by altering the words themselves and their arrangement.

I. I have spoken above of the steps to be taken to learn to name objects.
II. Steps to learn and to name the qualities of objects divide themselves into—
   a. Teaching the child to express himself clearly about number and form. Number and form, being the special elementary properties of all things, are the two comprehensive general abstractions of physical nature, on which all other means of making our ideas clear depend.

b. Teaching the child to express himself exactly about all the other qualities of things, besides form and number (about those that we know through our five senses as well as those that we learn, not by simple sense-impression, but through our powers of imagination and judgment).

The primary physical generalizations, number and form, that we have in accordance with the experience of ages, by using our five senses, learned to abstract from the qualities of things, must be early and familiarly brought to the child, not only as inherent characteristics of special things, but as physical generalizations. He must not only be able early to call a round or square thing, round or square, but he must, as soon as possible, be impressed with the idea of roundness or squareness as a unity, as a pure abstraction. This will enable him to connect all that he meets in nature round, square, simple, or complex, with the exact word that expresses this idea. Here also we see the reason why language must be considered as a means of expressing form and number, as distinguished from the way in which we may regard it as a means of expressing all the other qualities of objects, that Nature teaches us through our five senses.

I therefore begin, in the book for early childhood, to lead the children to a clear consciousness of these generalizations. This book contains a comprehensive survey of the ordinary methods, as well as the simplest way, of making the child understand the first properties of numbers.

Farther steps towards this end must, like the language-exercises, be reserved for a later time, and be connected with the special treatment of number and form. These, as elements of our knowledge, must be considered after a complete survey of the exercises in language.

The illustrations of the first instruction-book, the Mother's

Book for infants, are in all their variety, so chosen, that all kinds of physical generalizations that are learnt through our five senses, are spoken of, and mothers are enabled to make the child familiarly acquainted with the most exact expressions, without any trouble to themselves.

But in whatever relates to those qualities of things that are learnt not directly through our five senses, but through the intervention of our powers of comparison, imagination, and abstraction, I stick to my principle, of making no kind of human judgment apparently prematurely ripe ; but I use the unavoidable knowledge of such abstract words, as children of this age possess, merely as memory work, and as easy food for their fancy and power of guessing.

On the other hand, in respect to objects that can be learnt directly through our five senses, I take the following measures to enable the child to express himself accurately as soon as possible.

I take substantives distinguished by striking characteristics, known through our five senses, out of the dictionary and put the adjectives that express these characteristics next to them.　For example :—

Eel,　　slippery, worm-like, leather-skinned.
Carrion,　dead, stinking.
Evening,　quiet, bright, cool, rainy.
Axle,　　strong, weak, greasy.
Field,　　sandy, loamy, manured, fertile, profitable, unprofitable.

Then I invert the process, and find adjectives that describe the striking characteristics of objects, learnt through our senses ; then I put the substantive that has the characteristic described by the adjective next to it.　For example :—

Round,　ball, hat, moon, sun.
Light,　feather, down, air.
Heavy,　gold, lead, oak-wood.

Warm, stoves, summer days, flame.

High,   towers, mountains, trees, giants.

Deep,   seas, lakes, cellars, graves.

Soft,   flesh, wax, butter.

Elastic, steel springs, whalebone, etc.

I try, however, in no way to lessen the free play of the child's individual thought by the completeness of these illustrations, but only give a few illustrative facts that strike his mind, and ask directly : * "What else do you know like this ? " In most cases, the children find new facts within the sphere of their experience, and very often some that would not occur to the teacher. In this way the circle of their knowledge is made wider and more exact, than it could ever be through catechizing, or at least only by a hundredfold more skill and trouble.

In all catechising the child is fettered, partly by the limits of the precise idea about which he is catechized, partly by the form in which he is catechized, and lastly, but certainly, by the limits of the teacher's knowledge, and still more by the teacher's anxious care that he should not be drawn beyond the circle of his knowledge. Friend ! what terrible barriers for the child, that have been wholly removed by my method.

This done, I try to make the child, who is in many ways acquainted with objects of the world, still more clear about the objects so far known to him, by the further use of the dictionary.

For this purpose I divide this great witness of a former age under four headings.

    1. Descriptive Geography.

    2. History.

    3. Physical science.

    4. Natural history.

* This question is repeated in Ed. I.

But to avoid unnecessary repetition of the same word, and to make the form of teaching as short as possible, I divide these principal sections into forty sub-divisions, and show the children the names of objects in these sub-divisions only.

Then I consider the principal object of my sense-impression, myself, or rather the whole series of names that indicate myself in language; while I bring what the great witness of the ancients, language, says about men, under the following heads.

First head :—

What does it say of man, regarded as a *mere physical being*, in relation to the animal kingdom?

Second head :—

What does it say of him, as striving upwards through *the social state* to independence?

Third head :—

What does it say of him as struggling upwards, through the forces of his heart, mind, and skill, to a view of himself and his surroundings higher than the animal's? [6]

I divide these three heads into forty sub-divisions, and only bring them before the children in these sub-divisions.*

The first arrangement in these series, in both departments, about men, as well as material objects, should be simply alphabetical, without any meaning. They are to be used simply for making things gradually clear, by putting similar sense-impressions, and ideas gained by sense-impressions, together.

When this is done, when the witness of the ancients has been thus used to put all that exists into simple alphabetical order, the second question arises,—

How does the Art arrange these objects later, after closer inspection? Then a new work begins. The same series

* All these attempts were subsequently abandoned as the results of immature opinions.—P.

of words that the child knows perfectly well up to the seventieth or eightieth row, merely alphabetically, must now be shown him anew, in all these sub-divisions, and in all the classifications by which these subdivisions are further artificially divided, and he must be enabled to form sequences for himself, and to arrange them after the following plan.

The different classes, into which the objects are divided, are put at the head of each column, and indicated by numbers, abbreviations, or other convenient signs.

In the first reading lesson, the child must thoroughly learn the different classes of the principal divisions, and then, if he finds in the series of words the sign of the class to which it belongs, he is able at the first glance to see to which class the object belongs, and so, by himself, to change the alphabetical into a scientific nomenclature.

I do not know whether it is necessary to make the matter clearer by an example; it seems almost superfluous; but I will do it in consequence of the novelty of the form. One of the sub-divisions of Europe is Germany. Now the children are first made perfectly familiar with the division of Germany into 10 circles. Then the towns of Germany are first put before them, in reading, in alphabetical order; but afterwards every town is indicated by the number of the circle to which it belongs. As soon as they can readily read these towns, they learn the connection between these numbers and the sub-divisions of the chief headings, and, in a few hours the child is able to arrange the whole series of German towns according to the sub-divisions of the principal headings.

When, for example, he sees the following German towns with their numbers :—

Aachen, 8.	Acken, 10.	Aigremont, 8.
Aalen, 3.	Adersbach, 11.	Ala, 1.
Abenberg, 4.	Agler, 1.	Allenbach, 5.
Aberthran, 11.	Ahrbergen, 10.	Allendorf, 5.

Allersperg, 2.	Altenburg, 9.	Alkerdissen, 8.
Alschaufen, 3.	Altensalza, 10.	Amberg, 2.
Alsleben, 10.	Altkirchen, 8.	Ambras,1.
Altbunzlau, 11.	Altona, 10.	Amöneburg, 6.
Altena, 8.	Altorf, 1.	Andernach, 6,
Altenau, 10.	Altranstädt, 9.	
Altenberg, 9.	Altwasser, 13.	

he uses them in the following way.

Aachen is in the Westphalian circle. Abenberg in the Franconian circle. Acken in the Lower Saxon circle, etc.

So the child is enabled, at the first glance at the number or sign which belongs to the heading, to determine to what class every word of this series belongs and, as I said, to turn the alphabetical into a scientific nomenclature.

And here I find myself on the boundary where my own work ends, and where the powers of my children should have reached a point when they should be able in any kind of knowledge to which their inclination leads them, to use, independently, such helps as already exist; but which are of such a nature, that until now, only a privileged few could use them. *So far, and no further* do I wish to come. I did not and do not wish to teach the world art and science; I know none. 1 did and do wish to make the learning of the first beginning-points easy for the common people, who are forsaken and left to run wild; to open the doors of art, which are the doors of manliness, to the poor and weak of the land; and if I can, to set fire to the barrier that keeps the humbler citizens of Europe, in respect to that individual power which is the foundation of all true art, far behind the barbarians of the south and north, because, in the midst of our vaunted and valued general enlightenment, it shuts out one man in ten from the social rights of men, from the right to be educated, or at least from the possibility of using that right.

May this barrier burn above my grave in blazing flames. Now indeed I know that I only lay a weak coal in dank wet straw—but I see a wind, no longer afar off, and it will fan the coal; gradually the wet straw round me will be dried, will become warm, will kindle and burn. Yes, Gessner! however wet it is now round me, it will burn, it will burn!

But while I see myself so far advanced in the second special method of teaching language, I find I have not yet touched upon the third method, that should lead to the final end of education—the clearing-up of our ideas.

> c. Teaching the child to distinguish clearly by speech, the connection of objects with each other, in their varying conditions of number, time, and proportion; or rather to make still clearer the nature, properties, and powers of all objects that we have already learned to know by name, and have, to some degree, made clear by putting together their names and qualities.

Here the foundations on which real grammar should rest, appear, and in this way progress will be made towards the final end of education—the clearing up of ideas.

Here also I prepare the children for the first step by a very simple but psychological instruction in speech. Without letting fall a word about forms and rules, let the mother first repeat before the child simple sentences only, as exercises. These should be imitated, as much for the sake of exercising the organs of speech, as for the sake of the sentences themselves. We must clearly distinguish between these two objects—exercise in pronunciation, and learning words as language; and practise the first by itself, independently of the second. When the meaning and pronunciation are understood, the mother should repeat the following kinds of sentences :—

Father is kind.
The butterfly has gay wings.
The cow eats grass.
The fir has a straight stem.

When the child has said these sentences so often that the repetition is easy to him, the mother asks: Who is kind? What has gay wings? And then backwards: What is father? What has the butterfly? etc.

And then she goes on :—

Who or what are?
Beasts of prey are flesh-eating.
Stags are light of foot.
The roots are wide-spreading.

Who or what has ?   What has he or it ?
The lion has strength.
Man has reason.
The dog has a good nose.
The elephant has a trunk.

Who or what have?   What have they?
Plants have roots.
Fish have fins.
Birds have wings.
Cattle have horns.

Who wishes?   What does he wish?
The hungry man wishes to eat.
The creditor wishes to be paid.
The prisoner wishes to be free.

Who wish?   What do they wish?
Sensible people wish for what is right.
Foolish people wish for what they fancy.
Children wish to play.
Tired people wish to rest.

Who or what can?   What can he or it do?

The fish can swim.
The bird can fly.
The cat can climb.
The squirrel can jump.
The ox can toss.
The horse can kick.

Who can?   What can they do?

Tailors can sew.
Donkeys can carry.
Oxen can plough.
Pigs can grunt.
Men can talk.
Dogs can bark.
Lions can roar.
Bears can growl.
Larks can sing.

Who or what must be?   What must they be?

The draught-ox must be harnessed.
The horse must be ridden.
The ass must be loaded.
The cow must be milked.
The pig must be killed.
The hare must be hunted.
The right must be done.
Laws must be obeyed.

Who or what must do?   What must they do?

Raindrops must fall.
Fettered men must go together.
The vanquished must submit.
Debtors must pay.

Thus I go on through all the declensions and conjugations,

connecting this second step immediately with the first, and particularly dwelling upon the verbs, according to a plan of which I gave the following examples.

Verb and object simply connected.

Attend   to the teacher's words.

Breathe through the lungs.

Fell   a tree.

Bind   a sheaf, etc.

Then follows the second exercise in putting verbs together.

To tend. I *tend* the sheep. I *attend* to the teacher's words, to my duty and my property; *I *attend* to my duty and my work. I *contend* against wrong. I do not *pretend* to be better than I am. I *extend* my possessions. I *intend* to buy a house. I must *superintend* those men. So far as a child pays *attention* to anything, he is *attentive* or *inattentive.*

Breathe. I breathe hard, lightly, quickly, slowly. I breathe again, if I have lost my breath and recovered it. I breathe air in. The dying man breathes his last.

Then I go on and repeat these exercises with gradually extending additions, and so get to more complicated and descriptive sentences, *e.g.*—

I shall.

I shall preserve.

I shall preserve my health in no other way.

After all that I have suffered I shall preserve my health in no other way.

After all that I suffered in my illness, I shall preserve my health in no other way.

After all that I suffered in my illness, I shall preserve my health in no other way than by moderation.

* Literal translation impossible; an illustration is attempted. L. E. H.

After all that I have suffered in my illness, I shall preserve my health in no other way than by the greatest moderation.

After all that I have suffered in my illness, I shall preserve my health in no other way than by the greatest moderation and regularity.

After all that I suffered in my illness, I shall preserve my health in no other way than by the greatest moderation and general regularity.

All these sentences should be separately repeated in all the persons of the verb, *e.g.*—

I shall preserve.

Thou shalt preserve.

He shall preserve, etc.

I shall preserve my health.

Thou shalt preserve thy health, etc.

The same sentences should be repeated in other tenses.

I have preserved.

Thou hast preserved, etc.

With these sentences, thus deeply impressed upon the children, we take care to choose those that are particularly instructive, stimulating and suitable to their special case.

With these I give examples of descriptions of real objects, in order to strengthen and use the power given to the children by these exercises.

For example—

A bell is a wide, thick, round bowl, open below, usually hanging free, growing narrower towards the top, rounded above like an egg, and having in the middle a vertical and freely hanging clapper, that by a quick movement of the bowl is knocked from side to side, thus producing a sound we call ringing.

To walk is to move on step by step.

To stand is to rest upon the legs, with the body upright or vertical.

To lie is to rest on something, with the body in a horizontal position.

To sit is to rest on something, in such a position that the body makes two angles.

To kneel is to rest on the legs when they form an angle at the knee.

To courtesy is to let the body be lowered by bending the knee.

To bow is to bend the body forwards from an upright position.

To climb is to move up or down by clinging with the hands and feet.

To ride is to be carried sitting upon on animal.

To drive is to be carried in a moving vehicle.

To fall is to be forced to move from above downwards by one's own weight.[7]

To dig is to lift earth and turn it over with a spade.

I should like to conclude these exercises in language with a legacy[8] to my pupils, after my death. In this I put down as they occur to me, significant verbs which, at the most critical moments of my life, especially attract my attention to the subjects which they indicate. By this exercise I try to connect these verbs with truths about life, living knowledge gained by sense-impression, and soul-inspiring thoughts about all that men do and suffer, *e.g.*—[9]

To breathe. Man! thy life hangs upon a breath. When thou snortest like a madman, and swallowest the pure air of earth like poison into thy lungs—what dost thou but hasten to make thyself breathless and to deliver from thy snorting the men annoyed by it.

To improve the soil. In order to improve the soil, the earth was divided. Thus property arose, the right to which is only to be found in this purpose, and can never be opposed to it. But if the State allows to the proprietor or itself, an oppressive power over human nature, in opposition to this purpose, feelings are developed in the injured masses, the bad consequences of which can only be averted by a wise return to the spirit of the original limitations of the purpose, for the sake of which the earth, freely given by God to man, was divided by him into special plots.[10]

To express. Thou art angry because thou canst not always express thyself as thou wouldst. Do not be angry that thou art forced, even against thy will, to take time to become wise.

But it is time I ended this subject.

I have dwelt long upon language as a means of gradually making our ideas clear. It is indeed the first means. My method of instruction is particularly distinguished in this:—it makes greater use of language as a means of raising the child from vague sense-impressions to clear ideas, than has ever been done before. Also it is distinguished by the principle of excluding all collections of words, presupposing actual knowledge of language or grammar, from the first elementary instruction.

Whoever understands that Nature only leads from clearness about the individual to clearness about the whole, will understand that words must be separately clear to the child, before they can be made clear to him when joined together. Whoever understands this, will throw away at once all previous elementary instruction-books, as such, because they all presuppose knowledge of language in the child before they have given it him. Yes, Gessner, it is remarkable, even the best instruction-book of the past century has forgotten that the child must learn to talk before we can talk with him; this oversight is remarkable, but it is true. Since I know this, I no longer wonder that we cannot make other men out of the children than we do; for we have so far forgotten the wisdom and goodness of the ancients as to talk to them [of so many and such various things] before they can talk.   Language is an art—it is an infinite art, or rather it is the sum total of all arts, which our race has reached.   It is in a special sense, a giving-back of all impressions that Nature, as a whole, has made upon our race.   Thus I use it, and try by the associations of its spoken sounds to bring back to the child the very same impressions, which these sounds formed and gave rise to in the human race.   The gift of speech is infinite in itself, and becomes daily greater as it ever grows more perfect.   It gives the child in a short time, what Nature needed ages to give to mankind.   We say of an ox, what would he be if he knew his strength? and I say of man, what would he be if he [wholly] knew his power of speech and [wholly] used it?

The gap is great that has arisen in the maze, which we call human culture, because we have so far forgotten ourselves that we have not only done nothing to teach[11] humble folk to talk, but have made the speechless people dream their time away on abstract ideas, and while we made them learn empty words by heart, we have taught them to believe that they could reach real knowledge of things, and truth, in this way.

Verily the Indians could do no more to keep [12] their lowest classes of people in everlasting idolatry, and in that way, to breed a degraded race of men as sacrifices to their idols.

You may dispute the fact [that our lowest classes cannot speak, and are led astray by their apparent ability to speak]; I appeal to all clergy, magistrates, to all men who live among people who are oppressed in the midst of entire neglect, by such a terribly distorted paternal, sham-careful method, of teaching to speak.   Let him who lives among such people come forward and bear witness, if he has not experienced how troublesome it is to get any idea into the poor creatures. But every one agrees about this.   "Yes, yes,"[13] say the clergy, "it is so; when they come to us to be taught, they do not understand what we say, nor we what they answer, and we get on no farther with them until they have learnt the answers to our questions by heart." So say the magistrates; and they are right enough; it is impossible to make their justice comprehensible to these men. When they come out of a village, town-babblers are amazed at the want of speech of these people, and say, "We must have them in the house for years, before they even begin to understand orders given by word of mouth." Talkative town-folk who have learned to talk and chatter a bit behind the counter, think the most clever and sensible of these people, stupid though they may be, far more stupid than they really are. Good-for-noughts of every shade call out, each with his own grimace, "Lucky for us that it is so, trade would be worse if things were different."

Friend! men of business and all kinds of people, who have much to do with the lower classes in the country, for the sake of body and soul, express themselves alike on this subject. I might almost say, the people of rank in our High Comedy Theatre, speak thus in their boxes and stalls, about the condition of the people in the pit. They cannot help speaking so, because the people in the pit are, to a great degree, neglected in this respect. We cannot hide from ourselves that the lowest Christian people of our continent must in many places, sink into these depths, because we, in its lower schools, for more than a century, have given to empty words a weight in the human mind, that not only hindered attention to the impressions of nature, but even destroyed man's inner susceptibility to these impressions. I say again —while we do this, and degrade the lower class of Europe into "word and clapper folk," [14] as hardly any people have been degraded before, *we never teach them to talk.* It is, therefore, not surprising, that the Christianity of this century and this continent looks as it does. On the contrary, it is wonderful that good human nature, in spite of all the blundering of our "word and clapper" schools, has preserved so much inward strength as we often meet with in the lowest classes of the people. But, thank God! all follies and all apings find at last a counterpoise in human nature itself, and cease to be further harmful to our race when error has reached the highest point that we can bear. Folly and error carry in every garment the seeds of their decay and death, truth alone, in every form, bears the seeds of eternal life in itself.[15]

The second elementary means from which all human knowledge according to the nature of instruction must proceed, is

FORM.

The teaching of form is preceded by the consciousness of the sense-impression of things having form, the artificial representations of which, for the purpose of instruction, must be derived partly from the nature of the observing powers, and partly from the definite aim of teaching itself.

All our knowledge arises :—

1. From impressions made by everything that accident brings into contact with our five senses. This kind of sense-impression is irregular, confused, and has a very slow and limited scope.

2. From all that is brought to our senses through the interposition of the Art, and guidance of our parents and teachers. This kind of sense-impression is naturally more or less psychologically arranged, according to the degree of insight and energy of the parents and teachers [of each child], and is also more comprehensive and connected. His progress also, towards the end and aim of instruction, *clear ideas*, is in the same degree more or less rapid and safe.

3. From my will, [based on, and kept alive by the self-

activity of all my faculties] ; from my strong desire to obtain notions, knowledge and ability ; and from spontaneous efforts towards gaining sense-impressions. This kind of knowledge gained by sense-impression gives intrinsic value to our notions and brings us nearer to moral self-active education, by forming in us an independent vitality for the results of our sense-impressions.

4. From the results of effort, work at one's calling, and all kinds of activity, the object of which is not merely sense-impression. This manner of gaining knowledge connects my sense-impressions with my conditions and position, and brings the results into harmony with my efforts towards duty and virtue. It has, through the necessity of its course, as well as through its results, the most important influence on the accuracy, continuity, and harmony of my insight, as well as on the purpose aimed at—*making ideas clear.*

5. Lastly, by analogy. Knowledge gained by sense-impression teaches me the properties of things that have not been brought to my sense-impression, by their likeness to other objects that I have observed. This mode of observation (*Ansch.*) changes my advance in knowledge, which as the result of actual sense-impression, is only the work of my senses, into the work of my mind and all its powers; and I have, therefore, as many kinds of sense-impression as I have powers of mind. But now "sense-impression" has a wider meaning than in common speech. It includes the whole series of feelings that are inseparable from the very nature of my mind.[16]

It is important to learn the difference between these two

kinds of sense-impressions, in order to abstract the laws that
are proper to each.

Meanwhile, I return to my path.

From the consciousness of my sense-impression of the form
of things, arises the art of measuring. This, however, rests
immediately upon the *art of sense-impression (or Anschauung)*,
which must be differentiated from the simple power of
gaining knowledge, as well as from the simple kind of
sense-impression. All divisions for measurement and their
results are derived from these cultivated sense-impressions.
But even this art of sense-impression leads us, through comparison of objects, beyond the rules of the art of measurement, to free imitations of these proportions, that is, to the
art of *drawing*. Lastly we use the power given by the art
of drawing in the art of *writing*.

THE ART OF MEASURING

Presupposes an A B C of form (A B C of Anschauung),
that is to say, it presupposes an art of simplifying and
defining the principles of measurement by exact separation
of all inequalities that appear to the observer.

Dear Gessner, I will again call your attention to the empirical course that led me to this view of the subject; and
for this purpose, will add an extract from a passage in my
Report.[17] " Grant the principle," said I, " that sense-impression is the foundation of all knowledge, it follows inevitably, that accuracy of sense-impression is the foundation of
accurate judgment.

" But it is obvious, that in art education perfect accuracy
of observation must be a result of measuring the object to be
judged [or imitated], or of a power of perceiving proportion,
so far cultivated as to render measurement of the object
superfluous. Thus the capacity of measuring correctly,
ranks, in the art-education of our race, immediately after the

need of observation (*Ansch.*). Drawing is a linear definition of the form, of which the outline and surface are rightly and exactly defined, by complete measurement.

"The principle, that the exercise and capacity of measuring everything, must precede exercises in drawing, or, at least keep equal pace with them, is as obvious as it is generally overlooked. The usual course of our art-education is to begin with inaccurate observation and crooked structures, then to pull down and build up again crookedly ten times over, until at last, and late, the feeling of proportion is matured. Then we come, at last, to that which we should have begun with, *measurement.*[18] That is our art-course. Yet we are so many thousand years older than the Egyptians, and Etruscans, whose drawings all depend on perfect measurement, or are at bottom nothing but [simple statements of] such measurements.

"And now comes the question:—What means have we of educating the child in this foundation of all art, correct measurement of all objects that come before his eyes? Obviously by a series of measuring sub-divisions of the square, which are arranged according to simple, safe, and clear rules, and include the sum total of all possible sense-impressions.*

"True, the modern artists, in spite of the want of such measurements, have by long practice in their craft, *acquired* methods by which they have attained more or less ability in placing any object before their eyes and drawing it, as it really is in nature. It cannot be denied that many of them attained this power by toilsome and long-continued efforts. By the most confused sense-impressions, they reached a sense

* Remark for the new edition. This passage is, like many another, the expression of immature, unformed opinion of the first empirical inquiry, of an idea of elementary education only mistily conceived as a whole, and now only so far interesting as it shows the first empirical course that this idea took in myself and fellow-workers.—PESTALOZZI.

of proportion, so far cultivated as to render actual measurement superfluous. But there were almost as many varieties of method as men. No one had a name for his own, because no one knew it clearly ; therefore he could not properly impart it to his pupils. The pupil also was in the same state as his teacher, and was obliged, with extreme effort and long practice, to find out a method of his own, or rather the result of a method, and to acquire a correct sense of proportion. And so art stayed in the hands of the few happy ones who had time and leisure to gain this sense by circuitous ways ; and therefore no one could look upon it as an ordinary human business, or claim its cultivation as an ordinary human right. Yet it is one ; at least he cannot be contradicted who asserts that every man living in a cultivated State, has a right to learn to read and write. Then, evidently, the wish to draw and the capacity of measuring, which are developed naturally and easily in the child (as compared to the toil with which he is taught reading and writing) must be restored to him with greater art or more force, if we would not injure him more than the reading can ever be worth. But drawing, as a help towards the end of instruction, *making ideas clear*, is essentially bound up with the measurement of forms. When a child is given an object to draw, he can never use his art as he should, that is as a means of rising through vague sense-impression to clear ideas in all his education, until he can represent the proportions of the form, and express himself about them ; nor can his art have that real value that it might and should have, were it in harmony with the great purpose of education."

Thus in order to found the art of drawing, we must subordinate it to the art of measuring, and endeavour to organize as definite measuring forms the divisions into angles and arcs that come out of the fundamental form of the square, as well as its rectilinear divisions. This has been done, and I think I have organized a series of such measuring-forms,[19] the use of which makes the learning of all measurements, and the proportions of all forms easy to understand, just as the A B C of sounds makes the learning of language easy.

* This A B C of form (A B C of Anschauung), however, is an equal division of the square into definite measure-forms, and requires an exact knowledge of its foundation—the straight line in a vertical or horizontal position.

These divisions of the square by straight lines produce certain forms for defining and measuring all angles, as well as the circle and all arcs. I call the whole the A B C of Anschauung."

This should be presented to the child in the following way.

We show him the properties of straight lines, unconnected and each by itself, under many conditions and in different arbitrary directions, and make him clearly conscious of the different appearances, without considering their further uses. Then we begin to name the straight lines as horizontal, vertical, and oblique; describing the oblique lines first

---

* I must here remark that the A B C of Anschauung appears to be the only essential and true method of instruction for the just appreciation of the forms of things. But until now, this method has been entirely neglected and ignored, though we have a hundred such methods for arithmetic and language. Meanwhile, the want of such a method of instruction about form, is not to be regarded only as a defect in the structure of human knowledge, but as *the* defect in the foundation of all knowledge. It seems to me a defect in knowledge, at the very point, where language and number should be subordinate to it. My A B C der Anschauung will remedy this deficiency and secure instruction a basis, on which other methods of instruction must be built. I beg the men of Germany, who feel themselves entitled to judge, to look upon this point as the foundation of my method. The value or worthlessness of my attempt rests upon the rightness or wrongness of this foundation.—PESTALOZZI.

as rising or falling, then as rising or falling to right or left. Then we name the different parallels as horizontal, vertical, and oblique parallel lines; then we name the principal angles formed by joining these lines, as right, acute, obtuse. In the same way we teach them to know and name the prototype of all measure-forms, the square, which arises from joining together two angles, and its divisions into halves, quarters, sixths, and so on, then the circle and its variations, in elongated forms, and their different parts.

All these definitions should be taught to the children as results of measuring with the eye, and the measuring-forms named in this course as square, horizontal, or vertical oblong (or rectangle); the curved lines as circle, semi-circle, quadrant; first oval,[20] half-oval, quarter-oval, second, third, fourth, fifth, and so on. They must be led to use these forms as means of measuring, and to learn the nature of the proportions by which they are produced. The first means of obtaining this end is—

1. To endeavour to make the child know and name the proportions of these measure-forms.

2. To enable him to apply and use them independently.

The child will be already prepared for this purpose by the Mother's Book and many objects have been shown him that are square, round, oval, broad, long, narrow. Soon after the divisions of the A B C of Anschauung will be cut out in cardboard and shown him as quarter, half quarter, sixth of the square, and so on; and then again as circle, half and quarter circle, oval, half and quarter oval. In this way a dim consciousness will be produced beforehand, of the clear idea, that must hereafter be developed by learning the artistic appearance and the use of these forms. For this, too, they are prepared by the Mother's Book, in which the beginnings of a definite language of the forms, as well as the beginnings of number, which presupposes measurement, are given,

For this purpose they are led through the A B C of Anschauung, since the methods of this art, language and number, of which they are made dimly conscious by the Mother's
Book, are, in this A B C, made clear for the precise purpose
of measuring; and they are enabled to express themselves
clearly about number and measure in every form.

    3. The third means of attaining this end is by drawing
these forms themselves, by which the children (combining this with the other two methods) not only
gradually gain clear ideas about every form, but gain
accurate power of working with every form. In
order to attain the first end, we show them also the
proportions of the forms that are recognized in the
first course as horizontal and vertical rectangles, and
described in the second course, as *e.g.*, " the horizontal
rectangle 2 is twice as long as it is high: the vertical rectangle 2 is twice as high as it is long," and so
on through all the divisions. Here, too, the oblique
lines of several rectangles must be seen and described
by ratios for the sake of the different directions,
e.g.: horizontal rectangle, $1 \times 1\frac{1}{2}$, vertical rectangle,
$1 \times 2\frac{1}{3}$, $3\frac{1}{4}$, $1\frac{1}{6}$. For the same purpose the different
angles of the oblique lines, acute or obtuse, must be
defined as well as the divisions of the circle, and the
ovals arising from dividing the rectangle.

The power of measuring, thus developed in me by the recognition of such definite forms, raises my feeble observing
power to an art, subordinated to definite rules, from which
arises that just appreciation of all forms that I call the art
of sense-impression (or *Anschauung*). This is a new art that
should precede the usual, oldfashioned, well-known ideas of
art-culture, and serve as their general and essential foundation. By this means, every child, in the simplest way is enabled to judge rightly and express himself clearly about

every object in nature, according to its external * proportions and its relation to others. By this art-guidance he is enabled, whenever he looks at a figure, to describe and name, not only the proportion of height to breadth, but the proportion of every single deviation of its form from the square, in oblique lines and curves, and to apply the names which denote these deviations in our A B C of Anschauung. The means of attaining this power lie in the art of measuring; and will be still further developed in the child by the art of drawing, particularly the art of drawing lines. He will be brought to a point when he will be so familiar with the measure-forms, that they will become a kind of instinct. After perfecting the preliminary exercises, he need no longer put them before his eyes as an actual means of measuring the most complex objects; but without the help of [special] measurement, he can represent all their proportions, and express himself clearly about them.

We cannot say to what results the developed power may raise every child, even the weakest. No one shall say it is a dream. I have led children on these principles, and my theory is for me entirely the result of my decided experience. Any one may come and see. Certainly my children are only at the beginning of this guidance, but these beginnings show, so far, that it needs a peculiar species of man to stand near my children and not be convinced; and this is no less than extraordinary.

THE ART OF DRAWING

Is the power of representing to oneself the sense-impression made by any object, its outline and the characteristics contained within the outline, by means of similar lines, and of being able to imitate these lines accurately.

This art will become, beyond comparison, easier by the

* Ed. 1, Internal.

new method, because in every way it appears to be only an easy application of the forms that have not only been observed by the child already, but by practice in imitating, have developed in him a real power of measuring.

This is done in this way. As soon as the child draws the horizontal line, with which the A B C of Anschauung begins, readily and correctly, we try to find him, out of the whole chaos of objects seen and shown, figures whose outline is only the application of the familiar horizontal line, or at least only offers an imperceptible deviation from it.

Then we go on to the vertical line, then to the right angle, and so on. As the child, by easy application of these forms, becomes stronger, we gradually vary the figures. The results of these measures (which agree with the natural physical mechanical laws) on the art of drawing are as remarkable as those of the A B C of Anschauung upon the art of measuring. While in this way the children bring every drawing, even the first-beginning drawing, to perfection, before they proceed farther, a consciousness of the result of perfected power is developed in them, already, in the first steps of this art; and with this consciousness, an effort towards perfection and a perseverance towards completion, are also developed, which the hurly-burly caused by the folly and disorder of our unpsychological men and methods of art-education, never attempts or can attempt.

The foundation of progress, in children so taught, is not only in the hand, it is founded on the intrinsic powers of human nature. The exercise-books of measure-forms then give the sequence of means by which this effort, used with psychological art, and within physical-mechanical laws, raises the child step by step to the point on which we have already touched, when having the measure-forms actually before him becomes gradually superfluous, and when of the guiding lines in art, none remains but art itself.

THE ART OF WRITING.

Nature herself has subordinated this art to that of drawing; and all methods by which drawing is developed and brought to perfection in children, must then be naturally and specially dependent upon the art of measuring.

The art of writing can, as little as drawing, be begun and pursued without preceding developing exercises in measured lines, not only because it is a special kind of linear drawing and suffers no arbitrary deviation from the fixed direction of its forms, but also, if it is made easy to the child before drawing, it must necessarily spoil the hand (for drawing), because it stiffens it in particular directions before the universal flexibility for all the forms which drawing requires, has been sufficiently and firmly established. Still more should drawing precede writing because it makes the right forming of the letters incomparably easier, and saves the great waste of time spent in making crooked [and incorrect] forms again and again. The child enjoys this advantage in his whole education, from the very beginning of the art, he is made conscious of its power of perfection, and therefore from the first moment of learning to write, it creates the will to add nothing inharmonious, incorrect, and imperfect to the first steps already brought to a certain degree of accuracy, precision, and perfection.

Writing, like drawing, should be tried first with the slate pencil on a slate, until the child is *old enough* to make letters with a certain degree of accuracy with the pencil,—an age at which it would be extremely difficult to teach him to guide a pen.

Again, the use of the pencil before the pen in writing, and in drawing, is to be recommended, because, in any case, mistakes *can be easily erased* from the slate; while, on the contrary, one wrong word remaining on paper, often leads to a whole tribe of still worse mistakes than the first, and almost from the beginning of a line or page of writing to the end, there is a remarkable kind of progression from the mistaken deviation set up at the beginning of the line or page.

Lastly, I consider it an essential advantage of this method, that the child rubs out the perfectly good work also from the slate. No one can believe how important this is, if he does not generally know how important it is for the human race, that man should be educated without conceit, and not come to set a fictitious value on his own handywork too soon.

So I divide learning to write into two stages.

1. That in which the child becomes familiar with the forms of the letters and their combinations, independently of the use of the pen.
2. That in which his hand is practised in the use of the proper writing instrument, the pen.

In the first stage I put the letters in exact proportions before the child, and have prepared a copy-book by which the child, in harmony with this whole method and its advantages, may educate himself almost alone and without further help, in the power of writing. The advantages of this writing-book are :—

1. It dwells long enough on the beginning and fundamental forms of the letters.
2. It gradually joins the parts of the combined forms of letters to each other, so that the completion of the more difficult letters is only to be regarded as a gradual addition of new parts to the already practised beginnings of letters.
3. It exercises the child in combining several letters from the moment that he is able to copy one correctly, and he rises step by step to the combination of such words as consist simply of those letters, which he can copy correctly at that time.

4. Lastly, it has this advantage, it can be cut up into single lines, and so laid before the child, that the lines to be imitated by eye and hand, stand immediately over the letters of the copy.

In the second stage, when the child must be led to use the special writing instrument, the pen, he has already been exercised in the forms of the letters and their combinations, and is tolerably perfect. The teacher has then nothing further to do, but to complete the power of drawing these forms by the use of the pen, and make it the real art of writing.

Meanwhile the child, here too, must join on the further progress to the point up to which he has already practised. His first writing with the pen is merely his pencil progress over again, and with the first use of the pen he should begin with writing the letters just the same size as he drew them at first, and only gradually be exercised in copying the ordinary small writing.

All branches of instruction demand essentially psychological analysis of their methods, and the age should be exactly fixed at which each may, and ought to be, given to the child. As I work on this principle in all subjects, so in the art of writing, by always following it, and by using a slate pencil copy for children from four to five, I have come to the conclusion, that by this method even a bad teacher, or a very untrained mother, may be able to teach the children accurate and beautiful writing, up to a certain point without being able to do it herself. The *essential* purpose of my method here and elsewhere, is to make home instruction possible again, for people neglected in this respect, and to raise every mother, whose heart beats for her children, step by step, till at last she can follow my elementary exercises by herself, and be able to use them with her children. To do this, she need in every case be but a little step in advance of the children.

My heart beats high with the hopes to which these views ·lead me; but, dear friend, ever since I began to express any suggestion of the kind, men cry out at me from all sides, "*The mothers of this country will never do it.*" And not only men of the people, but even men who teach the people, men who teach the people Christianity, say scornfully to me, "You may run up and down our villages, you will find no mothers who will do what you ask of them." [They are quite right. It *is* so; but it *should* not be so; it *shall* not be so. Of a hundred men, who make this objection, hardly one knows why it is so, and still fewer know how to make it different.] Meanwhile I can answer these people with the utmost calmness: "*I will, with the means that are in my hand, enable heathen mothers* in the far north *to do* what I want, and if it is really true that *Christian mothers* in temperate Europe—that Christian mothers in *my fatherland* cannot be brought so far as I will bring heathen mothers in the wild north, at any time"—then I would cry out to these gentlemen who *now in this way slander* the people of our fatherland, whom they, and their fathers, have taught, instructed and guided hitherto: "You should wash your hands, and say aloud: 'We are guiltless of this monstrous barbarism of the people of temperate Europe. We are guiltless of this monstrous barbarism of the best natured, most docile of all European people, the Swiss.' Say out loud, 'We and our fathers have done what we ought to have done, to remove the unutterable misery of this barbarism from our country and our fatherland, and to prevent this unspeakable ruin of the first principles of morality and Christianity in our country and fatherland.'" I would answer the men who dare to say "Run up and down the country, *the mothers of the land* will not do it or wish to do it," and say, "You ought to cry out to these unnatural mothers of our fatherland as Christ once cried to

Jerusalem, 'Mothers! mothers! we would have gathered you together under the wings of wisdom, humanity, and Christianity, as a hen gathereth her chickens, *but ye would not.*'" If they dare do this, I will be silent and believe in their word and in their experience—and not in the mothers of the land, not in the heart that God has put into their breast. But if they dare not do this, I will not believe in them, but in the mothers of the land, and in the heart that God has put in their breast. I will declare the wretched talk, in which they throw away the people of the land as if they were the produce of a lower order of creation, a slander against the people, against nature and truth. I go on my way like a wanderer who hears the wind in a distant wold but feels it not. I go on my way for all this talk. Throughout my whole life, I have seen and known all kinds of such wordy men, wrapped up in systems and theories, *knowing nothing and caring nothing for the people;* and the individuals, who to-day slander the people in this way about this matter of education are more in this state than any others that I know. Such men think themselves upon a height, and the people far below them in the valley; but they are mistaken in both; and are like poor apes, hindered and made incapable, by the conceit of their miserable, nature, of judging rightly about the pure worth of real animal powers, or about true human talents. The brilliant polish, which these wordy men owe to their unnatural way of living, makes them incapable of understanding that they are mounted on stilts, and therefore *must come down from their miserable wooden legs,* in order to *stand as firmly as other folk, upon God's earth.* I pity them. I have heard many of these wretched wordy men say, with a mixture of nun-like innocence and rabbinical wisdom: " *What can be more beautiful for the people than the Heidelberg Catechism and the Psalter?* "—and I must take humanity into account even here, and recall to mind the causes of this error. Yes, friend! I will excuse them this error of the human mind, it has always been and will ever be so. Men are all alike, the scribes and their disciples were so too. Then I will not open my mouth again against the verbosity of their social dogmas, against the tinkling cymbals of their ceremonies, and the loveless and foolish frame of mind that they must, by their very nature, produce; but, with the greatest man who ever declared the cause of truth, of the people and of love victorious against the errors of the scribes, I will only say, "*Father, forgive them; for they know not what they do.*"

But I return. Learning to write appears to be, thirdly, a kind of learning to talk. In its nature it is only a peculiar and special exercise of this art.

As writing, considered as form, appears in my methods, in connection with measuring and drawing, and in this connection, enjoys all the advantages that are produced by the early development of these faculties, so it appears again as *a special kind of learning to talk* in connection with the very exercises, which have been used from the cradle upwards, for the development of this power.

The child enjoys just the same advantages that he has had already in the development of his speech, a faculty that has been developed and firmly fixed in him by the Mother's Book, the Spelling and the Reading Book.

A child taught by these methods, knows the spelling and first reading book almost by heart. He knows the fundamentals of orthography and language as one great whole, and when he has practised the forms of the letters, by means of the slate pencil and the first writing exercises, and is quite familiar with the individual features of the letters and their combinations, he needs for his further writing lessons *no more special copies.* He has the essence of copies in his head, by his readiness in speech and orthography; he writes

K

from his own experience, on the lines of the spelling and reading books, lists of words by which he confirms his knowledge of language, and uses his powers of memory and imagination.

The advantages of these graduated exercises in writing, connected with those used in learning to talk, are especially these :—

    1. They confirm the grammatical facility that the child already possesses, and impress its principles indelibly upon him. It must be so, since, following the direction of the reading book, in which nouns, verbs, adjectives, adverbs, etc., are arranged in separate columns, he is exercised in putting these words into their places, and so he learns to know at once, to which column any given word belongs, and to make for himself rules, which are applicable to these sequences.

    2. In the same way his power of gaining clear ideas generally is strengthened by speech (still according to the method); while as a writing-exercise, he can, with his dictionary, make lists of headings and signs of sub-divisions and some generalizations, collected by himself, on the relationships of all things.

    3. The means of gaining clear ideas by writing-exercises is confirmed, for not only is he exercised by writing, as by speaking, in *putting together* nouns, verbs and adjectives ; but by these exercises he gains independent power of discovering and adding his own knowledge or ideas to the many sequences ; the chief contents of which he has made his own in learning to talk.

For example, in the writing-exercise, he not only adds what in the reading book he has learned to call high, and pointed, but he is taught, and is pleased with the task, to think and add what objects, within his own circle of knowledge, have this form.

I give an example, which shows the children's power of discovering such illustrations.

I gave them the word *three-cornered* and they used it, with the help of a country schoolmaster, on the following examples.

Three-cornered : the triangle ; the plummet ; half a handkerchief ; the joiner's rule ; a kind of file ; the bayonet ; the prism ; the beechnut ; the scraper of an engraver ; the wound made by a leech ; the sword blade ; buckwheat seed ; the legs of the compass ; the lower part of the nose ; Good Henry's leaf* ; the spinage-leaf ; the ovary of the tulip ; the figure 4 ; and the ovary of the shepherd's purse.

They found several more three-cornered figures in tables, and windows with round panes, for which however they knew no names.

The same thing is done when they add adjectives to nouns. They add, for example, not only all the adjectives which they have learned from the reading book, to eel, carrion, evening, etc., but also those adjectives that their experience has shown them to be suitable. So, in the simplest way, by collecting the characteristics of things, they make themselves acquainted and familiar with the nature, essence, and properties of all things within their knowledge. Verbs also are treated in the same way. When, for example, they wish to explain *to observe* by adding nouns and adverbs, they will not only explain it, or support it by those which they find in the reading book, but will do as before.

The results of these exercises are far-reaching. They enable the children, from the descriptions learned by heart, *e.g.* the bell, to go, to stand, to lie, eye, ear, etc., which are fixed and general leading-strings for them, to express themselves clearly

* Chenopodium, Bonus Henricus, Goosefoot.

about every possible thing, whose form or substance they know, either by word of mouth, or by writing. But of course it must be understood, that this result is attained, not by isolated special writing-exercises, but by connecting these with the whole series of means, by which the method raises the pupils gradually to clear ideas.

This must be understood throughout the whole course of this teaching, when I say that learning to write is perfected not only as an art, but also as a calling, and that the child, in this way, may be enabled to express itself in words as easily and as naturally by this art, as by speech itself.

VIII.

The third elementary means of gaining knowledge is

NUMBER.

Now while sound and form lead us, by several subordinate methods, to the clear ideas and mental independence, which we aim at through them, arithmetic is the only means of instruction which is connected with no subordinate means. Wherever it applies it appears only as a simple result of that elementary faculty by which we make ourselves clearly conscious of the relations of more or less in all seen objects (*Ansch.*), and are enabled to represent these ratios with infinite accuracy.

Sound and form very often carry seeds of error and deception in themselves—number never. It alone leads to certain results, and if measurement makes the same claim, it can only support it by the help of arithmetic and in union with it. That is, it is sure because it calculates.

Now arithmetic is to be considered the means that aims most directly at the end of instruction, *clear ideas*, the most important of all means. It is obvious therefore, that this subject should always be pursued with special care and skill.

It is extremely important, that it should be put into such forms, as will enable us to use all the advantages afforded to instruction by deep psychology and a comprehensive know-ledge of the immutable laws of the physical mechanism.

I have, therefore, taken especial trouble to make arithmetic evident to the child's sense-impression, as the clearest result of these laws. I have not only tried to reduce its elements to that simplicity in which they appear in actual, natural sense-impressions, but also to connect, accurately and un-interruptedly, its further steps and all its variations with this simplicity of the beginning-points. I am convinced that even the extreme limits of this art can only be means of true enlightenment (that is a means of gaining clear ideas and pure insight) in so far, as they develope these in the human mind, in the same gradation, with which nature herself goes on from the first beginning-points.

ARITHMETIC

arises entirely from simply putting together and separating several units. Its basis, as I said, is essentially this. *One and one are two, and one from two leaves one.* Any number, whatever it may be, is only an abbreviation of this natural, original method of counting. But it is important, that this consciousness of the origin of relations of numbers, should not be weakened in the human mind, by the shortening ex-pedients of arithmetic. It should be deeply impressed with great care on all the ways in which this art is taught, and all the future steps should be built upon the consciousness, deeply retained in the human mind, of the real relations of things, which lie at the bottom of all calculation. If this is not done, this first means of gaining clear ideas will be de-graded to a plaything of our memory and imagination, and will be useless for its essential purpose.

It cannot be otherwise. When, for example, we just learn

by heart "three and four make seven," and then build upon this seven, as if we really knew that three and four make seven, we deceive ourselves, for the inner truth of seven is not in us, for we are not conscious of the meaning behind it, which alone can make an empty word a truth for us. It is the same with all branches of human knowledge. Drawing too, for want of being connected with its basis, measurement, loses the inner truth of its being, by which alone it can be raised to a means of leading us to clear ideas.

In the Mother's Book I begin my efforts to give the children an impression of the relations of numbers, as actual changes of more and less; these can be found in the objects before their eyes. The first tables of this book contain a series of objects, that give the child a clear sense-impression of one, two, three, etc., up to ten. Then I let the children look for those objects, that are represented on these tables as units, pairs of units, threes of units, and so on. Afterwards I let them find these same relations on their fingers, or with peas, stones or other handy objects, and I renew the knowledge hundreds and hundreds of times daily. For as I divide words into syllables and letters on the spelling-board, I throw out the question, "How many syllables has this word? What is the first, second, third?" and so on. In this way the beginning of calculation is deeply impressed upon the children, and they become familiar with its abbreviations, and with numbers, with full consciousness of their inner truth, before they use them, without the background of sense-impression before their eyes. Independently of the advantage of *in this way* making calculation the foundation of clear ideas, it is incredible how easy the art itself may be made to the child by this firmly based preparation through sense-impressions. Experience shows that the beginnings are only difficult because these [necessary] psychological methods are not so widely used as they should be. There-

fore I must be somewhat circumstantial in my description of
the methods to be applied here.

Besides the means already indicated, we use after them the
spelling-board also for counting. We put upon it each
tablet as a unit and we begin, when the children are learning
their letters, to make them learn the relations of numbers
also. We take a particular tablet and ask the child, "Are
there many tablets?" The child answers, "No; only one."
Then we add another and ask, "One and one—how many?"
the child answers, "One and one are two." Thus we go on,
adding only one at a time; afterwards we add two, three,
and so on.

When the child understands the addition of one and one,
up to ten, perfectly, and can express himself with absolute
ease, we put the letter-tablets in the same way upon the
board, but alter the questions, and say, "When you have
two tablets how many times *one* tablet have you." The
child looks, counts, and answers rightly: "If I have two
tablets, I have twice one tablet."

When by exact and often repeated counting of the parts
he has become clearly conscious how many units are in the
first numbers, we change the question again and say with
a similar arrangement of tablets, "How many times one is
two? How many times one is three?" etc., and then again,
"How many times is one contained in two? In three?"
etc. Then when the child is acquainted with the simple
beginnings of addition, multiplication, and division, and is
perfectly familiar with the nature of these forms of reckoning through sense-impression, we try to make him acquainted and familiar with the beginnings of subtraction, in
the same way, through sense-impression. This is done in
this way. From the ten tablets collected together, we take
away one, and ask: "When you have taken one away from,
ten how many are left?" The child counts, finds nine, and

answers, " When I take one away from ten, nine are left."
Then we take a second tablet away, and ask, " One less than
nine, how many?" The child counts again, finds eight, and
answers, " One less than nine is eight." So we go on to
the last.

This kind of explanation of arithmetic may now be set
down in writing in the following way in rows.

```
|   | |        | |         | |      etc.
  |   | | |      | | |      | | |     etc.
|    | | | |    | | | |               etc.
```

As the counting of each row is finished, the separate
numbers will be taken away in the same way; as follows:—

If, for example, we add 1 and 2 are 3, and 2 are 5, and 2
are 7, etc., up to 21, then we take two tablets away and say,
" 2 less than 21, how many?" and go on till no more are
left.

The consciousness of many, or few objects, that is produced by laying real, movable, actual things before the
child, is then confirmed in him by counting-tables, by which
he is shown similar sequences of relations, by means of
strokes and dots. These tables, like real objects, will be
used as guides to counting, as the Spelling Book is used
for putting up the words on the spelling-board. When the
child is accustomed to count with real objects, and with the
dots and strokes, put in their place, as far as these tables
(that are founded entirely on sense-impression) go, the knowledge of the real relations of numbers will be so confirmed
in him, that the short methods by means of ordinary numbers,
without sense-impression, will be incredibly easy to him
because his mental powers have not been dissipated [so
far as arithmetic goes] by confusion, discrepancies, and
guessing. We can say in a special sense that such counting
is an exercise for the reason, and not memory or routine

work. It is the result of the clearest most exact sense-impression and leads safely to clear ideas about these relations.

But as increase and decrease of all objects does not consist only of more or less units, but also in the division of units into several parts, a second form of counting arises; or rather a path is opened, by which every separate unit may be the foundation of endless divisions of itself, and endless divisions of the units contained in it.

As in the first kind of counting, that is of many or few whole units we have considered the number *one* as the beginning point of all calculation, and as the foundation of the *art of sense-impression* and all its changes; so now in the second kind of counting, a figure must be found which does the same for this kind of counting, as the number one does for the other.

We must find a figure that is infinitely divisible and that in all its divisions is like itself; a figure by which a kind of sense-impression of infinitesimal fractions, either as parts of a whole, or as independent undivided units, may be given. This figure must put every relation of a fraction, in relation to the whole, before the child's eyes as clearly and as exactly, as, by our method, in simple arithmetic, the number one is shown in the number three, exactly three times.

There is no possible figure that can do this except the square.

By this we can put sensibly before the child's eyes, the proportions of the divisions of the unit or the fraction, in their progressive sequences, from the common beginning-point of all notions of more or less, the number one, just as we showed him the increase or decrease of undivided units. We have prepared a table of sense-impressions of fractions that has 11 rows, each consisting of ten squares.[1]

The squares in the first row are undivided. Those in

the second are divided into two equal parts; those in the third into three, and so on up to 10.

This table simply divided, is followed by a second table in which these simple visible divisions go on in the following order. The squares, which in the first table are divided into two equal parts, are now divided into 2, 4, 6, 8, 10, 12, 14, 16, 18, 20 parts; those in the next row are divided into 3, 6, 9, 12, etc.

As the A B C of Anschauung consists of measuring-forms, which are founded generally on the ten-fold division of the square, it is obvious that we can use the common basis of the A B C of Anschauung, the square as the foundation of an A B C of Arithmetic; or rather, that we have brought the elements of form and number into such harmony, that our measure-forms can be used as the first foundation of relations of numbers; and the first foundations of the relations of numbers can be used as measure-forms.

So we have reached this: By our method we can teach children arithmetic, only by using the very same A B C that at first we used as the A B C of Anschauung in a narrow sense,[2] that is, as the foundation of measure, drawing, and writing.

The child will be made so fully conscious of the visible relations of all fractions by the use of these tables, that exercises in fractional arithmetic, in ordinary numbers, will be as incredibly easy as arithmetic with undivided units. Experience shows, that by this method, children attain readiness in these exercises, three or four years sooner than is possible without it. By these, as by the former exercises, the child's mind is preserved from confusion, discrepancies, and useless guesses, and here too we can say with decision:—The calculating power of such children is the result of the clearest, most exact sense-impression, and leads by its clearness to truth, and susceptibility to truth.[3]

IX.

Friend! When I now look back and ask myself: What have I specially done for the very being of education? I find I have fixed the highest, supreme principle of instruction in the recognition of *sense-impression as the absolute foundation of all knowledge.* Apart from all *special teaching* I have sought to discover the *nature of teaching itself;* and the *prototype,* by which Nature herself has determined the instruction of our race. I find I have reduced all instruction to 3 elementary means; and have sought for special methods which should render the results of all instruction in these three branches absolutely certain.

Lastly, I have brought these 3 elementary means into harmony with each other, and made instruction, in all three branches, not only harmonious with itself in many ways, but also with human nature, and have brought it nearer to the course of Nature in the development of the human race.

But while I did this I found, in necessity, that the instruction of our country, as it is *publicly and generally* conducted *for the people,* wholly and entirely ignores sense-impression as the supreme principle of instruction, that throughout it does not take sufficient notice of the prototype, within which the instruction of our race is determined by the necessary laws of our nature itself; that it rather sacrifices the *essentials of all teaching* to the hurly burly of *isolated teaching of special things* and kills the spirit of truth by dishing up all kinds of *broken truths,* and extinguishes the power of self-activity which rests upon it, in the human race. I found, and it was clear as day, that this kind of instruction reduces its particular methods neither to elementary principles nor to elementary forms; that by the neglect of sense-impression, as the absolute foundation of all knowledge, it is unable by any of its unconnected methods to attain the end of all instruction, clear ideas, and even to make those limited results, at which it solely aims, absolutely certain.

* This educational[1] position in which, at least, ten men against one are to be found in Europe, as well as the actual quality of that instruction which they enjoy, appears almost incredible at the first glance of the subject; but it is not only historically correct, it is psychologically inevitable; it could not be otherwise. Europe, with its system of popular instruction, was bound to sink into the error, or rather insanity, that really underlay it. It rose on the one hand, to a gigantic height in special arts and sciences, and lost on the other, all foundations of natural teaching for the whole race. No country ever rose so high on the one side, nor sank so low on the other. Like the image of the prophet, it touches the clouds with its golden head of *special arts and sciences;* but popular instruction, that should be the foundation of this *golden head,* is, like the feet of this gigantic image, the *most wretched, most fragile, most good for nothing clay.* This disproportion, ruinous for the human mind, between the advantages of the upper, and the misery of the lower classes, or rather the beginning-point from which this striking disproportion in the culture of our country dates, is the invention of the art of printing. The country, in its first astonishment about this new and boundless influence, this making of word-knowledge easy, fell into a kind of dizzy, quack-like trust in the universality of its effects. This was natural in the first generation after the discovery; but that the country, after so many ages, still lives in the same dizzy

* Even the good Lavater, caring for and honouring the positive condition of the world as nobody else did, knew and confessed this. He answered the question: What simple elements can be found for the Art, and particularly for the observation (*Ansch.*) of all things? *He knew none,* and it surpassed all belief how groundless the Art (of education) in Europe was.—PESTALOZZI.

state, and has let it grow to a soul-and-body-destroying nervous fever, without feeling ill! Really this could have happened in no country but ours.

But it needed another influence interwoven of monkish feudal, Jesuit, and government systems, in order to produce through this art *the result* it has had on Europe. With these surrounding circumstances, it is then really not only comprehensible how it came to take a positive position together with our arts and our popular instruction, but it is even clear, that under given circumstances it could produce no *lesser* art, but also no *better* instruction than it has actually produced. It is quite clear how it was *forced* to narrow the five senses of the country, and so to bind particularly, that instrument of sense-impression, the eye, to the heathen altar of the new learning, letters and books. I might almost say it was forced to make this universal instrument of knowledge a mere letter-eye, and us mere letter-men. The Reformation [by the weakening of its original spirit and the necessary resulting deification of dead forms and thoughts] completed what the art of printing began. Without putting its heart under the obvious stupidity of a monkish or feudal world, it has opened its mouth generally only to express abstract ideas.[2] This still more increased the inner atrophy of the world, making its men letter-beings, and brought it to such a point, that the errors of this condition cannot be dissolved by progress in truth, love and faith, but on the contrary, they can only be strengthened, while they seem to be dissolved, by the still more dangerous errors of infidelity, indifference and lawlessness.

As a devastating flood, checked in its career by a fallen rock, takes a new course and spreads its devastation from generation to generation, so European popular education, having once forsaken the even road of sense-impression, owing to the influence of these two great events, has taken generally a baseless, visionary course, increasing its human devastation year by year, from generation to generation. Now after ages it has culminated in the general *word-twisting*[2] of our knowledge. This has [led to the word-twisting of infidelity. This profound vice of word and dream is in no way fitted to raise us to the still wisdom of faith and love, but on the contrary to lead us to the word-twisting of sham and superstition and its indifference and hardness. In any case it is undeniable that this devouring word and book nature of our culture has] brought us to this —we cannot any longer remain as we are.

It could not be otherwise. Since we have contrived with deeply founded art, and still more deeply founded measures for supporting error, to rob our knowledge and our methods of instruction of all sense-impression, and ourselves of all power of gaining sense-impressions, the gilded, giddy pate of our culture could not possibly stand on any feet but those on which it does actually stand. Nothing else was possible. The drifting haphazard methods of our culture could in no subject attain the final end of public instruction, *clear ideas*, and *perfect facility* in what is essentially necessary for the people to know and to learn of all these subjects. Even the best of these methods, the abundant aids for teaching arithmetic, [mathematics,] and grammar must, under these circumstances, lose power, because, without finding any other foundation for all instruction, they have neglected sense-impression. So these means of instruction, word, number, and form, not being sufficiently subordinated to the one only foundation of all knowledge, sense-impression, must necessarily mislead our generation to elaborate these means of instruction unequally, superficially, and aimlessly, in the midst of error and deception ; and by this elaboration, weaken our inmost powers, rather than strengthen and cultivate them. We become necessarily degraded to *lies and folly*, and branded as miserable, weak, unobservant, wordy babblers, by the very same powers and the very same organism* with which the Art, holding the hand of Nature, might raise us up to *truth and wisdom.*

Even the knowledge gained by observation, (*Ansch.*) forced upon us by our circumstances and our business, in spite of our folly (because it is impossible for any error in the Art to snatch this wholly from mankind)—even this kind of knowledge, being isolated, becomes one-sided, illusory, egotistic and illiberal. There is no help for it. Under such guidance we are forced to rebel against whatever is opposed to this one-sided, illiberal kind of observation (*Ansch.*), and to become insensible to all truth that may be beyond the limited range of our untrained senses. There is no help for it. We are forced under these circumstances, to sink ever deeper from generation to generation into the unnatural conventionality, the narrow-hearted selfishness, the lawless ambitious violence resulting from it, in which we now are.

Dear Gessner! thus, and in no other way, can we explain how, in the past century, during the latter part of which this delusion rose to its greatest height, we were plunged into a dreamy, or rather raving condition of baseless, frantic presumption. This perverted all our ideas of truth and justice. Yielding to the violent agitation of our wild and blind natural feelings, we sank down and a general overturning spirit of sansculottism took possession of us all in one way or another and resulted, as it must needs result, in the inner disorganization of all pure natural feelings, and of all those means of helping humanity, which rest upon those feelings. This led to the disappearance of all *humanity* from political systems; this again to the dissolution of a few political

* Ed. 1. Mechanism.

systems which had ceased to be human.   But unfortunately
this did not work to the advantage of humanity.

   This, dear friend, is a sketch of my views on the latest
events.   Thus I explain the measures both of Robespierre
and Pitt, the behaviour of the senators and of the people.
And every time I reconsider it I come back to the assertion,
that the deficiencies of European instruction, or rather, the
artificial inversion of all natural principles of instruction,
has brought this part of the world *where it is now;* and
that there is no remedy for our present and future overturn
in society, morality and religion, except to turn back from
the superficiality, incompleteness, and giddy-headedness of
our popular instruction, and to recognise that *sense-impression
is absolutely the foundation of all knowledge;* in other
words, *all knowledge grows out of sense-impression and
may be traced back to it.*

X.

   Friend ! sense-impression, considered as the point at which
all instruction begins, must be differentiated from the art of
sense-impression or *Anschauung* which teaches us the relations
of all forms.   Sense-impression, as the common foundation of
all 3 elementary means of instruction, must come as long
before the art of sense-impression as it comes before the arts
of reckoning and speaking.   If we consider sense-impression
as opposed to the art of sense-impression or *Anschauung,*
separately and by itself, it is nothing but the presence of *the
external object before the senses* which rouses a consciousness
of the impression made by it.   With it Nature begins all
instruction.   The infant enjoys it, the mother gives it him.
But the Art has done nothing here to keep equal pace with
Nature.   In vain that most beautiful spectacle, the mother
showing the world to her infant, was presented to its eyes, *the*

Art has done nothing, has verily done nothing for the people, in connection with this spectacle.

Dear Gessner, I will here quote for you the passage that expressed this feeling about our Art more than a year ago.[1]

"From the moment that a mother takes a child upon her lap, she teaches him. She brings nearer to his senses what nature has scattered afar off over large areas and in confusion, and makes the action of receiving sense-impressions and the knowledge derived from them, easy, pleasant, and delightful to him.

"The mother, weak and untrained, follows Nature without help or guidance, and knows not what she is doing. She does not intend to teach, she intends only to quiet the child, to occupy him. But, nevertheless, in her pure simplicity, she follows the high course of Nature without knowing what *Nature* does through *her ;* and Nature does very much through her. In this way she opens the world to the child. She makes him ready to use his senses, and prepares for the early development of his attention and power of observation.

"Now if this high course of Nature were used, if that were connected with it which might be connected with it ; if the helping Art could make it possible to the mother's heart to go on with what she does instinctively for the infant, wisely and freely with the growing child ; if, too, the heart [and disposition] of the father were also used for this purpose ; and the helping Art made it possible for him to link, with the disposition and circumstances of the child, all the activities he needs, in order by good management of his most important affairs, to attain inner content with himself throughout his life, how easy would it be to assist in raising our race and every individual man in any position whatever, even amid the difficulties of unfavourable circumstances, and amid

L

all the evils of unhappy times, and secure him a still, calm, peaceful life. O God! what would be gained for men. But we are not yet so far advanced as the Appenzell woman, who in the first weeks of her child's life, hangs a large, many-coloured, paper bird over his cradle, and in this way clearly shows the point at which the Art should begin to bring the objects of Nature firmly to the child's clear consciousness."

Dear friend! Whoever has seen how the two and three-weeks old child stretches hands and feet towards this bird, and considers how easy it would be for the Art to lay a foundation for actual sense-impressions of all objects of Art and Nature in the child by a series of such visible representations, which may then be gradually made more distinct and extended—Whoever considers all this and then does not feel how we have wasted our time on Gothic monkish educational rubbish, until it has become hateful to us,—truly cakes and ale are wasted on him.

To me the Appenzell bird, like the ox to the Egyptians, is a holy thing, and I have done everything to begin my instruction at the same point as the Appenzell woman. I go further. Neither at the first point, nor in the whole series of means of teaching, do I leave to chance what Nature, circumstance, or mother-love may present to the sense of the child before he can speak. I have done all I could to make it possible, by omitting accidental characteristics, to bring the essentials of knowledge gained by sense-impression to the child's senses before that age, and to make the conscious impressions he receives, unforgetable.

The first *course in the Mother's Book* is merely an attempt to raise sense-impression itself to an art, and to lead children by all 3 elementary divisions of knowledge, *form, number* and *words*, to a comprehensive consciousness of all sense-impressions, the more definite concepts of which will constitute the foundation of their later knowledge.

This book will not only contain representations of those objects most necessary for us to know, but also material for a continuous series of such objects as are fit, at the first sense-impression, to rouse a feeling in the children of their manifold relationships and similarities.

In this respect the Spelling Book does the same thing as the Mother's Book. Simply bringing sounds *to the ear* and rousing a consciousness of the impression made *through the hearing,* is as much *sense-impression* for the child as putting objects *before his eye,* and rousing a consciousness of the impression made *through the sense of sight.* Founded on this, I have so arranged the Spelling Book that its first course is nothing but *simple sense-impression,* that is, it rests simply on the effort to bring the whole series of sounds, that must afterwards serve as the foundation of language, *to the child's sense of hearing,* and to make the impression made by them permanent, *at exactly the same age* at which in the Mother's Book I bring before his sense of sight the visible objects of the world, the clear perception of which must be the foundation of his future knowledge.

This principle, of raising sense-impression to an art, has a place, too, in our 3rd elementary means of knowledge. Number in itself, without a foundation of sense-impression, is a delusive phantom of an idea, that our imagination certainly holds in a dreamy fashion, but which our reason cannot grasp firmly as a truth. The child must learn to know rightly the inner nature of every form in which the relations of number may appear, before he is in a position to comprehend one of these forms, as the foundation of a clear consciousness of few or many. [2] Therefore in the Mother's Book I have impressed the first ten numbers on the child's senses (*Ansch.*) even at this age in many ways, by fingers, claws, leaves, dots, and also as triangle, square, octagon, etc.

After I have done this in all three branches, and have

made sense-impression the absolute foundation of all actual
knowledge, I again raise sense-impression in all three subjects to the art of sense-impression (*Anschauung*), that is
a power of considering all objects of sense-impression as
objects for the exercise of my judgment and my (Fert.) skill.

In this way I lead the child, with the 1st elementary
means of knowledge, *form.* Having made him acquainted,
in the Mother's Book, with manifold sense-impressions of the
objects and their names, I lead him to the A B C of the art
of sense-impression (*Anschauung*). By this he is put in a
position to give an account of the form of objects, which he
distinguished in the Mother's Book, but did not *clearly*
know.   This book will enable the child to form clear ideas
on the forms of all things by their relation to the square,
and in this way to find a whole series of means within
the compass of subjects of instruction, by which he may rise
from vague sense-impressions to clear ideas.

As to the 2nd primary means of knowledge, *Number*,
I go on in the same way. After I have tried by the
Mother's Book to make the child clearly conscious, before he can speak, of the ideas of *the first ten numbers*, I
try to teach him these expressions for few or many things, by
gradually adding *one unit to another*, and making him know
the nature of *two*, and then of *three*, and so on.   And thus
I bring the beginning of all reckoning to the clearest sense-
impression of the child, and at the same time make him un-
forgetably familiar with the expressions which stand for them.
Thus I bring the beginnings of arithmetic in general into sequences which are nothing but a psychological, certain, and
unbroken march onwards from deeply impressed judgments,
resting on sense-impression, to a little additional new sense-
impression, but mounting only from 1 to 2 and from 2 to 3.
The result of this course, ascertained by experience, is that
when the children have wholly understood the beginning

of any kind of calculation, they are able to go on without further help.

It is generally to be noticed with respect to this manner of teaching, that it tends to make the principles of each subject so evident to the children, that they can complete every step of their learning, so that in every case they may be absolutely considered [and used] as teachers of their younger brothers and sisters, as far as they have gone themselves.

The most important thing that I have done to simplify and illustrate number teaching is this : I not only bring the consciousness of the truth within all relations of numbers to the child, by means of sense-impression, but I unite this truth of sense-impression with the truth of the science of magnitudes, and have set up the square as the common foundation of the art of sense-impression **and of arithmetic.**

The third primary means of knowledge, *speech,* considered as an application of my principles, is capable of the greatest extension.

If knowledge of form and number should precede speech (and this last must partly arise from the first two), it follows that the progress of grammar is quicker than that of the art of sense-impression (*Anschauung*) and arithmetic. The impression made on the senses (*Ansch.*) by form and number *precedes* the art of *speech*, but the art of sense-impression and arithmetic *come after* the *art of speech (grammar).* The great peculiarity and highest characteristic of our nature, *Language,* begins in the power of making sounds. It becomes gradually developed by improving *sounds* to *articulate words*; and from *articulate words* to *language.* Nature needed ages to raise our race to perfect power of speech, yet we learn this art, for which Nature needed ages, in a few months. [In teaching our children to speak] we must follow exactly the same course Nature followed herein with the human race. We dare not do otherwise. And she unquestionably began with sense-impression. Even the simplest sound, by which man strove to express the impression that an object made on him, was an expression of a sense-impression. The speech of my race was long only a *power of mimicry and of making sounds* that imitated the tones of living and lifeless nature. From *mimicry* and *sound-making* they came to *hieroglyphics* and *separate words*, and for long they gave *special* objects *special* names. This condition of language is sublimely described in the first book of Moses, chap. ii., verses 19, 20: "The Lord God brought to Adam all the beasts of the earth, and all the birds under heaven, that he might *look upon them* and *name* them. And Adam gave every beast his name."

From this point speech gradually went further. Men first *observed* the striking differences in the objects that they *named*. Then they came to name properties; and then to name the differences in the *actions* and *forces* of objects. Much later the art developed of *making single words mean much*, unity, plurality, size, many or few, form and number, and at last to express clearly all variations and properties of an object, which were produced by changes of time and place, by modifying the form and by joining words together.

In all these stages, speech was to the race a *means* produced by art, not only of *representing* the actual process of making manifold ideas (*Intuitionen*) clear by the power of sound, but also of *making impressions unforgetable*.

Language-teaching is, then, in its nature, nothing but a collection of psychological means of expressing impressions (feelings and thoughts) and of making all their modifications that would be else *fleeting* and *incommunicable*, *lasting* and *communicable* by uniting them to words.

But in consequence of the constant likeness in human nature, this can only be done through the harmony between lan-

guage-teaching and the original course by which Nature herself developed our power of speaking to that art which is now
ours. That is, all instruction in language must be founded
on *sense-impression*. It must make mimicry superfluous
through the art of sense-impression (or observation) and *number-teaching*. It must supersede imitation of the *sounds of
animate and inanimate nature* by a series of *conventional
sounds*. Then it must gradually pass from *sound-teaching*,
or rather from general *exercises of the organs* in all human
sounds, to *word-teaching*, to *names*, to *speech-teaching*, to
grammatical declensions, inflections, and composition. But
in this class of gradation the child must maintain the slow
progressive step, which Nature has foreshown in the development of the grammar of the race.

But now come the questions: How have I *held firmly* to
this course of Nature in the three stages into which Nature
and experience have divided the development of language, in
respect to *sound-teaching*, *word-teaching*, and *speech-teaching?* How have I brought the forms of my method of
instruction in these subjects into harmony with the aforesaid
stages? I have given the highest scope, of which it is
capable, to *sound-teaching*, by firmly holding and distin-
guishing the *vowels*, as the special roots of all sounds, and
by gradually adding single consonants before and after the
vowels. In this way I have made it possible for the child in
the cradle to become conscious of all these speech-sounds and
their sequences. I have even made it possible to let an *inner*
sense-impression precede the *outer*, in the infant, by means
of this instruction, which shows the child arbitrary signs of
sounds. In this way I insure that the impression on the ear
should have the same start of the impression on the eye, that
it has in Nature's teaching of sound. Again, I have made
this subject easier to teach, by arranging the sequences of
sounds in this book, in such a way, that every succeeding

sound is as like as possible to the preceding, and is only
differentiated from it by the addition of *a single* letter.
Thus I rise from complete familiarity with syllables, to *word-
teaching*, to names ; and give the child a word in the first
reading book, in the " word-book," and again in sequences,
which by the greatest possible similarity of form, makes the
further steps of the reading book the easiest play, since this
word has been deeply impressed and made familiar by a constant addition of a few new letters to those already known.
Thus many sided sense-impression lies at the base of the
Mother's Book, of its speech-teaching, and of the meaning
of the words which the child has to speak.

The infinite range of knowledge gained by sense-impression, that nature brings to the child's consciousness at the
earliest age is, in this book, psychologically arranged and
concentrated, and the supreme law of Nature, by virtue of
which the *near* is always more firmly impressed upon the
child than the *distant*, is connected with the principle, which
is just as important for instruction, of letting the *essential
nature* of things make a far deeper impression on the children than their varying properties.   In this book, by concentration and psychological arrangement of objects, the
boundless range of speech, and knowledge gained by sense-
impression, it is made easy to the child to get a general view.
The separate objects of Nature only are countless, their
essential characteristics are not.   Therefore, when the objects
are arranged according to these characteristics, it can be
made easy for the child to get a general view.

I subordinate special language-teaching to this principle.
My [3] grammar is only a series of methods for enabling the
child to express himself accurately about all knowledge
gained by sense-impression, and its relations with number
and time.   I even use the art of writing, so far as it can be
considered as language-teaching, for this purpose, and have,

generally, tried to use all the means that Nature and experience have put into my hand, for the clearing up of ideas,
for this same purpose.

The empirical attempts I have contrived have chiefly served
to show me that our monkish instruction, by its neglect of all
psychology, has not only driven us in all subjects from this
final end of instruction, but has even robbed us of those
methods which Nature offers to us, without the help of the
Art for making our ideas clear, and has made the use of these
means impossible for us, by its pernicious effects on our
minds.

Friend! The annihilation of all real power in our country,
by this unnatural monkish instruction and all the misery
of its unconnected teaching, is incredible. Incredible, also,
is the degree in which all natural means of rising through
sense-impression to true knowledge, and all enticement to
strengthen ourselves for this purpose, has vanished from our
midst; because this unconnected teaching has dazzled us
with the charm of a language which we speak without having
knowledge founded on sense-impression, of the ideas which
we let fall from our mouths. I repeat:—The mass of our
public schools not only give us nothing, but, on the contrary,
they quench all that in us which humanity has without schools,
that which every savage possesses, to a degree of which we
can form no conception. This is a truth which is applicable
to no part of the world and no age but ours. A man, who is
instructed with monkish art to this wordy foolishness, is, so
far, less susceptible to truth than a savage, and more unfit
than he to make use of the guidance of Nature, and of what
she does herself to make our ideas clear. These experiences
have convinced me that the public school-coach throughout
all Europe must not only be driven better, it must be turned
round and put on quite a new road. I am convinced of this
by experience, that its fundamental error, the empty speech

of our age, and our onesided [superficial, thoughtless, sense-less] jabbering must be *brought to death and laid* in *the grave*, before it will be possible, by *instruction* and *language* to bring forth *truth* and *life* in our race.   Verily this is a hard saying, and I am inclined to say : " Who can hear it ? " But I am convinced by experiments that lie at the base of this statement, that in elementary language-teaching, we must reject all half measures ; all instruction-books (on this subject) must be set aside, which are based on the supposition[4] that a child can talk before he has learned to talk.   All instruction books, the words of which bear the evidence of a complete grammar in their terminations, their prefixes, and their combinations, as well as in the composition of phrases and sentences, are in this way rendered unfit to develop clearly in the child's mind a consciousness of the causes and means, which led to this completion.   Therefore I would, if I had influence, take apparently pitiless measures with these instruction-books in the school libraries ; or give up the attempt to bring language teaching into harmony with the course of Nature.[5]

Dear friend !   It is generally known that Nature, in the first stages of the development of language in the race, wholly and entirely ignores the complicated and artificial combinations of the complete grammar ; and the child understands these combinations as little as the barbarian.   Only gradually, by continuous practice in simple combinations, does he gain the power of understanding the *complicated*.   Therefore, my exercises in language, from the first, putting aside all science and all knowledge, that can only be aimed at through complete grammar, inquire into the elements of language ; and give the child the advantages of forming speech, in *exactly the same gradual way* in which Nature gave it to the human race.

Dear friend !   Will men misunderstand me here too ? [6] Will there be even a few, who wish with me, that I may succeed in checking and putting an end to the mad faith in words, that from the very nature of the subject, as well as from their artificial construction and combination, bear the stamp of incomprehensibility for the child; and being void of all sense-impression, by their inner emptiness, work towards the devastation of the human mind, and lead to faith in empty noise and sound. May I succeed in making noise and sound unimportant by language-teaching itself; and again, give sense-impression the preponderating influence which is due to it, by which alone speech may become the true basis of mental culture and of all real knowledge, and of the power of judgment resulting from it.

Yes, friend. [7] I know that for a long, long time there will be but few who do not misunderstand me, and who recognise that dreams, sound and noise are absolutely worthless foundations for mental culture. The causes for this are many and deep seated. The love of babble is so closely connected with respect for what is called *good society*, and its pretension to wide general culture, and still more with the livelihood of many thousands among us, that it must be long, very long, before the men of our time can take that truth with love into their hearts, against which they have hardened themselves so long. But I go on my way and say again: All science-teaching that is dictated, explained, analysed, by men, who have not learnt to think and to *speak in accordance with the laws of Nature*, all science-teaching of which the definitions are forced as if by magic into the minds of children like a *Deus ex Machinâ*, or rather are blown into their ears as by a stage-prompter, so far as it does this must necessarily sink into a miserable burlesque of education. For where the primary powers of the human mind are left asleep, and when words are crammed upon the sleeping powers, we make dreamers, who dream unnaturally and inconstantly, in proportion as the words, crammed into

these miserable gaping creatures, are big and pretentious.
[8] Such pupils dream of anything in the world except that they
are asleep and dreaming; but the wakeful people round them
feel all their presumption; and those who see most consider
them night wanderers, in the fullest and clearest sense of
the word.

The course of Nature in the development of our race is
unchangeable. There are and can be no *two good* methods of
instruction in this respect. There is but *one*—and this is the
one that rests entirely upon the eternal laws of Nature. But
of *bad* methods there are *infinitely many ;* and the badness of
every one *increases*, in proportion as it *deviates from* the
laws of Nature, and *decreases* in proportion as it *approaches*
to following these laws. [9] I well know that this one good
method is neither in my hands nor in any other man's, that
we can only approach it. But its completion, its perfection
must be the aim of him who would found human instruction
upon truth, and thereby content human nature, and satisfy
its natural claims. From this point of view, I declare, I
pursue this method of instruction with all the powers that are
in my hands. I have one rule for judging my own action,
as well as the actions of all those who strive for this end—*by
their fruits ye shall know them.*[10] Human power, mother-wit,
and common sense are to me the only evidence of the inner
worth of any kind of instruction. Any method, that brands
the brow of the learner with the stamp of completely stifled
natural powers, and the want of common sense and mother-
wit, is condemned by me, whatever other advantages it may
have. I do not deny that even *such* methods may produce good
tailors, shoemakers, tradesmen, and soldiers; but I do deny
that they can produce a tailor or a tradesman who is *a man*
in the highest sense of the word. Oh! if men would only
comprehend that the aim of all instruction is, and can be,
nothing but the development of human nature, by the

harmonious cultivation of its powers and talents, and the promotion of manliness of life. Oh, if they would only ask themselves, at every step in their methods of education and instruction,—" Does it further this end ? "[11]

I will now again consider the influence of clear ideas upon the essential development of humanity. *Clear* ideas to the child are only *those to which his experience can bring no more clearness.* This principle settles, firstly, the order of the powers and faculties to be developed, by which the *clearness* of all ideas can gradually be arrived at ; secondly, the *order* of *objects* by which exercises in definitions can be begun and carried on with the children ; lastly, the *exact time* at which definitions of *any kind* contain real truth for the child.

It is evident that *clear ideas* must be worked out, or cultivated in the child by teaching, before we can take for granted that he is *able* to understand the result of such training—the clear idea, or rather its statement in words.

The way to *clear ideas* depends on making all objects clear to the reason in their proper order. This order again rests on the *harmony* of all the arts, by which a child is enabled to express himself clearly about the properties of all things, particularly about the measure, number, and form of any object. [12] In this way, and no other, can the child be led to a comprehensive knowledge of the whole nature of any object, and become capable of defining it, that is, of stating its whole nature, with the utmost precision and brevity, in words. All definitions, that is, all such clear statements in words, of the nature of any object contain essential truth for the child, only so far as he has a clear, vivid background of sense-impression of the object. Where thorough clearness, in the sense-impression of the object to be defined, is wanting, he only learns to play with words, to deceive himself and blindly believe in words, whose sounds convey no idea to him, or give him no other thought than that he has just given out a sound.

In rainy weather toadstools grow fast on every dungheap; and in the same way definitions, not founded on sense-impression, produce, just as quickly, a fungus-like wisdom, which dies just as quickly in the sunlight, and which looks upon the clear sky as poison to it. The baseless, wordy show of such baseless wisdom produces men, who believe they have reached the end in all subjects, because their life is a tiresome babble about this end. They never reach it, never pursue it, because all their life it has not had that attractive charm for their observing powers (*Ansch.*) which is generally necessary to produce a manly effort. Our generation is full of such men. They lie sick of a kind of wisdom, that leads us *pro formâ* to the goal of knowledge, like cripples on the racecourse, without being able to make this goal their goal, until their feet are cured. The power of describing generally precedes definition. I can describe what is quite clear to me, but I cannot on that account define it. That is, I can say exactly what its properties are, but not what it is. I only know the object, the individual. I cannot yet point out its relations or its kind. Of that which is not clear to me, I cannot say exactly what its properties are, let alone what it is. I cannot describe it, much less define it. When a third person, to whom the matter is clear, puts words into my mouth, with which he makes it clear to *people in his own condition*, it is not on that account clear to me, but it is and will remain his clear thing, not mine, inasmuch as the words of another cannot be for me what they are for him—the exact expression of his own idea, which is to him perfectly clear.

This purpose of leading men, with psychological art, and according to the laws of their physical mechanism, to clear ideas, and to their expression, definitions, demands a gradation of statements about the physical world before definitions. This gradation proceeds from sense-impressions of separate objects to their names, from their names to determining their characteristics, that is the power of describing, and from the power of describing to the power of *specializing*, that is, of defining. Wisdom in guiding sense-impression is obviously the beginning-point, on which this chain of means for attaining clear ideas must depend ; and it is obvious that the final fruit, the end of all instruction, the clearness of all ideas, depends essentially on the complete power of its first germination.

Wherever, in the whole circle of all-working Nature, anything is imperfect in the germ, there it has lost the power of becoming perfect in its complete ripeness. Everything that is imperfect in the germ will be crippled in its growth, in the outward development of its parts. This is as true of the products of your mind, as of the products of your garden. It is as true of the results of a single idea gained by sense-impression, as it is certain of the condition of a grown cabbage.

The most important means of preventing confusion, inconsequence, and superficiality in human education, rests principally on care in making the first sense-impression of *things most essential* for us to know, as clear, correct, and comprehensive as possible, when they are first brought before our senses, for contemplation (*Ansch.*). Even at the infant's cradle we must begin to take the training of our race out of the hands of blind, sportive Nature, and put it into the hands of that better power, which the experience of ages has taught us to abstract from the eternal laws of our nature.

[13] You must generally distinguish between the laws of Nature and her course, that is, her single workings, and statements about those workings. In her laws she is eternal

truth, and for us, the eternal standard of all truth ; but in her modifications, in which her laws apply to every individual and to every case, her truth does not satisfy and content our race. The positive truth of the condition and circumstances of any individual case claims the same equal right of necessity, by virtue of eternal laws, as the common law of human nature itself. Consequently, the claim of necessity of both laws must be brought into harmony, if they are to work satisfactorily on men. Care for this union is essential for our race. The accidental is, by its existence and its consequences, as necessary as the eternal and unchangeable ; but the accidental must, from its very existence and its inevitable consequences, be brought into harmony with the eternal and unchangeable in human nature by means of the freedom of the human will.

Nature, on whom the inevitable laws of the existence and consequences of the accidental are based, seems only devoted to the whole, and is careless of the individual that she is affecting externally. On this side she is blind ; and being blind, she is not the Nature that comes, or can come into harmony with the seeing, spiritual, moral nature of men. On the contrary, it is only spiritual and moral nature that is able to bring itself into harmony with the physical—and that can, and ought to do so. The laws of our senses, by virtue of the essential claims of our nature, must be subordinated to the laws of our moral and spiritual life. Without this subordination it is impossible that the physical part of our nature can ever influence the actual final result of our education, the production of manliness. Man will only become man through his inner and spiritual life. He becomes through it independent, free, and contented. Mere physical Nature leads him not hither. She is in her very nature blind ; her ways are ways of darkness and death. Therefore the education and training of our race must be taken out of the hands of blind sensuous Nature, and the influence of her darkness and death, and put into the hands of our moral and spiritual being, and its divine, eternal, inner light and truth.

All, all that you carelessly leave to outer blind Nature sinks. That is true of lifeless nature as of living. Wherever you carelessly leave the earth to Nature, it bears weeds and thistles. Wherever you leave the education of your race to her, she goes no further than a confused impression on the senses, that is not adapted to your power of comprehension, nor to that of your child, in the way that is needed for the best instruction. In order to lead a child, in the most certain way, to correct and perfect knowledge of a tree or plant, it is not the best way, by any means, to turn him, without care, into a wood or meadow, where trees and plants of all kinds grow together. Neither trees nor plants here come before his eyes in such a manner as is calculated to make him observe their nature and relationships, and to prepare for a general knowledge of their subject by the first impression. In order to lead your child by the shortest way to the end of instruction, clear ideas, you must with great care, first put those objects before his eyes (in every branch of learning), which bear the most essential characteristics of the branch to which this object belongs, visibly and distinctly, and which are therefore fitted to strike the eye with the essential nature rather than the variable qualities. If you neglect this, you lead the child, at the very first glance, to look upon the accidental qualities as essential, and in this at least to delay the knowledge of truth, and miss the shortest road of rising from misty sense-impressions to clear ideas.

But if this error in your method of instruction is avoided, if the sequences of subjects in all branches of your instruction are brought to the child's sense-impression so arranged from the very beginning, that at the very first observation (*Ansch.*) the impression of the essential nature of an object

M

begins to overpower the impression of its qualities, the child learns, from the very first, to subordinate the accidental properties of an object to its essential nature. He is, undoubtedly, moving on the safe path, in which his power develops daily of connecting, in the simplest manner, all accidental qualities with his full consciousness of the essential nature of all objects and their inner truth, and so to read all Nature as an open book. As a child, left to itself, peeping into the world without understanding, sinks daily from error to error, through the confusion of separate scraps of knowledge which he has found while so groping; so, on the contrary, a child who is led on this road from his cradle, rises daily from truth to truth. All that exists, or at least all that comes within the range of his experience, unites itself clearly and comprehensively with the power already existing in him, and there is no error behind his views. No bias to any kind of error has been artificially and methodically organized in him, and the *nihil admirari*, which has hitherto been considered the privilege of old age, becomes, thanks to this training, the portion of innocence and youth. Having arrived at this, if he possesses fair average abilities, the child will necessarily reach the final goal of instruction, clear ideas,—it matters little for the time being whether these lead him to the conclusion that we know nothing, or that we understand everything. In order to reach this high end, to organize the means and secure them, and especially to give the first sense-impressions of objects that breadth and accuracy which they demand, in order to avoid deficiencies and error at the foundation, and to build our sequences of methods of gaining knowledge on truth, I have kept all these objects fully in view in the Mother's Book. Friend, I have succeeded; I have so far confirmed my powers of gaining knowledge through my senses by this book, that I foresee that children trained by it, may throw away the book, and in Nature and all that surrounds them, find a better guide to my goal than that which I have given them.

Friend, the book as yet is not; yet I already see it superseded by its own action.

Note for New Edition.

The Mother's Book, of which this is a dreamy account, never existed. At that moment I thought it easy to complete it. Its non-appearance is explained by the erroneous views in which I was then involved. This suggests a closer examination into the exact degree of truth I had then attained, with regard to my bold ideals, and the glaring deficiencies which were caused by immature judgment. It is now twenty years since these utterances, and yet I am hardly beginning to be able to give myself a clear account of the views here expressed. I must ask myself, "How have these twenty years passed in regard to these ideals?" and I rejoice to be able to say at last: However much they appeared to hinder my attempts to develop the vague ideas I then held, in that same degree they actually favoured this development, so far as it was attainable by a man of my character. Time has quenched my hopes, and I no longer stretch out my hand to pluck the moon from heaven, as a child does in his nurse's lap.

XI.

Dear Friend! The statement with which I ended my last letter is important, and I now repeat more emphatically, the training for the purpose of instruction which I spoke of just now, is only adapting the course of nature for that end; but there is a higher means possible of attaining it, a completion of this adapted course of nature, a course of pure reason. A training of pure reason is possible. It is possible for my nature to raise all that is uncertain in human sense-impression to the most definite truth. It is possible for my nature to separate sense-impression itself from the uncertainty of its origin in mere sensation, and to make it the work of the higher power of my being, that is of my reason. It is possible for the Art, thus ennobled by the hand of Nature, to make the wild man's living power of observation more than the mere mechanism of the senses. It is possible to add to this living power of observation my power of reason. It is possible to unite the restoration of this living power of observation with the most sublime study of my race, the study of absolute infallible truth.

Dear Friend! If my life has any value, it is that I have raised the square to be the foundation of a system of teaching by sense-impression, that the people never had before. Through it I have prepared a series of methods for the *basis of our knowledge* such as only existed before for speech and number, which are means of instruction subordinate to it, and which had never been worked out for form itself. In this way I have brought *sense-impression* and *judgment, sense-mechanism* and *the course of pure reason* into harmony with each other; and while, through this method, I have put aside the variegated hurly burly of thousands of separate truths, I have turned instruction back to truth.*

Friend! For upwards of twenty years I hardly knew to what the following passage, in the preface of "Leonard and Gertrude," would lead. "I take no share in all the strife of men about their opinions, but whatever makes them good, brave, true and honest, whatever can bring love of God and love of one's neighbour into the heart, and happiness and blessing into the house, that, I think, is above all strife, and is put into every heart for us all."

Now the course of my attempts makes me see, that this is very true of the kind of instruction, the knowledge and introduction of which I am striving after; in this too, I take no part in all the disputes of men. Purely as a means of developing all our powers and talents, by its *very nature*, it extends its influence and its results, not one step beyond that which is incontestable. Purely as a means of developing our powers, it is not the teaching of truths, but of truth. It is

* This beginning is omitted in Ed. 2, probably by an oversight.

not a combatant against error, it is the inner development of moral and mental powers, that are opposed to error. It is purely a guide to the faculty of recognising truth and error. The very nature of its effort is only to base the good cultivation of this faculty on psychological grounds, and to supply all its needs. Friend! I see both how far this expression leads, and how far distant I am from it. I recognise only the tracks of the means, by which it may be possible to reach this end as a whole. Yet faith in the possibility of reaching this end lives, undying, in my soul. But how, when, and through whom my anticipations can or will be fulfilled, I really know not. There is no presumption in my soul. In all my efforts, the results of which lead me to these expressions, I seek only to make easier and more simple the methods of instructing the lowest classes, in my immediate neighbourhood, whom I saw to be unhappy, discontented, and dangerous, in consequence of their wrong training. My heart was inclined to this effort from my youth up. From my youth up I have had opportunities, granted to few, of learning the causes of the moral, mental, and domestic degradation of the people, and the suffering, deserved or not, intimately connected with it. You may believe me I have borne some suffering and some wrongs with the people. I say it to excuse the apparent boldness of some of my assertions, for in my inmost soul lies only the ardent desire to help the people in the sources of their backwardness and the misery arising from it, not the least presumption, no thought of *being able* to do it. I pray you, consider all my apparently bold expressions in this light. When, for instance, I say distinctly, the development of all human powers proceeds from an organism, the action of which is absolutely certain, I do not say that the laws of this organism are clearly known by me, nor that I recognise their whole scope. When I say there is a course of pure reason in instruction, I do not say

I have proved and practised these laws in their full perfection. In the whole account of my doings I have tried far more to make the truth of my principles clear, than to bring my very restricted action to the standard of what might and must come, from the complete development of these principles, for the human race. I do not know myself; and I feel daily more and more how much I do not know.[1]

Whatever theory and judgment exist in my whole statement are absolutely nothing but the result of a limited, very laborious, and I must add seldom successful, series of experiments. I ought not and I will not conceal that if a man who had long ago sunk into weariness, and become a poor tired creature, who, until his hair turned grey, had been considered everywhere, absolutely impracticable by practical men, had not finally succeeded in becoming a schoolmaster, and if *Buss*, *Krüsi* and *Tobler* had not come with a power of helping his utter helplessness in all arts and activities (*Fert.*), as I never dared to hope, my theories on this subject would have died within me, like the glow of a burning mountain that can find no outlet. I should have sunk into my grave like a dreaming fool, on whom no charitable judgment would be passed, misunderstood by the good, and despised by the bad. My only merit, my desire, my incessant ever-growing desire for the *salvation of the people*, my laborious days, the sacrifice of my life, the murder of myself would have been given over to the mockery of rogues. I should not have had a friend, who dared to do justice to my despised shade. I could not have defended myself; I could not have done it. I should have sunk into the grave, angry with myself and despairing at my own misery and that of the people. Friend! sinking thus, I should only have retained the miserable power of complaining against my fate. I should,—I could not have helped it,—I should have imputed the guilt of my ruin to myself alone. The awful ideal of my life would have stood before my eyes, all in shadow, without any mitigating beam of light.

Friend! Imagine my feelings, my despair, this ideal of shadow, and the thought, that in my ruin I should [myself] have ruined the purpose of my life; and verily by my own fault I should have lost it. There is a God who gave it me again, after I had lost it. I failed over and over again like a child, even when it seemed that the means thereto were given into my hands. Ah! I behaved long like nobody else, and things went with me as with no one else. Not only did my utter want of developed practical skill and the entire incompatibility between the scope of my will and the limits of my power, impede from my childhood the attainment of my goal; but each year I became more unfit for everything that could really help towards its outward attainment, for that which was essentially necessary for the outward attainment of my end.

But is it my fault, that the course of a life constantly crushed, did not let me go on one bit of the way with an unbroken heart? Is it my fault, that all signs of interest on the part of the happy, or at least the not miserable, have been erased long ago from my soul, as the traces of an island sunk in the deep? Is it my fault, that men around me, around me so long! have seen nothing in me but a bleeding creature, crushed and thrown on the wayside, without consciousness,—in whom the aim of life, like an ear of corn among thorns, thistles, and marshy reeds, budded up very slowly, in constant danger of death and suffocation? Is it my fault, that the aim of my life now remains like a bare rock in the flood, from which the wasting waters have washed away every trace of the beautiful earth that once covered it?

Yes, Friend; it is my fault. I feel it deeply, and bow myself to the dust, not indeed before the judgment of bad men, buzzing round me like a disturbed nest of wasps, but before the ideal of myself, and of the inner worth to which I might have risen, if in the midst of the everlasting night of my forlorn life, I had been able to rise above my fate, and above the horror of days, in which all that cheers and elevates human nature, vanished; and all that confuses and degrades it, pressed round me unceasingly and constantly, falling with all its weight on the weakness of my heart, that found no support in my head, against the blows that broke on it. But it is my fault, friend. All my misfortune is my own fault. I could have done it; I ought to have done it; I might say I determined to do it. I did determine to raise myself above my fate—if that can be called a determination which I did not carry out. This much is true. I have grown old; the misery of my days has brought me near my grave, before the whole shattering of my nerves has completely destroyed my balance, and before the last revolt within me finally made me throw away myself and my sympathy with the human race.

Friend! A woman greater than any man, a woman, who was only ennobled, never degraded by the misfortunes of a life, that far outweighed my misery, saw long ago my despair of myself and answered my distracted words, "*It does not matter,*" with—"O Pestalozzi! if a man once utters that word of despair may God help him, he can help himself no more."

I saw the glance of sadness and anxiety in her eyes, as she spoke the word of warning; and, friend, if I had no more guilt in the final disappearance of my better self than that I could hear this word and forget it again, my guilt would be greater than that of all men who have never seen this virtue and never heard this word.

Friend! Let me now forget my action and my purpose for a moment, and give myself wholly up to the feeling of sadness that overwhelms me, because I still live and am no more my *self*. I have lost all; I have lost my *self*. Yet hast Thou, O Lord, preserved the desire of my life in me; and hast not destroyed the object of my pains before my eyes, as Thou hast destroyed the aim of a thousand men who ruined their own way, before their eyes and mine. Thou hast preserved the work of my life in the midst of my ruin, and hast cast an evening glow over my hopeless, dying old age; the lovely sight outweighs the sorrows of my life. Lord, I am unworthy of the faith and mercy that Thou hast shown me. Thou, Thou alone hast pitied the crushed worm. The bruised reed Thou hast not broken, and the smoking flax Thou hast not quenched. Till my death Thou hast not turned Thy eyes away from the offering, which from childhood I wished to make, and have never been able to make, to the forsaken in the world!

Note for the New Edition.

I read this letter, written twenty years ago, with heartfelt sorrow. It expresses my depression and my despair at the course of my life and the annihilation of my hopes, at the very moment when a new, living path for my purpose was opened. I cannot say how my heart beats, and how the impression of feelings long ago subdued, and raised again, is renewed. The words of self-accusation shake my soul, as the mitigation of these accusations confuse it. Gladly would I fall on my knees and pray, as I read this letter again, at a time, when after twenty years I again see a new, living path opened for my purpose. Reader! how I should feel encouraged, when after so many years I stand again at the point at which I stood then. I must repeat, speaking of my efforts and hopes, that without the almost miraculous assistance of Providence, without the co-operation of friends (in whom I recognised almost heroic power) I should undoubtedly again have come to a state in which my laborious days, the giving up of my life, and the sacrifice of my family would to-day have been given over to the mockery of a blind crowd!

Reader! How I gain fresh courage, as after so many years I read again the passage: "Friend, imagine my heart, my despair, and this ideal of shadow, and the thought, that in my ruin I had ruined the aim of my life." Then, reader, imagine how my heart soars up in thankfulness to God, who has preserved the desire of my life in me, and has not wholly destroyed the object of my pains before my eyes.

And yet, reader, if this had been, if I had really sunk into, and not only been nearly brought to despair, but had been wholly conquered by it, I should yet bear witness to-day, as in that letter, half accusing myself of my misfortunes, and sink forbearing, forgiving, thanking and loving into the grave. But, reader, how my heart beats high when I can say, as twenty years ago, "The Lord hath helped." How my heart beats as I repeat the words of that letter: "Thou, O Lord! hast preserved the desire of my life, and hast not destroyed the object of my pains before my eyes, as Thou hast destroyed the desire of thousands who spoilt their own path, before their eyes and mine. Thou hast preserved the work of my life in the midst of my ruin. Thou hast cast an evening glow over my hopeless old age, and the sight of its beauty compensates for my sufferings. Lord, I am unworthy of Thy loving kindness and faithfulness. Thou, Thou alone hast had pity for the crushed worm; Thou, Thou alone hast left the bruised reed unbroken, and the smoking flax unquenched. Thou hast not rejected the sacrifice that from childhood I would have made for the poor and forsaken in the land, and have never made."

Reader, forgive the repetition of the same words in the same page. But the ardent desire of my heart will not permit me to oppose this new feeling of salvation and happiness, that must be expressed and put down in words, that I wrote twenty years ago. I must use them to express the feelings of the present hour with the words of to-day. You will, I know, willingly forgive this repetition.

XII.

In my last letter my feelings would not allow me to say more. I put my pen away, and I did well. What are words when the heart bows itself in dark despair, or rises in highest rapture to the clouds?

Friend, what are words even apart from these heights and depths!

In the eternal nothingness of the most sublime characteristic of our race, human speech, and then again in its sublime power, I see the mark of the external limitation of the shell in which my cramped-up spirit pines. I see in it the ideal of the lost innocence of my race, but I see in it also the ideal of the shame which the memory of this lost holiness always awakens in me, so long as I am not wholly unworthy. This feeling, so long as I have not sunk in the depths, ever revives within me the power of seeking what I have lost, and of saving myself from ruin. Friend, so long as man is worthy of the sublime characteristic of his race, speech, so long as he uses it as a powerful means of expression, and for the maintenance of his human superiority, with a pure desire to ennoble himself and humanize himself by it, it is a high and holy thing. But when he is no longer worthy; when he no longer uses it as a powerful expression of his human superiority, and with no pure desire to humanize himself, it will be nothing but a natural inexhaustible source of illusion, the use of which will lead to the loss of his manliness, to effeminacy and brutality. It will be to him the first and most powerful means of completely ruining his moral and spiritual nature, and the first source of his domestic misery, civil wrong-doing and wrong suffering, and the public crime arising from it. Meanwhile he, most skilfully, makes it into a cloak for all this ruin and crime. It is incalculable how deeply the depravity of our language has spread, how deep a hold it has on all the aspects of the world of our time, how its tone is to be found in good society, at court, in the law courts, in books, in comedies, in periodicals, in daily papers,—in short, it is everywhere in our midst, with all its dissolute force. It is notorious that now, more than ever before, it is encouraged from the cradle; it is inspired by the school; it is strengthened through life; I might even say, it speaks from the pulpit and the council-chamber, down to the tavern and the beershop; it is heard among us everywhere. All the sources of human depravity and sensuality find a centre in it, in which they collect and unite for their common interest, and become infectious. By this, and this only, can we explain the terrible fact, that the depravity of language grows with the depravity of men. Through it, the wretched become more wretched; through it the night of error becomes

still darker; through it the crimes of the wicked still increase.   Friend! the crimes of Europe are still increasing
through idle talk.   It is connected with over-civilization,
and its results are influencing the condition of all our
feelings, thoughts and actions.   It is connected with the
far-reaching increase of our *slavery*.   It is intimately connected with the equally far-reaching loss of independence,
not only in the common, lower classes of the country, but of
our so-called gentry, notables, and persons of importance;
and it is also connected with the increasing degeneration
of our middle class, the recognised first and most essential
support of all true political power, and civil happiness.
The daily increasing list of publications is only an insignificant symptom of this great evil of our time.   But the public
and private placards, increasing daily in number and size,
on the corners of our walls, are often more significant indications of this evil than the swollen list of publications.
But in any case we cannot guess to what this chattering
degeneracy will lead a generation, which has already
reached the state of so many countries in our part of the
world, by its weakness, confusion, violence, and inconsequence.[1]

But I return to my path.   In my experimental inquiries into
the subject, I started from no positive notion of teaching—
I had *none*—I ask myself simply, " What would you do, if
you wished to produce in a single child, all the *knowledge*
and *ability (Fert.* [2]) that it needs, in order, *by wise care of its
essential concerns, to attain to inward content ?*

But I see now that in the whole series of my letters to you,
I have only considered the first portion of the subject, the
training of the child's *judgment* and *knowledge ;* but not
the training of his *activities (Fert.* [2]), so far as these are not
especially activities brought out by instruction [in knowledge
and science].   And yet the activities that a man needs to

attain inner content by their possession, are not actually limited to the few subjects that the nature of instruction forced me to touch upon.

I cannot leave these gaps untouched. Perhaps the most fearful gift that a fiendish spirit has made to this age is *knowledge without power of doing (Fert.) and insight without that power of exertion or of overcoming* that makes it possible and easy for our life to be in harmony with our inmost nature.

Man! needing much and desiring all, thou must, to satisfy thy wants and wishes, *know* and *think*, but for this thou must also [*can* and] *do.* And knowing and doing are so closely connected, that if one cease the other ceases with it.[3] But this harmony between thy life and thy inmost nature can only be, if the *powers of doing (Fert.)* (without which it is impossible to satisfy thy wishes and wants) are cultivated in thee with just the same art, and raised to the same degree of perfection, as thy insight into the objects of thy wants and wishes. The cultivation of these activities rests then on the same organic[4] laws as the cultivation of knowledge.

The organism[4] of Nature is one and the same in the living plant, in the animal, whose nature is merely physical, and in man, whose nature is also physical, but who possesses will. In the threefold results which Nature is capable of producing in me, she is always the same. Her laws work either physically upon my physical nature, in the same manner as upon animals generally, or secondly, they work upon me so far as they determine the *sensuous basis of my judgment and will.* In this respect they are the sensuous basis of my opinions, my inclinations, and my resolutions. Thirdly, they work upon me so far as *they make me capable of that practical skill (Fert.)*, the need of which I *feel* through my instinct, *recognise* through my insight, and the learn-

ing of which I *command* through my will.   But in this
respect also, the Art must take the cultivation of our race out
of the hands of Nature, or rather from her accidental attitude
towards each individual, in order to put it in the hands of
knowledge, power and methods which she has taught us
for ages, to the advantage of the race.

Certainly men never lose the feeling for the necessity of
being cultivated in the activities required in ordinary life,
even in the deepest decadence caused by over-refinement and
artificial training.[5]   Still less does the individual man lose
this consciousness.   Natural instinct, in all moral, mental,
and practical things, drives him with its whole force into
paths of life, in which this consciousness of need increases
and develops daily.   This tends in every way to take his
improvement out of the hands of blind Nature, and out
of the one-sided, over-refined and artificial training of his
senses, in this case intimately connected with the blind-
ness of Nature, and put it into the hands of those intelligent powers, methods and arts which have been raising our
race for ages.   But in every case bodies of men succumb
to the claims of sensuous nature, and its over-refined and
artificial training, far, far more than individuals.   This
is true even of governments.   They succumb as bodies,
masses or corporations to the claims of our sensuous nature
and its atrophy, far more than individuals, or even the
individual members of the corporations.   It is certain, in
matters in which a father would not easily act wrongly
towards his son, or a teacher towards his pupils, a government may very easily act wrongly towards its people.
It cannot well be otherwise.   Human nature acts with far
greater gentleness and purer power on each individual,
than it ever can on masses, corporations, or communi-
ties of men, whatever they may be.   The first common
instinct of human nature remains, and keeps itself infinitely

purer and more powerful, in the individual, than in any corporation or community. Instinct stimulates no body or community of men as it can and does stimulate the individual. It loses the basis of harmony, from which its influence on the whole compass of human powers, may and should start and aspire. It is undeniable, that whatever is holy and divine in instinct expresses itself in the individual by its harmonious influence on all natural powers. This holy and divine quality in instinct becomes crippled and ineffectual (whatever form its one-sidedness may take) in every case where it influences any mass or body of men in their collective capacity, and by this very influence produces in them an *esprit du corps* with its deadening influences. Instinct affects masses of men of whatever kind with the same deadening force that every kind of union among men produces in itself ; and wherever this is the case, there its influence on truth and justice, and in consequence, on national enlightenment and national happiness is inevitably hindered. This distinction, between the effect of instinct upon individuals, and upon bodies of men, is of the highest importance and deserves far more attention than it gets. It throws, when we understand it, decided light on many phenomena of human life, particularly on many actions of governments, which else would be incomprehensible. It also explains why we must not expect too much of governments with regard to the care of the individual, of the education of the people, and everything on which the common weal depends—things which can only be accomplished by individuals. No, it is an eternal truth, easily explained by human nature, and shown in all the history of the world, that what can be done by the life and energy of individuals in the state, that is by the people, cannot be done so well by the government. We cannot expect it, much less demand it. The only thing we can ask is that the individual should not be allowed to sink down into want of power and will. Governments ought to try and guard against this want of power in the individual, in those matters in which he could accomplish and contribute anything himself to forward the public good ; and should neglect nothing that every individual needs for the cultivation of his intelligence, disposition, and abilities, in order as an individual to be able to do his part for the public good.   But it grieves me to say that the governments of our time are not strong and living enough for the practical skill required for this end.   It is undeniable, that the people of our part of the world do not enjoy the practical help that each man needs for the cultivation of his intelligence, disposition, and ability (*Fert.*), in order, on the one hand, by wise care of his own business, to attain inner self-content, and on the other to facilitate, provide and secure to the state all that it needs, in order, as a state, to find help, and assistance in its millions of individuals, for that which it can only maintain through the good condition of the moral, mental and practical powers of these individuals. [6]

HERE IS A GREAT GAP.*

All abilities, on the possession of which depend all the powers of knowing and doing, that are required by an educated

* *Note Pestalozzi.*—Much as I have wished and resolved to leave the original edition of this work unaltered, and to give free course to the stream of my opinions and thoughts at that time, I have here suppressed a long passage that expressed my feelings about the position of the people and our country at that time, although the *horrible events* of the twenty years, between the first and second edition, have in many ways confirmed these opinions.   I was obliged to suppress them.   I now regard the condition of the people with more sorrow than zeal ; and my views of remedies for the evils of the time tend rather to more sorrow than to the eloquence of youthful zeal, the shrill expressions of which, with whatever reserve of love, truth and justice, rather extinguish than kindle the holy, eternal, inner nature of love.

mind and a noble heart, comes as little of itself as the *intelligence* and *knowledge* that man needs for it. As the cultivation of mental powers and faculties pre-supposes a psychologically arranged gradation of means, adapted to human nature, so the cultivation of the faculties which these powers of doing (*Fert.*) presuppose, rests on the deep-rooted mechanism of an A B C of *Art ;* that is on universal laws of the Art, by following which the children may be educated by a series of exercises, proceeding gradually from the simplest to the most complicated. These must result, with physical certainty, in obtaining for them a daily increasing facility in all that they need for their education. But this A B C is anything but *found.* It is quite natural that we seldom find anything that nobody looks for. But if we would seek it, with all the earnestness with which we are wont to seek any small advantage in the money-market, it would be easy to find, and when found, would be a great blessing to mankind. It must start from the simplest manifestations of physical powers, which contain the foundations of the most complicated human practical ability [7] (*Fert.*). Striking and carrying, thrusting and throwing, drawing and turning, encircling and swinging, etc., are extremely simple expressions of our physical powers. In themselves, essentially different, they contain, all together and each separately, the foundations of all possible actions (*Fert.*), even the most complicated, on which human callings depend. Therefore, it is obvious that the A B C of actions must start altogether from early psychologically arranged exercises in these actions, all and each. This A B C of limb exercise must, naturally, be brought into harmony with the A B C of sense exercises, and with all the mechanical practice in thinking, and with exercises in form and number-teaching.

But as we are far behind the Appenzell woman and her paper bird, in the A B C of Anschauung, so are we far behind the greatest barbarians in the A B C of actions, (gymnastics) (*Fert.*), and their skill in striking and throwing, thrusting and dragging.

We want a graduated series of exercises, from their simplest beginning to their highest perfection, that is, to the utmost delicacy of nerve power, which enables us to perform with certainty and in a hundred different ways, the actions of thrusting and parrying, swinging and throwing. We want, too, actions exercising hand and foot in opposite, as well as in the same directions. All these, as far as popular instruction is concerned, are castles in the air. The ground is clear. We have spelling schools, writing schools, catechism (Heidelberger) schools only, and we want — *men's schools.* [8] But these can be of no use to those whose whole idea is to keep things as they are, to the jobbery, and injustice, that are so readily maintained by this idea, nor to the nervous state of the gentry whose interests are involved in this contemptible state of *laissez-faire.* [But I almost forget the point at which I began.]

The mechanism of activities takes the same course as that of knowledge, and its foundations, with regard to self-education, are perhaps still more far-reaching. In order to *be able*, you must *act;* in order *to know*, you must, in many cases, *keep passive;* you can only see and hear. Hence, in relation to your activities, you are not only the centre of their cultivation, but in many cases, you determine their ultimate use—always within the laws of the physical mechanism. As in the infinite range of lifeless nature, its situation, needs and relations have determined the special characteristics of every object; so in the infinite range of living nature that produces the development of thy faculties, situation, needs and relations determine the sort of power (*Fert.*) that you specially need.

[9] These considerations throw light on the mode of developing

our activities, and also on the character of the activities when developed. Every influence, that in the development of our powers and activities, turns us away from the centre point, on which rests the personal responsibility of every- hing that man is bound throughout his life to do, to bear, to attend and provide for, must be regarded as an influence opposed to wise manly education. Every influence leading us to apply our powers and activities in a way that turns us away from this central point, and thus weakens or robs the activities of the special character, which our duty towards ourselves requires of us, or puts us out of accord with them, or in some way or other makes us incapable of serving our fellow-men or our country, must be regarded as a deviation from the laws of nature, from the harmony with myself and my surroundings. Therefore it is a hindrance to my self-culture, to the training for my calling, and to my sense of duty. It is a delusive and self-destructive deviation from the pure and beautiful dependence of my relations in life on my real character. [10] Every kind of instruction or education, every kind of life, every use of our trained powers and talents in life, which bears in itself the seeds of such discord be-tween our education and our actions and the real character of our being, our relations and our duties, must be guarded against by every father and mother, who have their children's life-long peace of mind at heart, since we must seek the sources of the infinite evil of our baseless *sham-enlighten-ment*, and the misery of our *masquerade revolution*, in errors of this kind; since both find a place alike in the instruction, and in the life, of our educated and uneducated people. The necessity of great care for the psychological manner of developing and cultivating our powers of doing (*Fert.*), as well as the psychological training for the development of our power of knowing, is obvious. This psychological training for the development of our powers of knowing is based on an A B C of Anschauung, and must lead the child, by this fundamental clue, to the fullest purity of clear ideas. For the cultivation of the activities, on which the sense-foundation of our *virtue* rests, we must seek for an A B C for developing this power and on its lines a sense-cultivation, a physical dexterity of those powers and activities which are needed for the life-duties of our race,[11] which we must recognise as *leading strings in the nursery of virtue,* until our senses, ennobled by this training, need the leading-strings no longer. In [12] this way a general kind of education, suitable to the human race, can be developed, for training those practical abilities which are necessary for the fulfilment of the duties of life. It goes from *complete power of doing to the recognition of law,* just as the education of intelligence goes from *complete sense-impression to clear ideas,* and from these to their expression in words, to definitions. Therefore it is, that as *definitions before sense-impression* lead men to presumptuous chatter, so word-teachings about virtue and faith, preceding the realities of living sense-impressions, lead men astray to similar confusion about them. It is undeniable, that the presumption of these confusions, by virtue of the inner profanity and impurity that lie at the bottom of all presumption, leads even the virtuous faithful generally to the common vice of presumption. I believe also (experience speaks loudly on this view, and it must be so) that gaps in the early sense-cultivation of virtue have the same consequences, as gaps in the early sense-cultivation of knowledge.[13]

But I see myself at the beginning of a far greater problem than that which I think I have solved. I see myself at the beginning of this problem :—

"How can the child, considering the nature of his disposition, and the changeableness of his circumstances and relations, be so trained that whatever is demanded of him in the course of his life by necessity and duty, may be easy to him, and may, if possible, become second nature to him?"

I see myself at the beginning of the task of forming in the child, in its baby clothes, a satisfactory wife, the helpmeet of her husband, a good and vigorous mother, who fulfils her duties well. I see myself at the beginning of the task of making the child, in its baby clothes, the satisfactory husband of the woman, and a strong father, filling his place well.

What a task, my friend! To make the spirit of his future calling a second nature to the son of man. And what a still higher task to bring the sense-means of facilitating the virtuous and wise disposition of mind, into the blood and veins, before the hot desires for sensual pleasures have so infected blood and veins as to make virtue and wisdom impossible.

Friend! This problem is also solved. The same laws of the physical mechanism that develop in me the sense-foundations of knowledge, are also the sense-means of facilitating my virtue. But, dear friend, it is impossible for me to go into the details of this solution now. I reserve it for another time.

XIII.

Friend! As I said, it would have led me too far to enter into details of the principles and laws upon which the cultivation of the practical abilities (*Fert.*) in life depend. But I will not end my letters without touching on the keystone of my whole system, namely this question,—How is religious feeling connected with these principles, which I have accepted as generally true for the development of the human race?

Here also I seek the solution of my problem in myself,

and I ask: " How is the idea of God germinated in my soul? How comes it that I believe in God, that I throw myself in His arms, and feel blessed when I love Him, trust Him, thank Him, follow Him?

I soon see that the feelings of love, trust, gratitude, and readiness to obey, must be developed in me before I can apply them to God. I must love men, trust men, thank men, and obey men before I can aspire to love, thank, trust, and obey God. For whoso loveth not his brother, whom he hath seen, how can he love God whom he hath not seen?

Then I ask myself: How do I come to love, trust, thank, and obey men? How come those feelings in my nature on which human love, human gratitude, human confidence rest, and those activities by which obedience is formed? And I find: " *That they have their chief source in the relations that exist between the baby and his mother.*

The mother is forced by the power of animal instinct to tend her child, feed him, protect and please him. She does this. She satisfies his wants, she removes anything unpleasant, she comes to the help of his helplessness. The child is cared for, is pleased. *The germ of love is developed in him.*

Now put an object that he has never seen before his eyes; he is astonished, frightened, he cries. The mother presses him to her bosom, dandles him, and diverts him. He leaves off crying, but his eyes are still wet. The object appears again. The mother takes him into her sheltering arms and smiles at him again. Now he weeps no more. He returns his mother's smile with clear unclouded eyes. *The germ of trust is developed in him.*

The mother hastens to his cradle at his every need. She is there at the hour of hunger, she gives him drink in the hour of thirst. When he hears her step he is quiet, when he sees her he stretches out his hands. His eye is cast on her breast. He is satisfied. Mother, and being satisfied, are one and the same thought to him. *He is grateful.*

The germs of love, trust and gratitude soon grow. The child knows his mother's step; he smiles at her shadow. He loves those who are like her; a creature like his mother is a good creature to him. He smiles at his mother's face, at all human faces; he loves those who are dear to his mother. Whom his mother embraces, he embraces; whom his mother kisses, he kisses too. *The germ of human love, of brotherly love is developed in him.*

Obedience in its origin is an activity whose driving-wheel is opposed to the first inclinations of animal nature. Its cultivation rests on art. [1] It is not a simple result of pure instinct, but it is closely connected with it. Its first stage is distinctly instinctive. As *want* precedes love, *nourishment* gratitude, and care trust, so *passionate desire* precedes obedience. The child screams before he waits, he is impatient before he obeys. Patience is developed before obedience, he only becomes obedient through patience. The first manifestations (*Fert.*) of this virtue are simply passive; they arise generally from a consciousness of hard necessity. But this, too, is first developed on the mother's lap. The child must wait until she opens her breast to him; he must wait until she takes him up. *Active* obedience develops much later, and later still, the consciousness that it is good for him to obey his mother.

The development of the human race begins in a strong passionate desire for the satisfaction of physical wants. The mother's breast stills the first storm of physical needs, and creates *love;* soon after *fear* is developed. The mother's arm stills *fear.* These actions produce the *union* of the feelings of love and trust, and develop the first germ of *gratitude.*

Nature is inflexible towards the passionate child. He beats wood and stone, Nature is inflexible, and the child *ceases to beat* wood and stone.   Now the mother is inflexible towards his irregular desires.   He rages and roars—she is still inflexible.   He *leaves off crying*, he becomes accustomed to subject his will to hers.   *The first germs of patience, the first germs of obedience are developed.*

Obedience and love, gratitude and trust united, develop the first germ of conscience, the first faint shadow of the feeling that *it is not right* to rage against the loving mother ; the first faint shadow of the feeling that the mother is not in the world *altogether for his sake ;* the first faint shadow of a feeling that everything in the world is not altogether for his sake ; and with it is also germinated the feeling that *he himself* is not in the world for *his own sake* only.   The first shadow of duty and right is in the germ.

These are the first principles of moral self-development, which are unfolded by the natural relations between mother and child.   But in them lies the whole essence of the natural germ of that state of mind, which is peculiar to human dependence on the Author of our being.   That is, the germ of all feelings of dependence on God, through faith, is in its essence, the same germ which is produced by the infant's dependence on its mother.   The manner in which these feelings develop is one and the same.

In both, the infant hears, believes, follows, but in both, at this time, it *knows* not what it believes and *what it does.* Meanwhile, at this time, the *first grounds* of its faith and actions begin to vanish.   Growing independence makes the child let go his mother's hand.   He begins to become conscious of his own personality, and a secret thought unfolds itself in his heart,—"*I no longer need my mother.*"   She reads the growing thought in his eyes; she presses her darling more firmly to her heart, and says, in a voice he has not yet heard, "Child, there is a God whom thou needest, who taketh thee in His arms when thou needest me no longer, when I can shelter thee no more. There is a God who prepares joy and happiness for thee when I can no more give them thee." Then an inexpressible something rises in the child's heart, a holy feeling, a desire for faith, that raises him above himself. He rejoices in the name of God, as soon as he hears his mother speak it. The feelings of love, gratitude and trust that were developed at her bosom, extend and embrace God as father, God as mother. The practice (*Fert.*) of obedience has a wider field. The child, who believes from this time forwards in the eye of God as in the eye of his mother, does right now for *God's sake*, as he formerly did right for his *mother's sake*.

Here, in this first attempt of the mother's innocence and the mother's heart to *unite the first feeling of independence with the newly developed feeling of morality through the inclination to faith in God*, the foundations are disclosed on which education and instruction must cast their eyes, if they would aim, with certainty, at ennobling us.

As the first germination of love, gratitude, trust, and obedience was a simple result of the *coincidence of instinctive feelings* between mother and child, so the *further development* of these germinated feelings is a *high human art*. But it is an art, the threads of which will be *lost* in your hands, if for one moment you lose sight of the origin from which the web springs. The danger of this loss to the child is great, and comes early. He lisps his mother's name, he loves, thanks, trusts and follows. He lisps the name of God, he loves, thanks, trusts and follows. But the motives of gratitude, love and trust vanish with the first appearance of the idea: *He needs his mother no more.* The world that now surrounds him appears to him in a new light, and entices him with its pleasure, saying, " *You are mine now.*"

The child cannot but hear this voice. The instinct of the infant is quenched in him; the instinct of *growing powers takes its place*, and the germ of morality, *in so far as it begins in feelings that are proper to the infant*, suddenly withers up, and must wither, if at this moment, no one attaches to the golden spindle of creation the threads of his life, that is the first throbbing of the higher feelings of his moral nature.

Mother, mother! the world is now beginning to wean your child from your heart; and if at this moment no one connects his nobler nature with the new revelation of the world of sense, it is all over. Mother, mother, your child is torn from your heart. The new world becomes his mother, *the new world* becomes his god, *sensual pleasure* becomes his god, *self-will* becomes his god.

Mother, mother! he has lost you, he has lost God, he has lost himself. The touch of love is quenched for him. The germ of *self-respect* is dead within him. He is going towards destruction, striving only after sensual enjoyment.

Mankind, mankind! Now with this transition when the feelings of infancy vanish in the first consciousness of the charm of the world, independent of the mother—now when the ground, in which the noblest feelings of nature germinate, begins for the first time to tremble under the child's feet; now when the mother begins to be no more what she once was to her child; now when the germ of trust in the new aspect of the world is developed in him, and the charm of this new manifestation begins to *stifle and devour* his trust in his mother, who is no more what she once was to him, and with it his trust in an unseen and unknown God— as the wild web of tangled roots of the poisonous plant stifle and devour the finer web of roots of the noblest plants,— now, mankind! Now at this moment of transition between the feelings of trust in mother and God, and those of trust in the new aspect of the world and all that therein is,— now at this parting place, you should use all your art and all your power to keep the feelings of love, gratitude, trust and obedience pure in your child.

God is in these feelings, and the whole power of your moral life is intrinsically connected with their preservation.

Mankind! at this time when the physical causes of the germination of these feelings in the infant cease, your Art should do everything to bring to hand *new methods of stimulating them, and to let the attractions of the world only come before the mind of your growing child in connection with them.*

Now for the first time you *cannot trust Nature,* but must *do everything* to *take* the reins out of her blind *hands* and put them into the hands of principles and powers, in which the experience of ages has put them. The world that appears before the child's eyes is not God's first creation, it is a world spoilt alike for the innocent enjoyment of the senses, and for the feelings of his inner nature. It is a world full of war for the means of gratifying selfishness, full of contradiction, full of violence, presumption, lying and deceit.

Not God's first creation but *this* world decoys the child to the giddy dance of the whirlpool of the abyss, whose depths are the home of lovelessness and moral death. Not God's creation, but the brute force and art of bringing about its own ruin, is what *this* world puts before the child's eyes.

Poor child! your dwelling-room is your world; but your father is bound to his workshop, your mother is vexed to-day, has company to-morrow, and has whims the next day. You are bored; you ask questions; your nurse will not answer. You want to go out; you may not. Now you quarrel with your sister about a toy.—Poor child! what a miserable, heartless, heart-corrupting thing your world is! But is it anything more when you drive about in a gilded carriage under shady trees? Your leader deceives your mother. You suffer less, but you become worse than all sufferers. What have you gained? Your world is become a heavier load to you than any pain.

This world is so rocked to sleep in the ruin of a perverse and oppressive opposition to the laws of Nature, that it has no mind for being the means of preserving purity in the heart of man; on the contrary, it is as careless, at the critical moment, of the innocence of our race, as a heartless second wife of her step-child. A carelessness, that in a hundred cases to one, *causes and must cause* the wreck of the last means that are left us for ennobling our race. At this time the child has no counterpoise that can be opposed to the phenomena of the world, and the one-sided charm of its impressions on the senses, and so its conceptions, both through their one-sidedness and through their vividness, maintain a decided preponderance over the impressions of *experiences* and *feelings* which *lie at the base* of the moral and spiritual improvement of our race. Henceforth an infinite and infinitely living field is opened up for selfish and degraded passions. On the other hand, the way to that state of mind, on which the powers of his intelligence and enlightenment rest, is lost; that path to the narrow gate of morality is blocked up; the whole sensuousness of his nature must take a direction separating the *path of reason* from that of *love*, and the *improvement* of *the mind* from the *impulse towards faith in God*, a way that more or less makes selfishness the one driving wheel of all his actions, and thereby determines the result of his culture to his own destruction.

It is incomprehensible that mankind does not recognise this *universal source of ruin*. It is incomprehensible that it is not the one *universal aim of their Art* to stop it, and to *subordinate* the education of our race to *principles* which do not destroy the *work of God*, the feelings of love, gratitude and trust already developed in infancy, but which must at this dangerous time tend specially to care for those *means of uniting our moral and spiritual improvement* implanted in our nature by God Himself, and to bring education and instruction into harmony, on the one side, with those *laws of the physical mechanism* according to which our God raises us from vague sense-impressions to clear ideas, and on the other, with *those feelings of my inner nature*, through the gradual development of which my mind rises to recognise and venerate the *moral law.* It is incomprehensible that mankind *does not begin to bring out a perfect gradation of methods for developing the mind and feelings*, the essential purpose of which should be, to use the advantages of instruction and its mechanism for the preservation of moral perfection, to prevent the selfishness of the reason by preserving the purity of the heart from error and one-sidedness; and above all, to *subordinate* my sense-impressions to my convictions, my eagerness to my benevolence, and my benevolence to my righteous will.

The causes which make this subordination necessary, lie deep in my nature. As my physical powers *increase*, their *preponderance*, by virtue of the laws of my development, *must vanish*, that is, they must be *subordinated* to a higher law. But every step of my development must be completed before it can be subordinated to a higher purpose. This subordination of that which is already complete, to that which is to be completed, requires above all, pure *holding fast* to the *beginning-points* of all knowledge, and the most exact continuity in gradual progress from these beginning-points to the final *completion.* The primary law of this continuity is this : the first instruction of the child should never be the business of the *head* or of the *reason ;* it should always be the business of the senses, of the *heart*, of the *mother.*

The second law, that follows it, is this : human education goes on slowly from exercise of the senses to exercise of the judgment. It is for a long time the business of the *heart*, before it is the business of the *reason*. It is for a long time the business of the *woman* before it begins to be the business of the *man*.

What shall I say more?—With these words the eternal laws of nature lead me back to your hand, *mother!* Mother! I can keep my innocence, my love, my obedience, the excellences of my nobler nature with the new impressions of the world, *all, all* at *your side* only. Mother, mother! while you have still a hand, a heart for me, let me not turn away from you. If no one has taught you to know the world as I am forced to learn it, *then come, we will learn it together*, as you ought, and I must. Mother, mother! we will not *part from each other* at the moment when I run into danger of being drawn away from you, from God, and from myself, by the new phenomena of the world. Mother, mother! *sanctify the transition from your heart to this world, by the support of your heart.*

Friend! I must be silent. My heart is moved, and I see tears in your eyes. Farewell!

XIV.

Friend! I go further now and ask myself: What have I done to work against the evils that affected me throughout my life, from a religious point of view? Friend! If by my efforts I have in any way succeeded in preparing the road to the goal at which I have been aiming, that is to take human education out of the hands of blind Nature, to free it from the destructive influence of her sensual side, and the power of the routine of her miserable teaching, and to put it into the hands of the noblest powers of our nature, the soul of which is faith and love; if I can only in some slight degree succeed in making the Art of education begin in the sanctuary of home, more than it now does, and to put new life into the religious instinct of our race, from this tender side ; if I should only have partly succeeded in bringing nearer to my contemporaries the withered rootstock of mental and spiritual education, and an Art of education in harmony with the noblest powers of heart and mind ; if I have done this, my life will be blessed, and I shall see my greatest hopes fulfilled.[1]

I will dwell a moment longer on this point. The germ, out of which the feelings that are essential to religion and morality spring, is the same from which the whole spirit of my method of teaching arises. It begins entirely in the natural relation, which exists between the infant and its mother, and essentially rests on the Art of connecting instruction, from the cradle upwards, with this natural relation, and building it with continuous Art upon a state of mind that resembles our dependence on the Author of our being. When the physical dependence of child on mother begins to vanish, my method uses all possible means to prevent the germ of the nobler feelings, that arose from this dependence, from withering away ; and as the physical causes cease, it supplies new sources of vitality. At the important moment of the first separation of the feelings of trust in mother and God, and of reliance on the phenomena of the world, it applies all possible power and Art, so that the charm of the new phenomena of the world shall always appear to the child in connection with the nobler feelings of his nature. It uses all its power and Art to let these phenomena come before his eyes as God's *first creation*, not merely as a world full of lying and deceit. It limits the one-sided charm of the new phenomena by stimulating dependence upon mother and God. It limits the boundless free play of selfishness, to which the destructive phenomena of the world lead my animal nature, and does not allow the path of my reason to divide absolutely from the path of my heart, nor the improvement of my mind to separate me absolutely from my impulse of faith in God.

The whole spirit of my method is not only to renew the bond between mother and child, with the disappearance of its physical cause, but to put a methodical series of means, that is an Art, into her hand by which she can give permanence to this relation between her heart and her child, until the sense-methods of making virtue easy, united with the sense-methods of acquiring knowledge, may be able, by exercise, to ripen the independence of the child, in all that concerns right and duty.

It has made it easy for every mother, whose heart is her child's, to keep him not only at the critical period from the danger of being drawn away from God and love, to save his soul from dreadful withering, and himself from being given up to unavoidable bewilderment, but also to lead him by the hand of her love and with pure, supporting, noble feelings into God's best creation, before his heart is spoilt for the impressions of innocence, truth and love by all the lying and deceit of this world.

For the woman who makes my method her own, her child is no longer confined within the miserable and limited sphere of her own actual knowledge. The Mother's Book opens to her for her child the world which is God's world. The purest love opens her mouth for all that the child sees through her. She has taught him to lisp the name of God on her bosom, now she shows him the All-loving in the rising sun, in the rippling brook, in the branches of the trees, in the splendour of the flower, in the dewdrops. She shows him the All-present in himself, in the light of his eyes, in the flexibility of his joints, in the tones of his voice, in everything she shows him God; and wherever he sees God his heart rises, wherever he sees God in the world he loves the world. Joy in God's world is interwoven with joy in God. He includes God, the world, and his mother in one and the same emotion. The torn bond is joined together again. He loves his mother more now than when he lay upon her breast. He stands now a step higher. He is now raised through the very same world, by which he would have been bewildered, if he had not learned to know it through his mother. The mouth that smiled on him so often from the day of his birth, the voice that from the day of his birth has so often foretold joy to him, this voice now teaches him to talk. The hand that pressed him so often to her heart now shows him pictures, whose names he has often heard. A new feeling germinates in his breast. He becomes conscious by words of what he sees. The first step of the gradation of the union of his spiritual and moral improvement is open. The mother's hand opens it, the child learns, knows, and names; he wishes to know more, to name more. He forces the mother to learn with him; she learns with him, and both mount daily to knowledge, power and love. Now she attempts with him the elements and grounds of art, straight and curved lines. The child soon outsteps her—the joy of both is equal, new powers develop in his mind, he *draws, measures, reckons.* The mother showed him God in the aspect of the world, now she shows him God in his drawing, measuring, reckoning, in all his powers. He now sees God in his self-perfection. The law of perfection is the law of his training. He recognises it in the first perfect drawing, in one straight or curved line—yes, friend, with the first perfect drawing of a line, with the first perfect pronunciation of a word, the first idea of the high law: "Be ye also perfect, as your Father in heaven is perfect" is developed in his breast. And since my method rests essentially on constant efforts towards the perfection of single things, it works powerfully and constantly to impress the spirit of this law *deeply* in the child's breast from the cradle upwards.

To this first law of your inner perfection, a second is united, intrinsically interwoven with the first. This is,— Man is not in the world for his own sake only; he can only perfect himself through the perfection of his brethren. My method seems exactly fitted to make these two laws, united, second nature to the children, almost before they know right from left. The child of my method can hardly talk before he is his brother's teacher, and his mother's helper.

Friend! It is not possible to join the bonds of the feelings on which true reverence for God rests, more tightly than it is done by the whole spirit of my method. By it I have preserved the mother for the child, and procured permanence for the influence of her heart. By it I have united God's worship with human nature, and secured their preservation by stimulating those emotions, from which the impulse of faith is germinated in our hearts. Mother and Creator, mother and Preserver, become through it, one and the same emotion for the child. By it the child remains longer *his mother's child;* he remains by it longer *God's child.* The gradual development of his mind and heart united rests longer on the pure beginning-points from which their first germs sprang. The path of his love of man, and his wisdom is familiarly and sublimely opened. By it I am the father of the poor, the support of the wretched. As my mother *leaves* her healthy children and *clings* to the sickly, and *takes double care* of the wretched because she *must, being the mother*, because she stands in God's place to the child, so must *I, if the mother. is in God's place* to me, and God fills my heart in the *mother's place.* A feeling like the mother's feeling impels me. Man is my brother, my love embraces the whole race, but I cling to the *wretched*, I am *doubly* his father; to act *like God* becomes my *nature.* I am a child of God; I believed in my mother, her heart showed me God. God is the God of my *mother*, of *my heart* and *her heart.* I know no other God. The God of my *brain* is a *chimæra.* I know no other God but the God of my *heart.* By faith in the God of *my heart* only I feel a man. The God of my *brain* is an *idol.* I ruin myself by worshipping him. The God of my *heart* is my God. I perfect myself in His love. Mother, mother! you showed me God in your *commands*, and I found Him in *obedience.* Mother, mother! when I forget *God* I forget *you*, and when I *love* God I am in *your place* to your infant. I cling to your *wretched ones*, and *those who weep*, rest in my arms as in their *mother's.*

Mother, mother! as I love you so I love God, and duty is *my highest good.* Mother! when *I forget you, I forget* God, and the wretched ones *no longer* rest in my arms; I am *no longer* in God's place to the sufferer. When I forget you I forget *God.* Then live I, like the lion, for *myself* and in self-confidence use my powers for *myself against my own race.* Then is there no sense of fatherhood in my soul, then no *sense of God* sanctifies my obedience; and my apparent *sense of duty* is a vain deception.

Mother, mother! as I love you, so love I God. *Mother* and *obedience, God* and *duty* are one and the same to me— *God's will*, and the *best* and *noblest*, that I can imagine, are one and the same to me. I live then no more for *myself;* I lose myself in *my brethren*, the children of my God—I live *no more for myself*, I live for Him who took me in my mother's arms, and *raised* me with a father's hand above the dust of my mortal coil to His love. And the more I love Him, the Eternal, the more I honour His commandments, the more I *depend on Him*, the more I *lose myself and become His*, the more does my nature become *divine*, the more do I feel in harmony with my inner nature and with my whole race. The more I love Him, the more I follow Him, the more do I hear on all sides the voice of the Eternal, " Fear not, I am thy God, I will never forsake thee; follow My commandments; My will is thy salvation." And the more I follow Him, the more I love Him and thank Him, the more I trust the Eternal, the more I know Him *who is and was and shall be evermore*, the Author of my being, needing me not.

I have recognised the Eternal *in myself.* I have *seen* the way of the Lord, I have *read* the laws of the Almighty in the dust, I have *sought* out the laws of His love in my heart—I *know* in whom I *believe.* My trust in God becomes infinite through my self-knowledge, and through the insight germinated in it, of the laws of the moral world. The idea of the Infinite is interwoven in my nature with the idea of the Eternal. I hope for eternal life. And the more I love Him, the Eternal, the more I hope for eternal life. The more I trust, the more I thank and follow Him. The more faith in His eternal goodness becomes a truth to me, the more does my faith in His eternal goodness become a witness of my immortality.

I am silent again, Friend !—What are words to express a certainty that springs from the heart ? What are words on a subject in which a man, whose head and heart alike deserve my respect, thus expressed himself : ' There is no perception of God from mere knowledge ; the true God lives only for faith, for childlike faith."

> " What is dim to the wisdom of the wise,
> Is clear and simple unto childlike eyes."

Then only the heart knows God, the heart that rising above care for its own finite being embraces mankind, be it the whole or a part?

" This pure human heart requires and creates for its love, its obedience, its trust, its worship, a personified type of the highest, a high, holy will, which exists as the soul of the whole spiritual world.

"Ask the good man,—Why is duty your highest good? Why do you believe in God? If he gives proofs, only the schools are speaking in him. A more skilful intellect beats all these proofs down. He trembles a moment, but his heart cannot deny the Divine; he comes back to Him, blessing and loving, as to his mother's bosom.

"Then whence comes the good man's conviction of God? Not from the intellect, but from that inexplicable impulse which cannot be comprehended in any word, or any thought, the impulse to glorify and immortalize his being in the higher imperishable being of the whole.—*Not me, but the brethren.—Not the individual—but the race.* This is the unconditional expression of the divine voice within the soul. In comprehending and following it lies the only nobility of human nature." [2]

APPENDIX.

"THE METHOD, A REPORT BY PESTALOZZI."*

I AM trying to psychologize the instruction of mankind; I am trying to bring it into harmony with the nature of my mind, with that of my circumstances and my relations to others. I start from no positive form of teaching, as such, but simply ask myself :—

"What would you do, if you wished to give a single child all the knowledge and practical skill he needs, so that by wise care of his best opportunities, he might reach inner content ?"

I think, to gain this end, the human race needs exactly the same thing as the single child.

I think, further, the poor man's child needs a greater refinement in the methods of instruction than the rich man's child.

---

* "The Method, a Report by Pestalozzi," published by Niederer, with other posthumous works by Pestalozzi, in the *Allgemeine Monatschrift für Erziehung und Unterricht*, edited by J. P. Rossel, Aix-la-Chapelle, 1828. Vol. ix., pp. 66–80, 161-174. — This work is in the Library of the Teachers' Guild, London.—These papers were also published separately under the title of "Pestalozzische Blätter," of which one volume and part of another were published. A copy is in the Musée Pédagogue, Paris.

Niederer says, in the Introduction : "The following original treatise, hitherto unprinted, contains Pestalozzi's report to a Society which had been formed to support his efforts for education at the time of his return from Stanz to Burgdorf. It is Pestalozzi's own work, and he has signed the copy, from which this is taken, with his own hand.

"This precious document takes us back again to Pestalozzi's standpoint when he created the method. In this his views are fully expressed, and it contains the germ which developed later into the theory of elementary human education ; but it also contains the errors and mistakes which hindered the progress of his work."

Seyffarth, who republishes it, Vol. 18, says : "It seems that Niederer made no alteration in this treatise, for he has added notes to the text, which he did not do when he made alterations." But there is reason for thinking that it has been touched by Niederer. See note at end. pp. 207-8.

199

NATURE, indeed, does much for the human race, but we have strayed away from her path. The poor man is thrust away from her bosom, and the rich destroy themselves both by rioting and by lounging on her overflowing breast.

The picture is severe. But ever since I have been able to see I have seen it so; and it is from this view that the impulse arises within me, not merely to plaster over the evils in schools, which are enervating the people of Europe, but to cure them at their root.

But this can never be done without subordinating all forms of instruction to those eternal laws, by which the human mind is raised from physical impressions on the senses to clear ideas.

I have tried to simplify the elements of all human knowledge according to these laws, and to put them into a series of typical examples that shall result in spreading a wide knowledge of Nature, general clearness of the most important ideas in the mind, and vigorous exercises of the chief bodily powers, even among the lowest classes.

I know what I am undertaking; but neither the difficulties in the way, nor my own limitations in skill and insight, shall hinder me from giving my mite for a purpose which Europe needs so much. And, gentlemen, in laying before you the results of those labours on which my life has been spent, I beg of you but one thing. It is this:—Separate those of my assertions that may be doubtful from those that are indisputable. I wish to found my conclusions entirely upon complete convictions, or at least upon perfectly recognised premises.

The most essential point from which I start is this:—

Sense impression of Nature is the only true foundation of human instruction, because it is the only true foundation of human knowledge.

All that follows is the result of this sense impression, and the process of abstraction from it. Hence in every case where this is imperfect, the result also will be neither certain, safe nor positive; and in any case, where the sense impression is inaccurate, deception and error follow.

I start from this point and ask :—"What does Nature herself do in order to present the world truly to me, so far as it affects me? That is,—By what means does she bring the sense impressions of the most important things around me, to a perfection that contents me?" And I find,—She does this through my surroundings, my wants, and my relations to others.

Through my surroundings she determines the kinds of sense

impressions I receive. Through my wants she stimulates my activities. Through my relations to others she widens my observation and raises it to insight and forethought. Through my surroundings, my wants, my relations to others, she lays the foundations of my knowledge, my work, and my right-doing.

And now I ask myself :—" What general means of the Art * has the experience of ages put into the hands of humanity to strengthen this influence of Nature in developing intelligence, energy and virtue in our race?" And I find these methods are speech, the arts of drawing, writing, reckoning and measuring.

And when I trace back all these elements of the human Art to their origin, I find it in the common basis of our mind, by means of which our understanding combines those impressions which the senses have received from Nature, and represents them as wholes, that is, as concepts.

It is evident from this statement that in any case, where systematic training does not keep pace with the actual sense impressions of Nature, that the Art by its over-hasty work upon the human mind, becomes a source of physical atrophy, that must inevitably result in one-sidedness, warped judgment, superficiality and error. Every word, every number, is a result of the understanding that is generated by ripened sense impression.

But the gradual process, by which sensuous impressions become clear conceptions, goes up to the limits of the spontaneous working of the understanding—which is independent of the sensibility (receptivity)—in harmony with the laws of the physical mechanism.

Imitation precedes hieroglyphics ; hieroglyphics precede culti-vated language, just as the individual name precedes the generic.

Further, it is only through this course, in harmony with the mechanism of the senses, that culture brings up before me the sea of confused phenomena (*Ansch.*) flowing one into another, first as definite sense impressions, and from these forms clear concepts.

Thus all the Art (of teaching) men is essentially a result of physico-mechanical laws, the most important of which are the following :—

1. Bring all things essentially related to each other to that connection in your mind which they really have in Nature.

---

* The Art of Teaching : our Science and Art of Education.

2. Subordinate all unessential things to essential, and especially subordinate the impression given by the Art to that given by Nature and reality.

3. Give to nothing a greater weight in your idea than it has in relation to your race in Nature.

4. Arrange all objects in the world according to their likeness.

5. Strengthen the impressions of important objects by allowing them to affect you through different senses.

6. In every subject try to arrange graduated steps of knowledge, in which every new idea shall be only a small, almost imperceptible addition to that earlier knowledge which has been deeply impressed and made unforgetable.

7. Learn to make the simple perfect before going on to the complex.

8. Recognise that as every physical ripening must be the result of the whole perfect fruit in all its parts, so every just judgment must be the result of a sense impression, perfect in all its parts, of the object to be judged. Distrust the appearance of precocious ripeness as the apparent ripeness of a worm-eaten apple.

9. All physical effects are absolutely necessary; and this necessity is the result of the art of Nature, with which she unites the apparently heterogeneous elements of her material into one whole for the achievement of her end. The Art, which imitates her, must try in the same way to raise the results at which it aims to a physical necessity, while it unites its elements into one whole for the achievement of its end.

10. The richness of its charm and the variety of its free play cause the results of physical necessity to bear the impress of freedom and independence. Here, too, the Art must imitate the course of Nature, and by the richness of its charm and the variety of its free play, try to make its results bear the impress of freedom and independence.

11. Above all, learn the first law of the physical mechanism, the powerful, universal connection between its results and the proportion of nearness or distance between the object and our senses. Never forget this physical nearness or distance of all objects around you has an immense effect in determining your positive sense impressions, practical ability and even virtue. But even this law of your nature converges as a whole towards another. It converges towards the centre of our whole being, and we ourselves are this centre. Man! never forget it! All that you are, all you wish, all you might be, comes out of

yourself. All must have a centre in your physical sense impression, and this again is yourself. In all it does, the Art really only adds this to the simple course of Nature.—That which Nature puts before us, scattered and over a wide area, the Art puts together in narrower bounds and brings nearer to our five senses, by associations, which facilitate the power of memory, and strengthen the susceptibility of our senses, and make it easier for them, by daily practice, to present to us the objects around us in greater numbers, for a longer time and in a more precise way.

The mechanism of Nature as a whole is great and simple. Man! imitate it. Imitate this action of great Nature, who out of the seed of the largest tree produces a scarcely perceptible shoot, then, just as imperceptibly, daily and hourly by gradual stages, unfolds first the beginnings of the stem, then the bough, then the branch, then the extreme twig on which hangs the perishable leaf.

Consider carefully this action of great Nature, how she tends and perfects every single part as it is formed, and joins on every new part to the permanent life of the old.

Consider carefully how the bright blossom is unfolded from the deeply hidden bud. Consider how the bloom of its first day's splendour is soon lost, while the fruit, at first weak but perfectly formed, adds something important every day to all that it is already. So, quietly growing for long months, it hangs on the twig that nourishes it; until, fully ripe and perfect in all its parts, it falls from the tree.

Consider how Mother Nature, with the uprising shoot, also develops the germ of the root, and buries the noblest part of the tree deep in the bosom of the earth; then how she forms the immovable stem from the very heart of the root, and the boughs from the very heart of the stem, and the branches from the very heart of the boughs. How to all, even the weakest, outermost twig she gives enough, but to none useless, disproportionate strength.

The mechanism of physical human nature is essentially subject to the same laws by which physical Nature generally unfolds her powers. According to these laws all instruction should graft the most essential parts of its subject firmly into the very being of the human mind; then join on the less essential gradually, but uninterruptedly, to the most essential, and maintain all the parts of the subject, even to the outermost, in one living proportionate whole.

I now go further, and ask:—How has Europe applied these

laws of the physical mechanism to all matters of popular education? What has Europe done to bring the elementary means of human knowledge, that the work of ages has put into our hands, into harmony with the real nature of the human mind, and the laws of the physical mechanism? What use has this generation made of these laws in the organization of its teaching institutions, in its speaking, drawing, writing, reading, reckoning and measuring?

I see none. In the existing organization of these institutions, at least so far as they affect the poorer classes, I see no trace of any regard for the general harmony of the whole and for the psychological gradations required by these laws.

No, it is notorious! In the existing methods of popular instruction these laws are not only ignored, but generally rudely opposed.

And when I ask again :—What are the unmistakable consequences of thus rudely despising these laws? I cannot conceal from myself the physical atrophy, one-sidedness, warped judgment, superficiality, and presumptuous vanity that characterize the masses in this generation, are the necessary consequence of despising these laws, and of the isolated, unpsychological, baseless, unorganized, unconnected teaching, which our poor race has received in our lower schools.

Then the problem I have to solve is this :—How to bring the elements of every art into harmony with the very nature of my mind, by following the psychological mechanical laws by which my mind rises from physical sense impressions to clear ideas.

Nature has two principal and general means of directing human activity towards the cultivation of the arts, and these should be employed, if not before, at least side by side with any particular means. They are singing and the sense of the beautiful.

With song the mother lulls her babe to sleep; but here, as in everything else, we do not follow the law of Nature. Before the child is a year old, his mother's song ceases; by that time she is, as a rule, no longer a mother to the weaned child. For him, as for all others, she is only a distracted, over-burdened woman. Alas! that it is so. Why has not the Art of ages taught us to join the nursery lullabies to a series of national songs, that should rise in the cottages of the people, from the gentle cradle song to the sublime hymn of praise? But I cannot fill this gap. I can only point it out.

It is the same with the sense of the beautiful. All Nature is full of grand and lovely sights, but Europe has done nothing to awaken in the poor a sense for these beauties, or to arrange them in such a way as to produce a series of impressions, capable of developing this sense. The sun rises for us in vain; in vain for us he sets. In vain for us do wood and meadow, mountain and valley spread forth their innumerable charms. They are nothing to us.

Here, again, I can do nothing; but if ever popular education should cease to be the barbarous absurdity it now is, and put itself into harmony with the real needs of our nature, this want will be supplied.

I leave these means of directing the Art generally, and turn to the forms by which special means of education, speaking, reading, drawing and writing should be taught.

Before the child can utter a sound, a many-sided consciousness of all physical truths exists already within him, as a starting-point for the whole round of his experiences. For instance, he feels that the pebble and the tree have different properties, that wood differs from glass. To make this dim consciousness clear, speech is necessary. We must give him names for the various things he knows, as well as for their properties.

So we connect his speech with his knowledge, and extend his knowledge with his speech. This makes the consciousness of impressions which have touched his senses clearer to the child. And the common work of all instruction is to make this consciousness clear. This may be done in two ways.

Either we lead the children through knowledge of names to that of things, or else through knowledge of things to that of names. The second method is mine. I wish always to let sense impression precede the word, and definite knowledge the judgment. I wish to make words and talk unimportant on the human mind, and to secure that preponderance due to the actual impressions of physical objects (*Ansch.*), that forms such a remarkable protection against mere noise and empty sound. From his very first development I wish to lead my child into the whole circle of Nature surrounding him; I would organize his learning to talk by a collection of natural products; I would teach him early to abstract all physical generalizations from separate physical facts, and teach him to express them in words; and I would everywhere substitute physical generalizations for those metaphysical generalizations with which we begin the instruction of our race. Not till after the foundation of human knowledge, (sense impressions of Nature,) has been fairly laid and secure would I begin the dull, abstract work of studying from books.

But even my A B C book is only a collection of easy stories by which every mother is enabled with the sound of the letter to make her child acquainted with the most important facts of his physical nature.

Supplement No. 1 contains the letter T of this A B C book.

Before the child knows the forms of the letters by sight, before his organs begin to make articulate sounds, I let the root-forms of all German syllables be repeated so often and so carefully before his developing organs, that he learns to imitate them easily and distinctly. When this is done, I let him see first single letters, then two or three together, letting him hear the sound as he looks at them, and when he has fixed the order in which they are placed in his memory, he pronounces 2, 3, or 4 together like one.

The examples of the series by which this is done are in Supplement No. 2. I also depend here on the physical effects of completeness, and have given this stage of sense-impression a fulness that it has never had before.

Words of one or more syllables are placed letter by letter on the board. For instance, take the word Soldatenstand. We first put:—

	S and ask, How do you say that?			Answer, S
then O	„	„	„	now? „ SO
„ L	„	„	„	„ „ SOL
„ D	„	„	„	„ „ SOLD
„ A	„	„	„	„ „ SOLDA
„ T	„	„	„	„ „ SOLDAT
„ E	„	„	„	„ „ SOLDATE
„ N	„	„	„	„ „ SOLDATEN
„ ST	„	„	„	„ „ SOLDATENST.

Frequent repetition of building up the same word is absolutely necessary to make the formation and pronunciation perfectly fluent to the child.

When the children can form and pronounce the word with ease, it should be shown them in syllables, and imitated by them until they feel, themselves, which letters on the board belong to each syllable. I number the syllables, and ask: What is the first, the second, and so on? and out of the order of their sequence—the sixth, the first, the fourth, and so on? Then, for the first time, I let them spell it. Changing the letters of a word to be spelt; taking one or more of them away, adding others, and dividing it up into false syllables strengthens the observation of the children, and their increased power enables them to re-arrange the very hardest words by themselves.

By this method the formation of words becomes evident to children; their organs of speech are exercised to pronounce the hardest words easily; in a short time they reach an incredible facility in this business, usually so tiresome; and from one word often learn a number of independent words, as in the above example.

Lastly, we use the separate letters as a basis for beginning arithmetic, according to a systematic series of number-relationships, which is shown in Supplement No. 3.

Regardless of confusion and error, Nature lays her whole wealth before the eyes of the inexperienced child, and the child in her great warehouse hears the whole wealth of language before he has an idea of a single word. But sound and tone are deeply impressed upon him, and the connection in which he daily hears the words soon gives him a vague sense of what they mean.

Here, too, I imitate the course of Nature. My first reading book for the child is the dictionary; the sum of our ancestors' testimony about all that exists. Language, as one great whole, is in this first reading book, that rises through a series of repetitions, of imperceptible grammatical additions, to be an encyclopedic register of facts. No. 4 contains a specimen of this reading book in its original simplicity. No. 5 contains a specimen of simple grammatical additions.

No. 6 contains the classification of words according to the similarity of their meaning.

No. 7 contains exercises in language-teaching, in the use of verbs and substantives together.

Writing is only a kind of linear drawing applied to certain arbitrary forms, and must be subject to the general laws of linear drawing. Nature confirms this principle. The child is able to make the elements of linear drawing his own, two years before he is in a position to guide that delicate instrument, the pen, well. Therefore I teach the children to draw before thinking of writing, and by this means they form the letters more perfectly than they would otherwise do at this age.

The success depends entirely on the very simple principle, that whoever can divide an angle accurately and draw an arc round it, has already the foundations for the accurate drawing of all letters in his hand. The following figure contains the characteristic lines of the art of writing.*

* Seyffarth omits the last sentence and diagram, he may have good rea-

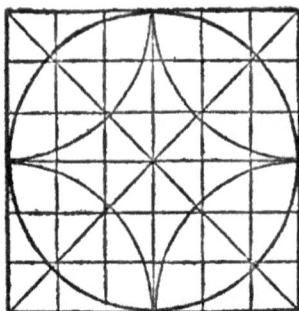

The principle from which I start is this :—

Angles, parallels and arcs comprise the whole art of drawing. Everything that can possibly be drawn is only a definite application of these three primary forms. We can imagine a perfectly simple series arising out of these primary forms, within which an absolute standard is to be found for all drawing; and the æsthetic beauty of all forms can be evolved from the nature of these primary forms.

No. 9 contains a few drawings, mathematical and æsthetic.

No. 10 contains mathematical definitions of the primary forms of all the letters.

No. 11 gradated exercises in writing with the slate pencil. The beginnings of geometry are closely connected with these.

No. 12 contains examples of the way in which I try to sharpen the child's eyes.

No. 13 contains attempts to make clear to them the principles of this subject.

Numbers are abstractions from magnitudes, therefore it is necessary that the elements of geometry should precede the first principles of arithmetic, or, at least, should be taught at the same time.

Here, too, I begin with sense impressions, and make the divisions of numbers by showing first, few or more real things; then groups of dots so that the child does not take arbitrary

sons. It is supposed to be Buss's A B C of Anschauung—Form. See Letter III. Note I. If it really occurs here in the original text, Pestalozzi must have made it. When this Report was written he had not met Buss. I cannot yet satisfactorily trace its origin. Biber calls it the alphabet of form, and uses it to illustrate Buss's account, he says "it was never published, and soon superseded," p. 205. He evidently did not know Niederer had published it three years before. Although he had his information through Krusi and Niederer, we follow Rossel. Seyffarth apparently thinks that Niederer has added it, and therefore leaves it out.

forms as numbers, but can revise and test by the actual dots the actual relations of numbers.

In No. 14 are a few examples of this method of calculating.

In this way, gentlemen, I try to follow in elementary instruction the mechanical laws by which man rises from sense impression to clear ideas.

All Nature is bound to this course of action. She is bound to rise step by step from the simple beginning.

I follow in her path. If the child knows simple bodies—air, earth, water, fire—I show him the effects of these elements on bodies that he knows, and as he learns the properties of several simple bodies, I show him the different effects obtained by uniting one body to another, and lead him always by the simplest course of sense impression to the boundaries of the higher sciences. Everything must be put into forms that make it possible and easy for any sensible mother to follow this instruction. But I would also wish that my children, taught in this way, should not let themselves be led astray by the presumptuous ignorance of schoolmasters.

I maintain that my method will lead them as early as their seventh year to seek the man, who is master of any branch of knowledge, and to be able to judge about it independently and freely.

But we neither know what education is, nor what the child is.

The details of human sense impression from which his knowledge arises, are in themselves imperceptible, and left to Nature, unarranged, they are chaotically confused. But the important part of this boundless chaos is small in each department, and when accurately arranged, can easily be surveyed. On the other hand, the child's power of apprehension when used psychologically is infinite; but we must in all subjects use the work of our forefathers, which has not only brought the details of our sense impressions nearer to our consciousness through language, but has arranged their infinite details, and has brought them for definite purposes into orderly sequence.

It is obvious that we must not neglect the preliminary work of former ages as if we were apes and never meant to be men. Here my course rises to the final destiny of the child; but I look on it only within the limits of physical mechanism, the scope of which I would inquire into and try to follow, and I find myself once more at Nature's law, that my sense impressions, my efforts, and my ends are closely connected with the physical nearness or distance of the objects that determine my will.

It is true that a child, who runs about for an hour, looking for a tree that grows before his door, will never know a tree. The child, who in his dwelling room finds no stimulant to effort, will scarcely find any in the wide world; and he who finds no stimulus to human love in his mother's eyes may travel the world through and find no motive for benevolence in human tears.

The natural man becomes an angel when he avails himself of the incentives to wisdom and virtue that naturally and closely surround him. He becomes a devil when he neglects them, and ranges over all mountains to seek them at a distance. It must be so. When the objects of the world are removed from my senses they are, so far, sources of deception and error, and even of crime. But I say again, this law of the physical mechanism revolves about a higher one, it revolves about the centre of your whole being, that is yourself. Self-knowledge, then, is the centre from which all human instruction must start.

But this has a double nature.

No. 15 shows, (1) how much I try to use the knowledge of my physical nature as the foundation of human instruction.

(2) How much I try to use the knowledge of my inner individuality; the consciousness of my will to further my own welfare; and of my duty to be true to my inner light. But in the sphere of the child's physical experience, there are not enough motives for standpoints. Therefore, Nature has inspired him with trust in his mother, and upon this trust founded willing obedience, within the limits of which the child has acquired those habits, the possession of which will make the duties of life easier.

Nourished on his mother's breast, reading love in her every glance, dependent for each want of his life upon her, obedience in its first origin is a physical necessity for him, its performance an easy duty, and its result the source of his pleasure.

Even so is man. He finds in the whirl of existence and in his material experiences no sufficient motives for subjecting himself to that alone which the duties of his life require of him.

To fill this gap Nature has implanted in his bosom trust in God, and upon this trust founded willing obedience, within the limits of which he daily acquires those habits, the possession of which alone makes a lasting effort towards inner nobility possible. He, too, is nourished at the bosom of Nature, and finds all his joys resting on her lap; but just as much is he dependent on stern necessity. Therefore for him obedience to truth and justice, obedience to the Author of his being, who has no need of him, is also in its origin a physical necessity of his condition, its fulfilment an easy duty, and its result the source of all his joy.

I, then, lay the keystone of my instruction upon the early development of the natural motive to fear God; for though I am thoroughly convinced that religion is badly used as an exercise for the understanding and as a subject of instruction for children, yet I am equally convinced that as the affair of the heart it is a necessity for my nature even at the tenderest age; that as such it cannot too early be awakened, purified or elevated. From Moses to Christ all the prophets have tried to connect this sentiment with the innocence of the childlike mind, and to develop and nourish it through sense impression of all Nature.

I follow their path. My whole instruction is nothing but a series of illustrations of the wisdom and greatness of my nature in so far as it has not been degraded by me.

Through an eye, opened by infinite preparation of the Art, I show the child the world, and he no longer dreams of God, he sees Him; he lives in contemplation (*Ansch.*) of Him. He prays to Him.

Supplement No. 16 contains an example of my series of verbs, from the simple combination of which every process and action of Nature that specially concerns man is made clear,—what he does in common with inanimate Nature and what he does in common with the brute.

I do not think it possible to find illustrations by which the natural man can be more surely raised to worship God and to reverence himself and his own worth. It is my inmost wish too, to found my instruction on this foundation of human tranquility. For I am convinced that a child brought up without trust in God is a motherless waif; and a child out of tune with this trust is an unhappy daughter who has lost her mother's heart.

But it is time I ended. Gentlemen, this is the first sketch of my principles and method of instruction, and I offer it to your free criticism.

PESTALOZZI.

BURGDORF, *June 27th*, 1800.

NOTES TO PREFACE AND LETTER I.

(G) Refers to Roger de Guimps' *Life of Pestalozzi*, Translated by J. Russell, B.A.
(London: Swan Sonnenschein & Co., 1890).

[1] The preface was added to the second edition, *Collected Works*, Vol. 5, Cotta, Stuttgart and Tübingen, 1820.—The first edition (1801) has no preface.—This gives us Pestalozzi's views twenty years after the first publication of the book; it should therefore be read, as prefaces often are, after the work itself.

[2] Ith, Johannsen, and Niederer.

Ith, J. von, wrote *Official Report of the Pestalozzian Institute and the New Method of Teaching*. Bern and Zürich, 1802. This was one of the first works published on the new method of Burgdorf.

Johannsen published a *Criticism of the Pestalozzian Method*. Jena and Leipzig, 1804.

Neiderer, editor of Pestalozzi's collected works, was one of Pestalozzi's principal fellow-workers at Yverdun, and had great influence over him. His first work, *The Pestalozzian Institute and the Public*, with a preface by Pestalozzi, was published at Yverdun in 1811, *Pestalozzi's Educational Undertaking in its Relation to the Culture of the Age*, 2 vols., Stuttgart and Tübingen, 1812–13.

[3] Gruner, Von Türk, and Chavannes.

Gruner published *Letters from Burgdorf about Pestalozzi, his Method and his Institute.* 1804, Ed. 2, 1806, Frankfort.

Von Türk was of a noble family in North Germany. He gave up a good position in the magistracy of Oldenburg, and went to Yverdun to study Pestalozzi's work and methods. He was the author of *Contributions to Information about German Elementary Schools* and *Letters from München-Buchsee on Pestalozzi and his Educational Method*, 2 vols., Leipzig, 1806. He was appointed Counsellor of State at Potsdam, and worked zealously for thirty years in propagating and applying Pestalozzi's method. (G., p. 252.)

Chavannes, D. A.   *An Account of the Elementary Method of H. Pestalozzi, with an account of the works of this celebrated man, his Institute, principles, and fellow-workers.* Paris, 1805. Ed. 2, 1809.

[4] The letters are not numbered by Pestalozzi, but they are distinctly divided. See Mr. Quick's copy of Ed. 1, 1801. Teachers' Guild Library, London. There are fourteen letters, but Seyffarth divides Letter seven, and so makes fifteen. This has caused some little confusion;

but there is really no difference in the text. They are addressed to Heinrich Gessner, publisher, Zürich, son of Solomon Gessner, the poet. He was a member of the "Patriotic Party," a society of young men founded 1762, whose object was to improve the condition of the people.

⁵ Lavater, Johann Kasper, Zürich, 1741–1802. Died Jan. 2, from effects of a bullet-wound received on Sept. 22, 1799, when the French entered Zürich, while he was helping wounded soldiers in the street. Preacher, philosopher, poet, and prose writer. Best known to us by his work on physiognomy. Member of Patriotic Party; warm friend of Pestalozzi. His *Views on Eternity*, in Letters to J. G. Zimmermann, were published, Zürich, 1768, 4 vols.

Zimmermann, Johann Georg. Brugg, Canton Aargaü, 1728–95. Physician and philosophical writer. His *Observations on Solitude* is well known.

⁶ Iselin Isaak, author and publisher, Basle, 1728–82, published a journal entitled *Ephemerides of Humanity*. In 1776, Pestalozzi published in it *An Appeal to the Friends and Well-wishers of Mankind for kind Support of an Establishment for giving poor Children Education and Work in the Country*. Iselin warmly supported the appeal. Pestalozzi's *Evening Hour of a Hermit* also appeared first in this journal, May, 1780. Iselin especially directed the attention of the readers of the *Ephemerides* to Pestalozzi's efforts, and tried to support him in every way. Pestalozzi always remembered him gratefully. "In the good hot working days, when apparently I was wasting my strength, he was the only one upon whom I could lean, covered as I was with dust and sweat, and find refreshment in my pains. Oh, my friend! perhaps without you I should have sunk in the depths and been lost in the mire of my life." (*Beck;* and G., p. 75, note.)

⁷ Ed. 1, p. 3, 4, instead of "But I was young," etc., has the following beginning with the oft-quoted passage, not in Ed. 2. "Long years I lived surrounded by more than fifty beggar children. In poverty I shared my bread with them. I lived like a beggar in order to learn how to make beggars live like men.

"My ideal of their training included work on the farm, in the factory and the workshop. In all three branches I was full of high and sure instinct for what is great and important in this plan, and even now I know of no error in the principles. Yet, on the other hand, it is quite true that in all three branches I wanted skill to deal with details, and a mind that could devote itself to trifles. I was not rich enough, and I was too forsaken, to remedy what was wanting in me by sufficient collaboration. My plan was wrecked, but I had learned in the struggle immeasurable truth, and my conviction of the truth of my plan was never stronger than at the time when it was ruined. My heart still moved on unshaken towards the same end. In my own misery I learned to know the misery of the people and its sources, more and more; I knew them as no happier man can know them. I suffered," etc. (See G., chap. v. pp.52–72, for account of the experiment at Neuhof, which began in the winter of 1774.)

[8] "Leonard and Gertrude." The first volume of this work appeared 1781, and was a great success. In the form of a story Pestalozzi shows how the people in Bonal were reformed by education. Gertrude, the mother of seven children, wife of Leonard, a mason, is the educator. But these things are an allegory : Bonal is the world, and Gertrude the typical mother-educator. Pestalozzi likes to connect his work, and Gertrude here is only a name for the ideal mother who educates, as in his previous work. We forget sometimes, perhaps Pestalozzi himself forgets, that this work is "a guide to mothers in educating their children." Few mothers can undertake the entire education of their children; but the mother is the child's first teacher and guide; her natural methods of teaching, prompted by sympathy and love, are adapted to the little child, and her influence is generally stronger than any other. "The mother, untrained, follows nature in pure simplicity without knowing what nature does through her, and nature does very much through her. She opens the world to the child, she makes him ready to use his senses, and prepares for development of attention and observation" (Lett. X.). Two women, both servants, are said to have been models for Gertrude. Babeli, servant to Pestalozzi's mother (G. 2–4), and Elizabeth Naef, who found Neuhof in disorder and worked hard to provide for Pestalozzi and his family. Of her Pestalozzi said, "She is an image of Gertrude" (G., pp. 69–70, 79–88).

[9] *Inquiries into the Course of Nature in the Development of the Human Race.* This study of the evolution of man was written at Neuhof at Fichte's suggestion. Published, 1797. Niederer, writing to him early in 1801, says, "I look upon it as containing a most valuable discovery; I may call it indeed the germ of your whole method" (G., pp. 110–112).

[10] "Gallimaufry," nonsense, hodge-podge. *Winter's Tale,* Act iv. sc. 3.

[11] "Stanz burnt.—Legrand." Stanz, market town, Canton Unterwalden, destroyed by French, Sept. 9, 1798. Legrand, Jean Lue, 1755–1838. Belonged, with Iselin and other reformers, to the "Patriotic Party." Became a member of the Grand Council of Bern, in 1783, and President of the Swiss Directorate, 1798, but held office for only part of a year. Became acquainted with Oberlin, the famous pastor of Ban-de-la-Roche, in 1812. Settled near him in 1814, and devoted the remaining years of his life wholly to popular education.

[12] "Pronouncing sounds," etc. Herbart, as early as May, 1801, promised his friend Halem, who was planning a literary journal under the name of *Irene,* an article on Pestalozzi. The letter accompanying the article is dated Dec. 24, 1801, and the article appeared early in 1802.

Herbart met Pestalozzi for the first time at Zürich. "In Zürich

I met neither Lavater nor Hegel, but chance brought me in contact with the celebrated Pestalozzi." (Letter, Jan. 28, 1798.)

The second time he visited him was at Burgdorf; but Pestalozzi says that here " he crowed his A B C daily from morn till night, and went on in the same empirical way " that he had followed at Stanz. Herbart says: " I saw him in his schoolroom. A dozen children, from five to eight years old, were called into school at an unusual hour in the evening. I feared they would be sulky, and that the experiment which I had come to see would be a failure. But the children came with no signs of reluctance; a lively activity lasted continuously to the end. The noise of the whole school speaking together—no, not the noise—it was a pleasant harmony of words, quite intelligible, in measured time, like a chorus, as powerful, and as firmly united, and so clearly arising from what had been learned, that I had some difficulty not to change from a spectator and observer into a learner and child. I went round among them to hear if any were silent or speaking carelessly; I found none. The children's pronunciation did my ears good, although their teacher has the most incomprehensible organ in the world, and their tongues cannot be well trained by their Swiss parents." (Herbart, *Päd. Schriften*, vol. i. p. 88, 1880.)

[13] In June, 1799, the French were driven out of Uri into Unter-walden by the Austrians, and the orphanage was converted into a French hospital. On June 8th, 1799, sixty children were sent away, leaving only twenty. Pestalozzi intended to return, but the Government was unfavourable, and the orphanage after some time was closed. (G., 142–146.)

[14] The first " *Letter from Stanz*" was written at Gurnigel, between June 8 and the end of July, 1799, and was printed in 1807. It will be found entire in de Guimp's Life, pp. 147–171. It should be compared with this account. At that time, he says here, "I was not certain of the foundations of my procedure." His " *Account of the Method* " to the Society of Friends of Education, June 27, 1800, is the first attempt to state his principles. (See "The Method," last paragraph.)

[15] [ ] These brackets include additions made in Ed. 2. All have not been indicated in this way. Some are very slight, and others are difficult to separate in a translation. They may be found in most German editions. Rarely words or passages in Ed. 1. have been left out of Ed. 2. The most important omission is given in note 7. The most important additions made are to this passage, and give us Pestalozzi's views twenty years later, they may be considered as his last words in the book.

When the notes are from Ed. 1, the reference figures are placed where the cue can be most easily found.

[16] " Anschauung" we have usually translated "sense-impression." When another equivalent is used we have indicated it by (*Ansch.*)

" Sense-impression " is frequently used by Mr. Sully. "Sense-impressions are the alphabet by which we spell out the objects presented to us." (*Teacher's Handbook of Psychology*, ch. viii., 1886). It was one of the most suitable words, but we are indebted to Mr. J. Russell for fixing it. The first draft of the translation of this work was made before his translation of R. de Guimp's *Life of Pestalozzi* was published, but he suggested this term, and said he had used it. "Intuition "was impossible; instead of conveying it hides Pestalozzi's meaning, and it has caused much mischief. Mr. F. C. Turner shows in the following note that "intuition" has not the same meaning for us that "Anschauung " had for Pestalozzi.

" The language of Pestalozzi presents considerable difficulties to the translator. He tells us (Letter VI.) that he "is incapable of philosophic thought." His words do not always express his full meaning, but that is partly because his thought is still growing and imperfect. A year earlier he did not really know the foundation of his method, and his expressions, like his thought, are in some ways still immature, changing and confused. His sentences are often over-burdened with qualifications and saving clauses, characteristic of him. Sometimes he uses words with local meanings differing from their usual signification.

The greatest difficulty, however, is in dealing with that word which is the keystone of his whole theory, *Anschauung*. Its meaning has grown under his hands, and it connotes for him much more than it ever did before. It has, and can have, no satisfactory English equivalent. The early writers and translators used the word " *intuition*," and quite recently Mr. Quick, in the new edition of his *Educational Reformers*, has sanctioned its use. It has the advantage of being etymologically an equivalent of Anschauung, but so have *contemplation* and *inspection*, by which no one would propose to translate it. It has, moreover, the fatal objection of connoting a philosophical idea and theory, which is far removed from Pestalozzi's Anschauung. To show this, we give the most authoritative account we can find of the two words.

ANSCHAUUNG.

Contemplatio, intuitio, experientia.

"Anschauung ist eine sich unmittelbar auf den Gegenstand als einzelnen sich beziehende Erkenntniss." Anschauung is a knowledge which is directly obtained from a special object.

"Anschauung ist eine Vorstellung so wie sie unmittelbar von der Gegenwart des Gegenstandes abhängen würde." Anschauung is a mental image, such as would be produced directly by the presence of the object. (Kant, *Kritik der reinen Vernunft*.)

"Ein unmittelbares Bewusstsein heisst Anschauung." A direct consciousness is called Anschauung.

"Sie sollen es fassen nicht im Denken sondern in lebendiger

Anschauung." You must grasp it not in thought, but in vivid Anschauung. (Fichte.)

—Grimm's *Deutsches Wörterbuch.*

INTUITION.

1. Mental perception of anything; immediate knowledge.

"The truth of these propositions we know by a bare, simple intuition of the ideas, and such propositions are called self-evident."

2. Knowledge not obtained by deduction of reason, but instantly accompanying the ideas which are its object.

"All knowledge of causes is deductive, for we know nothing by simple intuition, but through the mediation of the effects, for the causality itself is insensible." (Glanville.)

"Discourse then was almost as quick as intuition." (South, *Sermons.*)

> " He these single virtues did survey
> By intuition in his own large breast." (Dryden.)

—Latham's *Johnson's Dictionary.*

It is evident that the two words have not the same connotation, and that the English word "intuition" does not imply the presence of the object before the senses with the same strictness that Anschauung does in the mouths of Kant and Pestalozzi.

Pestalozzi uses the word—"Anschauung."

1. For the *knowledge* obtained by the direct contemplation of the object before the senses—*sense-impression.*

2. (*a*) For the *mental act* by which the above knowledge is obtained—*observation.*

(*b*) And for the *mental faculties* by which it is obtained—*the senses.*

(*c*) And again, for *objects of the world*, about which such knowledge is gained—*seen objects.*

Allied to this is the meaning in the following passage:—

"Culture brings up before me the sea of confused *phenomena* (*Ansch.*) flowing one into the other." (*The Method*) So also *Anschauung-bücher*, picture books, Letter I.

(*d*) Objects seen possess form, number, colour, light, and shade, etc. Pestalozzi considers that *form* is common to all, and so he frequently uses Anschauung as a synonym for FORM, not for form alone, but for form plus something else. The nearest equivalent for *A B C der Anschauung* is alphabet of form, though the expression is often used in other and wider senses. As Pestalozzi found drawing impossible without measurement, the *A B C of Anschauung* was used for measurement also. Therefore *A B C of Anschauung* meant form, and a means of measuring form (MEASURE-FORM).

3. For knowledge obtained by contemplation of ideas already in the mind, which have not necessarily been derived from the observation of external objects. This meaning seems at first to contradict the foregoing; but it is obvious, on reading the passages in which this meaning occurs, that Pestalozzi regarded the ideas in

question as possible objects of an internal or subjective observation, *e.g.* "knowledge gained by *sense-impression* teaches me the properties of things that have not been brought before my *senses* by their likeness to other objects that I have observed. This mode of *observation*," etc. (Letter VII.) For this meaning the word *intuition* can appropriately be used.

4. Es (der Kind) lebt in seiner Anschauung (d. h. Gottes). "The child lives in *contemplation* of God." (*The Method*.)

The word *intuition* is used by Pestalozzi, but not as an equivalent of Anschauung, unless it be for meaning 3. "I lived entirely upon convictions that were the result of countless, though for the most part forgotten intuitions" (Letter I.) "Speech was a means . . . of representing the actual process of making ideas (Intuitionen) clear." (Letter X.) In both these passages it means something different from Anschauung; it means Anschauungen with the mental process which combines them into unity of idea superadded." (F. C. T.) "Intuitive ideas given by nature and art" (p. 36), is nearer Anschauung.

[17] Burgdorf, town in canton Bern. Here he resumed his interrupted work towards the end of July, 1799. (G., p. 173 seq.)

[18] Gurnigel, a beautifully situated, much frequented bath, ¾-hour below the summit of Mt. Gurnigel, 9 miles west of Thun.

[19] Rengger, Stapfer, Schnell, and Dr. Grimm.

Rengger, Albert, 1764-1835, educated as a theologian; became tutor to Emanuel von Fellenberg, afterwards studied medicine. After some years abroad he settled in Bern, 1789. Became Minister of the Interior, 1798.

Stapfer, Phillipe Albert, 1766-1840, Professor of Philosophy and Philology, Bern, Minister of Arts and Sciences. He alone remained steadfast to Pestalozzi when he left Stanz, and exerted himself to find a place where he might carry on his experiments. Stapfer wished to found a Teacher's Institute. Fischer submitted his plans to him, and Stapfer proposed to the Directorate that they should give up the castle of Burgdorf to him. In July, 1799, Fischer went to Burgdorf as superintendent of the schools and institutes that he had just organized. Stapfer opened a new field of work to Pestalozzi at Burgdorf; he sent a report to the Directory, July 23, 1799; on the same day they granted him part of Castle Burgdorf as a dwelling, and a fixed position as a teacher, with a salary of Livres 160. (Seyffarth, *Introduction*.) He founded the Society of Friends of Education, June, 1800; in July, 1800, a further grant was made to Pestalozzi through his efforts, of as much of the Castle of Burgdorf as he needed, a garden and wood. (G., p. 201.) Sept., 1800, was ambassador to Paris. At the end of the Republic, 1803, he retired into private life, and lived in France 37 years.

Schnell, J., Prefect of Burgdorf. He published a pamphlet, perhaps the first on the subject, giving a complete exposition of Pestalozzi's views, about October, 1800. Reprinted in *Pestalozzi-Blatter*, Zurich, 1888. (G., 174–206.) The first edition of *Wie Gertrud* closed with an extract from a letter of Dr. Schnell.

Dr. Grimm, an influential citizen of Burgdorf, and a warm friend of Pestalozzi.

[20] Hintersassen, or Hintersedler, were non-burgesses, who possessed, besides a house, a garden or a bit of field. They were also small suburban peasants. Their children attended the school of a worthy shoemaker, Samuel Dysli, who carried on his trade in his spare time as well as when with the children. His instruction consisted in teaching the children to read in a mechanical, tedious manner, and in hearing the Heidelberg Catechism. The room belonged to him, and he worked at his trade in it. His teaching apparatus consisted of the *Spelling and Name Book* (Fibel), *The Beginnings of Christian Doctrine* (Siegfried), *The Heidelberg Catechism*, and the usual *Psalter*. The school contained seventy-three scholars of all ages. (G., 175.)

Morf obtains much information about the wretched condition and entire absence of culture among Swiss teachers in Pestalozzi's time from the official list of questions which teachers had to answer in writing, about their personal relations, their former occupations, their future work, their nomination, etc. One teacher, Meyer of Schöfflesdorf, could not answer the questions because he " could not write very well." Another, Meyer of Kloten, " in summer, when he has no school, earns his bread by bricklaying. He used to be a watchman in the town; he now works in the garden, and is a rope-maker."

"We find hardly any trace of a proper schoolroom. The choice of a teacher often depended, not on his ability, but on his having a room, his family remained in it and carried on their domestic duties during school hours. Often neighbours brought their spinning wheels, finding more warmth and entertainment there than at home. . . . Reading and learning by heart were the pupils' only tasks. The big ones were learning aloud, so there was a constant hubbub in the school. Class teaching was not thought of. One report says :—' The vanity of parents makes them wish their children to appear clever. A child is considered clever if he can shout the whole catechism without a blunder. If he knows the 119th Psalm and can rattle off a few chapters of the Bible (never mind the sense), he is a wonder. To read the Bible through is the highest point.'" See also Seyffarth, *Introduction to " Wie Gertrud*," Vol. XI.

Schools of this kind were not confined to Switzerland. Possibly some exist still, changed it may be in appearance, but unchanged in principle. Psalm and catechism are gone, but mere word memory work remains.

[21] "The ' Heidelberg ' was in danger."

The Heidelberg or Palatinate Catechism was compiled and published by the Heidelberg theologians, Zacharias Ursinus and Kaspar

Olevianus in 1563 by command, and with the co-operation of Prince Elector Friedrich III. of the Palatinate. It was and is the most popular elementary book of religious instruction in the schools of the Swiss Evangelical Confession. The little book has a preponderant doctrinal character, and was therefore not suited for Pestalozzi's teaching.

[22] This was the Spelling and Reading School kept by Miss Margaretha Stähli the younger. It was attended by 20–25 boys and girls, aged 7–8. This must not be confused with the girls' school kept by Miss Margaretha Stähli the elder.

[23] "A B C of Anschauung." We are obliged to use Anschauung here, so that objects seen, observation, sense-impression, form, measurement, "intuition," and the other meanings included in it, may retain the unity Pestalozzi intended. It was while working out his first attempts at the A B C of Anschauung that the whole scheme of a united method appeared. Here Anschauung is used in a wide general sense; it soon develops and differentiates. The various meanings will be noted as they appear.

[24] Ed. 1, p. 30. "I shall work none. I am not pre-ordained for this. I will have nothing to do with miracles, real or pretended."

[25] Ed. 1, p. 32. "'Vous voulez méchaniser l'éducation.' He hit the nail on the head, and put the word into my mouth that exactly described the nature of my purpose." Pestalozzi soon afterwards found that he had not quite understood Gleyre.

In the second edition the word "mechanical" is sometimes changed to "organic." The new element in his conception of mind is its entire self-activity. The self-contained power of orderly working, or mechanism of the physical nature or body. Mind works in harmony—body and mind are one (p. 31, l. 29). "A machine having its own power of going within itself." De Guimp says whenever he speaks of *mechanism* he means *organism*. "That the mind and heart of man no less than his body develop according to organic laws, is indeed the fundamental principle of his doctrine" (G., p. 185), but he uses *mechanical* sometimes with its own meaning.

[26] "The Art," frequently refered to hereafter, is distinguished by a capital from art generally; it is our "Science and Art of Education," which is here first put on a psychological and scientific basis.

[27] Ed. 1, p. . "And in all three branches." An interesting little slip. Pestalozzi anticipates the elements, number, form, and language, which he describes later; in Ed. 2 he corrects this.

[28] Ed. 1, p. 36. "In order to make those ideas, which are to be imparted by language, clear to the children beforehand by well-chosen, well-executed drawings."

Pestalozzi here says *drawings*, but in the second edition "*real things*, models and drawings." The paragraph bears evidence of

revision. Anschauung or *picture*-books should precede A B C books
to make ideas clear by means of well-chosen *real* objects. At first he
showed the children large drawings for them to observe and describe.
This is one of his A B C's of Anschauung. "I made much progress
in what was called the A B C of Anschauung," says Ramsauer.
De Guimps adds this note: "Exercises in which the children made
their own remarks on the object placed before them" (p. 209) our
"object-lesson." At Burgdorf it is an A B C of Anschauung the
foundation of *all* studies. The observation, thought, and expression
are all the child's; with us the object lesson is isolated, and in this
way, almost obsolete. We *tell* what should be seen, thought, and said.
This A B C of Anschauung involves expression by words as "obser-
vätion" is sometimes used by us. It includes *expression by the child*
of what *it sees and thinks.*

One day at Burgdorf when they were looking at a drawing of a
window, a child said, "Could we not learn as well from the window
itself?" Another time a similar remark was made. "The child is
right," said he, and put the drawings away, and studied from objects,
but he does not exclude drawings.

Some have naturally supposed that as objects are the sources of
ideas and knowledge, objects only should be given for drawing
studies. In Belgium "they reject absolutely the practice of drawing
from prints. . . . As soon as a child can draw lines, he is set to
produce geometrical forms, plane surfaces, and solid bodies." (M.
Couvreur, Conference on Education, "Health Exhib.," Liter., Vol.
XIV., p. 259). But the child's nature should be considered also, and
children prefer to draw from copies, even the usual dead copies, but
copies made with them, by the living teacher or the mother are the
best. Historically, direct imitation of objects comes later. Possibly
drawings may have value as well as objects. If they are useful as
copies for drawing, they may be useful as helps to observation.

[29] Ed. 1, p. 37. "And came soon to know the hardest names of the
least known animals in Buffon's *Natural History,* and to notice and
distinguish clearly points in them as well as in plants and men.
But yet this test was not decisive for the beginning point of instruction. This boy had already three unused years behind him, and I
am convinced," etc.

[30] Ed. 1, p. 39. "I cease describing, lest I should come again upon
the picture of the schoolmaster, and the terrible contrast between
their nature, their action, their state, and their misery, and that of
lovely nature. But, friend, tell me," etc.

[31] Ed. 1, p. 42. "While I was thus on the track of the first beginning points of all instruction for the children who should be educated
by it from the cradle, and all power for the method itself, I took
means with the school children who fell into my hands, not having
been formed by it in direct opposition to my principles," etc.

[82] Pestalozzi came in many ways into opposition with himself; he tried to cram in when he ought to have "drawn out." Nature's method alone is right, he says, and then gives this unnatural parrot-like repetition of "dull, uncomprehended words or wildest nonsense, absurdly hard, complicated and entirely incomprehensible." We must always remember he has only really reached clear ideas about his principles within this year, and it is not wonderful that he opposes himself; the habits and thoughts of his life are not all reformed and regenerated at once. Possibly, too, something may be said in favour of such test exercises.

[83] Fischer, 1772, 1800, was a pupil of Salzmann, in Schnepfenthal. Was appointed Secretary of the Science and Art Department by Stapfer in 1798. In 1799, with Stapfer's consent, he attempted to organize a course of training for teachers in Castle Burgdorf, but failed. In 1800 he left Burgdorf, and went back to his post as secretary. He died on the 4th of May, 1800.

Fischer's letter was printed in full by Steinmüller, to whom it was addressed in his *Helvetischer Schulmeisterbibliothek*, vol. i. pp. 216, seq. St. Gallen, 1801. The first and last two paragraphs, which were not quoted by Pestalozzi, are given here.

"BÜRGDORF, *Dec.* 20th, 1799.

You have a right to expect that I should at least send you some account of Pestalozzi and his undertakings. I propose soon to publish a much fuller account, and to call the attention of schoolmasters to his methods. In the meanwhile you will be interested to have a short *exposé* of the principles of it, and this I send you in the following few remarks."

*   *   *   *   *

By this plan, of which I have drawn up an abstract from experiments carried on before my eyes, Pestalozzi is endeavouring to gain and to maintain the interest of the government and of all schoolmasters by uncontrovertible results; he hopes, and has reason to hope, that his experiments in Burgdorf, where they find support and prosper, will do more to make known the value of what he is doing than his efforts at Stanz, which were on a very limited scale, and were crushed by a hundred local and personal obstacles. There he was over-weighted with work and oppressed by religious and political animosities, open or concealed. In Burgdorf he is in a more congenial mental atmosphere; and as the work is less heterogeneous, he is more capable of concentrating himself on working out his scheme on a liberal scale.

Meanwhile, Pestalozzi understands that he is wanting in much positive knowledge and in practical skill in using his machinery. The latter defect he makes up for in a great degree by his indefatigable experiments, and in this way not only are many parts of the methods hitherto in use subjected to criticism, but also many forms and details of methods are found and adapted at once to the new point of departure.

He hopes by the friendly aid of his helpers and fellow-workers to be able to fill in the gaps which he has had to leave in his school-books; or rather, he will try with their aid to arrange, simplify, and clear of unimportant matter, the choice, terminology and arrangement of that which is essential.

It is inspiring to every discoverer who has his heart in his work that it shall, and can be perfected by the help of strangers, and so Pestalozzi will rejoice to see his rough casting filed down and polished up by others."

[34] Steinmüller took great interest in Pestalozzi, and applied to Fischer to learn more of his method of teaching. Fischer answered, Dec. 6, 1799. On Dec. 31, Steinmüller wrote to thank him, and says, "Oh, how true it is that the teacher without psychology does his work as badly as an old woman doctoring." Steinmüller in 1803 criticised Pestalozzi's views and methods in a small pamphlet, *Remarks upon Pestalozzi's Method of Instruction.* It is especially directed against exaggerated praise of the method, and disputes to some degree the claim of novelty of Pestalozzi's ideas.

Morf publishes a collection of his letters to Fischer taken from the Swiss Archives at Bern, giving an account of his life.

[35] How steadfastly Pestalozzi hoped in mothers, appears clearly in this passage. In the first edition he wrote, "Before we get to 1803" (p. 61). This hope was not fulfilled, and yet in the second edition he expressed it again, but this time it is "before I am buried."

LETTER II.

[1] Krüsi, Tobler and Buss. Krüsi, 1775 ; 1844, Appenzel.

His career from an errand boy to a fellow-worker with Pesta-lozzi is given in the text. His situation in Gais brought him plenty of work, and 2½ gulden a week. For self-culture, he zealously studied the works of Basedow, Salzmann, and others, and tried to use in school what he learned this way, as well as by his own obser-vations and experiences from nature and life. He was an active, thoughtful teacher, with a lovable disposition, the effects of which were soon recognised. At Steinmüller's suggestion he went to Fischer at Burgdorf, 1799, with the orphans from Gais, and after Fischer's death he joined Pestalozzi, with whom he worked out the sense-impression-teaching of word and number (*Sprach-und-Rechen-unterricht*). He accompanied him to Münchenbuchsee, and also to Yverdun. He parted from him with great regret in 1817, and founded an educational establishment of his own, which soon became known. In 1822 he undertook the direction of Hans Karl Zell-weger's school in Trogen, and in 1833 the direction of the Teacher's

Seminary in Gais. He died there, after successful work, July 25, 1844. Gruner says he was "a man whose unassuming soul and quiet talent was formed by much experience. He has a gentle disposition, is calm, indefatigable, active and firm. He knows his pupils and child-nature generally, and how to treat children." (G., pp. 190-203.)

His son, Hermann Krüsi, taught in England and America, and his *Progressive Course of Inventive Drawing on the Principles of Pestalozzi* was published here by W. F. Ramsey, 1850.

Tobler, Johann, Georg., 1769; 1843. From Trogen, in Appenzell, Ausserhoden, went to Basle, 1792, to be trained for the Church, but soon gave up theology for teaching. He was a tutor for five years, and became director of a girls' school in Basle, 1799. In 1800 his friend Krüsi introduced him to Pestalozzi, with whom he stayed seven years. In 1807 he founded an industrial school at Mühlhausen, that soon numbered 600 scholars; this was closed in 1811. In 1812 he became master of a private school in Glarus, but left in 1817, on account of the famine. After again being a tutor for three years he became director of an educational institute founded by himself; this he gave to his eldest son in 1831. His last years were spent in Basle, where he died at the house of his youngest son, who had a boys' school at Nyon. Tobler helped Pestalozzi in his writing. His written works consist chiefly of Children's and Popular books. (*Riegel.*)

Buss, of Tübingen, tells his own history in the text. Afterwards he taught drawing in Bern; Gruner thus describes him. "Buss has extraordinary talents, particularly for art. He is born to teach by sense-impression. He has indefatigable zeal, energy and skill. Like Krüsi he has absolute authority over his pupils, and manages them well, showing admirable patience in teaching them." (*Riegel.*)

[2] Johann Hübner, rector, Hamburg, 1688-1731, wrote a Biblical History, 1714 *Twice Two and Fifty Selected Bible Stories*. Each story was followed by "plain questions." These questions were so compiled that they fitted in with the words of the story, and could only be answered in the same words. Pestalozzi called this *Catechising* as opposed to *Socratising*. He makes a great distinction between them. "Catechisms, a mere parrot-like repetition of dull uncomprehended words." "Socratising real development of thought, mental power and expression by means of questions." He objected to Fischer's socratising because it was not prepared for and preceded by sense-impression or observation of objects, at this time new to him. "Consider no human judgment ripe that is not clearly the result of complete sense-impression of all parts of the object to be judged." (IV.) He would rather hold back the judgment until the child had *really seen with its own eyes* the object about which he should express himself *from all sides and under different conditions*. But he believes even now strongly in Socratising. "I found weakness nowhere except in myself and in the art of using what already exists. I tried to force in where it is only possible to draw out from within the child

that which is in him and is only to be developed from what is within him and cannot be put into him." (Letter I.) Later he is not less than Fischer its supporter. " All true, all real educative instruction must be drawn out of the children." (Letter I.)

[3] Ed. 1, p. 74. "Afterwards Krüsi tried to combine socratising and catechising. But this combination by its very nature leads no further than the squaring of the circle that a wood-cutter," etc.

[4] Ed. 1, p. 77. "With time and industry, it is possible to ask many questions easily about many subjects."

[5] Ed. 1, p. 84. "I have said, fearlessly, that it is not opposed to God or religion to lead up to clear ideas, and endeavour to teach children to talk before we cram their memories with the affairs of positive theology and its never-to-be-settled disputes."

[6] Ed. 1, p. 88. "All these views, connected with the harmony daily becoming clearer between my methods of instruction and nature, fully convinced him that all knowledge lay in the union of these methods, so that a teacher need only *learn how to use them* in order to raise himself and his pupils by their means to all knowledge that can be aimed at by teaching.

[7] Slates. Pestalozzi was led by his limited means to use slates and slate pencils. This very practical invention made writing, drawing and arithmetic common subjects of instruction at a time when the more expensive paper could not have been used. He speaks first of using slates at Burgdorf. They were of great service, but he never mentions the invention or application as his own. Tobler's statement here is allowed to stand, and is therefore sanctioned by Pestalozzi. Chalk too was used. "For drawing we were given only slates and red chalk." (Ramsauer's account; G., p. 181.)

LETTER III.

[1] Ed. 1, p. 107. "Show Wieland the *A B C der Anschauung* and ask him if he ever found stronger proofs of powers thrown away."

Wieland, author of *Oberon*, was friendly to Pestalozzi. His *German Mercury*, Dec., 1801, contains the first notice of *Wie Gertrud*. It is warmly recommended. In it he says, "Pestalozzi promises much, but judging from the first fruits lying before us, he is a man to keep his word."

Buss's A B C of Anschauung is an A B C of Form, of linear form. He gives us in the text its purpose. "Children should read outlines of forms as they read words, and name the parts, curves and angles, with letters, so that lines combined in the outline of an object may be as clearly expressed as words by letters." This he did not reach. Biber gives a diagram, p. 205, "for the better understanding of what is said," and says "it was never published, for it was soon superseded by more matured labours," but this diagram was published, 1828, by Niederer. It is incorporated in his version of the Report; but if it is Buss's A B C, it could not have existed when Pestalozzi

Q

made that Report of the Method. (For diagram see p. 208, " *The Method.*") In Letter VII. the ellipse is included, but it is not even mentioned here. The smaller squares or chequers for measurement became hereafter an A B C of measure-forms. They are the origin of the chequers in the Kindergarten, and are now used in our Board Schools for various purposes of design. Fragments of the unity he sought and strove for are used for the unconnected teaching, that he protested against, and yet they are applied at last to the hand-training he from first to last earnestly worked to establish.

[2] Duke Carl Engen of Würtemburg founded a military training at Castle Solitude in 1771—"the Carl's School." In 1775 this was removed to Stuttgart, enlarged and made into an academy. Schiller was educated here.

[3] Ed. 1, p. 119. "In the weakness and superficiality of the instruction I had received in art. For this reason I failed to grasp its principles. I threw all my energy into the special department in which Pestalozzi wanted my help."

[4] Ed. 1, p. 126. "How men have language, in order by knowing the names of objects to be able more easily to distinguish one from another."

[5] Ed. 1, p. 127. "However, I estimated the whole method only through the medium of a department and its effects upon it. In this way I came step by step to see and understand its effects upon other branches. I found now by the clue given by my art-teaching how it might be possible," etc.

[6] Ed. 1, p. 129. "Which alone make the Art difficult to the human race because they undermine the foundation which it has in man and lead him away from Nature, who asks nothing of us that is not easy, if we only seek it in the right way from her hands only."

Richter says, "We see, even this account of one of Pestalozzi's fellow-workers is altered in the second edition in one or two places. Did Pestalozzi do this? It is doubtful. It is more likely that Jos. Schmid, who brought out 'the collected works,' made these changes, for he has been proved to have made arbitrary alterations sometimes. Some other changes in the second edition are due to Schmid. But that Pestalozzi did sometimes make alterations appears from the preface in which he says that he left the book 'almost unaltered,' in fact *most* of the alterations are limited to forms of expression. In some, however, and particularly in the more important alterations, Pestalozzi's authorship is undoubted, as is evident from their character."

This note of Richter's illustrates the way in which the best editors speak of Schmid, while the latter part neutralizes the beginning, "most of the alterations are limited to forms of expression." Yes, they are often so slight that we could not well represent them in translation. For instance, "villages in Bohemia" become "castles in Spain" in the second edition; "dem Auge" becomes "in dem Auge," etc., etc. Some are evidently corrections. But if the more

important additions are evidently Pestalozzi's own, the lesser alterations and corrections may also be his; besides the original communi-
cation of Buss may have been written under circumstances which
justified these slight alterations by Pestalozzi. No Schmid theory
is needed to explain them.

LETTER IV.

[1] Rousseau and Basedow.

Rousseau, Jean Jacques, 1712-1778. The Revolution last century
began a new era. It was not like the Renaissance—a return to
an older civilization, with its art and literature, but a return to
nature. A new faith was growing, and the need was felt for cultivating the intellect instead of subjugating it to priestly authority.
It was a struggle for liberty of thought, speech, and inquiry.
Rousseau was the man of his time, prepared by special education
and mental condition for it. "It was his work more than that of
any other man that France arose from decay and found irresistible
energy," says Mr. Morley. "For twelve years," he says himself,
"his heart made hot within him by the idea of the future happiness
of the human race and the honour of contributing to it," he wrote
those works which, Mr. Morley says, "gave Europe a new gospel"
and a new education. One of these works, perhaps the best, is
Emile. By some means he had the very education himself that
he suggested for "Emile," that of nature. All his life he was outside
the rules of civilization, "an untamed natural man," a vagabond,
Quick says. Here are a few fragments from *Emile:*—

"Everything is good as it leaves the hands of the Creator, everything
degenerates in the hands of man," are the first words in *Emile.*
"We do not understand children; we fix on what concerns men to
not what children can learn. Begin by studying children; most
assuredly at present you do not understand them. I wish some
judicious hand would give us a work on the art of studying children."
At present we do not know its elements. Let childhood ripen in
children. Their energies overflow; allow their activities free scope;
let them run about and make a noise. "The lessons schoolboys
learn of each other in play are a hundred times more useful to them
than those which the master teaches in school." "Exercise the child's
body, senses, and all his faculties. Avoid learning by heart memory
may be exercised on things seen and heard. Nothing but words are
taught, and things not useful; signs are useless without ideas;
without observation of things there can be no clear ideas. The child
should not be coerced. If your head always directs the child's, his
own will become useless. The very first thing he takes on trust or
learns from others without being convinced he loses part of his
understanding. My object is not to furnish his mind with knowledge, but to teach him the method of acquiring it himself. He is
not to know because he is told, but because he has himself com-

prehended—he should not learn, but discover. Avoid telling. Things are themselves the best explanations. The grand thing to be educed is self-teaching. Progress should be in proportion to strength. We acquire more clear, certain notions of ourselves than of others who teach us. Learn without effort. Do not keep a boy poring over a book; let him learn a trade, let him work with his hands."

"Nature wills that children should be *children* before they are *men*. If we seek to pervert this order, we shall produce forward fruits, without ripeness or flavour, and though not ripe, soon rotten: we shall have young *savans* and old children. Childhood has ways of seeing, thinking, feeling, peculiar to itself; nothing is more absurd than to wish to substitute ours in its place."

These quotations will give some idea of the new Education founded by Rousseau, and worked out by Pestalozzi, Froebel and others. Strangely enough, it agrees with the Renaissance in the place given to the child. We must study the child, learn its nature, if we would teach it. "We must conquer nature by obeying her." Employ the child's activity. Let it learn from things, not books; it is an observer and a doer. Self-activity helps self-teaching. Knowledge comes by the action of our mind, not from what it is told. The real teacher is within. Teach the method of acquiring knowledge. Exercise faculty, and by so doing develop it. (See Quick's *Educational Reformers*, Ed. 1890.)

Basedow, John Bernard (1723-1790), was one of the earliest to feel Rousseau's influence and to apply his principles. Kant had said that revolution not reform was wanted in education, and Basedow attempted it. "Everything according to nature" is his great principle. Treat children as children. They love motion and noise, here is a hint from nature. Even in play children may learn names of things. (Both Rousseau and Basedow agree with Froebel.) They should be acquainted with the world through the senses first—should learn from nature. Reduce mere memory work. Educate the whole being—the body by gymnastics, the mind by study of things. Coercion is wrong; children should be free. Educate the natural desires and direct them, but never suppress. In 1774 he opened an Institute at Dessau, called the Philanthropin. At first it was successful but, owing to disputes with his associates, he withdrew in 1778 to Magdeburg, where he taught privately till his death, 1790. His method had considerable influence in Germany. (Räumer, *Geschichte der Pädagogik;* Quick's *Educational Reformers;* Payne's *Lectures on the Science and Art of Education*.)

[2] Ed. 1, p. 134. "But they violently put out the eyes of those who dare to raise their heads to peep at the splendour of the highest story."

[3] Ed. 1, p. 138. "And, Gessner, my experiments went further: they have thriven and become ripe fruit."

It is interesting and significant of Pestalozzi's conception of the subject to see how the expression is altered in the second edition.

⁴ Report. This Report is so important that it is printed as an appendix. In it Pestalozzi first states his great fundamental principle of *Anschauung.* At first he limited his purpose to *improving* details in existing schools, and when he left Stanz, he says at the beginning of his letter that even his old plans for educating the people began to wither. But this Report marks a new epoch. He is now a *Reformer of Education,* not an *Improver of Instruction.* What he observed at Stanz had germinated and developed, and the first printed expression of the method of Burgdorf is this Report. The next is *Wie Gertrud.*

⁵ Ed. 1, p. 145. " This physical nearness or distance determines all that is positive in your sense-impression, your technical training, and even in your virtue.

LETTER V.

¹ Pestalozzi's frequent use of the word " wesentlich," *essential,* is due to scientific and philosophical ideas now no longer held. From Plato downwards the qualities of objects were divided into two classes, essential and accidental. To some extent this corresponds to the distinction drawn by Mill between connotative and nonconnotative qualities, *i.e.* those qualities which help to decide the classification, and so are implied in the use of the name, and those that do not. (F. C. T.)

² Ed. 1, p. 150. " This mechanism of your nature."

In two places in this paragraph " mechanism " has been altered in the second edition to " organism."

LETTER VI.

¹ *Form* is one of the key-words in Kant's philosophy. To put the matter simply, the manner in which we think is determined by the nature of our minds, and it is impossible for us to think of any object except as existing in time and space. Time and space, therefore, are not to us properties of the external world, but the form in which alone it can be thought. Although Pestalozzi does not use the word strictly in the Kantian sense, his use of it is coloured thereby. Following Grimm, we get those meanings that have any bearing on the use of the word in *Wie Gertrud.*

  1. Outline of figure, shape.
    " A just appreciation of all form." (*P.*)
  2. As opposed to matter.
  3. The vessel or mould in which a work is made.
  5. (Technical.) The frame in which type is set.
    (*Metaph.*) " must be fitted into *forms.*" (*P.*)
  6. The form of a legal process (rel. to 2).
    " Ein Widerspruch in der besten Form." (*Kant.*)
    A contradiction in the best form.

8. General for *manner.*

"Aber in den heitern Regionen
Wo die reinen Formen wohnen
Rauscht des Jammers trüber Sturm nicht mehr." (*Schiller.*)

9. Visualization, sense representation of phenomenon.

"The Kingdom of God can be represented in the visible form of a church."

Pestalozzi's special meanings, which do not exactly correspond to any of the above, though they follow immediately upon them, are—

(*a*) Model, type. *Urform,* prototype.

"The form discloses itself independent like the human race." (*P.*)

"All instruction is nothing but this; it is derived from the typical form of human development." (*P.*)

"Everything depends on the exact knowledge of this prototype." (*P.*)

(*b*) Method imposed by the facts of human nature.

"The Art leads us no further than the spirit of that *form* by which the race is raised from vague sense-impressions to clear ideas." (*P.*)

"The *form* or rather the different methods of teaching languages." (*P.*)   F. C. T.

[2] The Elements were not reached when *The Method* was written.

LETTER VII.

[1] *Sound teaching.* His natural means of teaching at Stanz was the living voice; and here he begins with *sounds,* not with *names,* or *forms* of letters. The child should be able to repeat the sounds easily before the forms are put before his eyes. Phonetics he had not reached. "Always connect a consonant with a vowel, because it cannot be pronounced alone." "We here see," says Seyffarth, "the beginning of the method of teaching by sound, instead of the more difficult method of spelling."

[2] *Spelling Book.* "Hints on Teaching Spelling and Reading," published 1801. Pestalozzi calls this the "Spelling Book." It consists of syllables and words, from which other words can be made by adding letters or syllables before or after. "But when Pestalozzi more fully comprehended the *method of spelling,* he felt it was deficient and unnatural, and tried to improve it. He combined sentences about real objects with the spelling course, exercised the children in spelling by ear before he taught them the symbols in writing, and arranged the letters in groups, which he used by degrees. Movable letters, pasted on cards, spread through his influence. But he fell into the error of putting a certain number of letters together in the most complicated manner, without troubling himself whether the words thus produced were used in speaking or not; and by so doing encouraged the use of sounds without meaning, against which he so strongly protests. For instance, he put O T I N together in the following ways: *nito, toin, into, onit, toni, tino, tion*" (Schindler, *Theoretical and Practical Handbook for First School Teaching. Quoted by Beck*).

³ Ed. 1, p. 171. "These should be repeated daily by the child who is learning to spell, in the presence of the child in the cradle, that the latter may become conscious of these sounds through constant repetition," etc.

⁴ *Singing.* This method was soon applied to singing by Nägeli and Pfeiffer. There is no study in this country where his influence has been greater, or his method used so effectively as in the teaching of singing. The Rev. John Curwen, founder of the Tonic Solfa method, said at a discussion on Pestalozzi at the Education Society, that he came on purpose to testify how much and how deeply he was indebted to him; and Mrs. J. S. Curwen tells me he was always ready to acknowledge it, and that before he attempted to teach singing he was familiar with Pestalozzi's method, and used it.

⁵ *The Mother's Book* never existed, so Pestalozzi himself says. (Note, Letter X.) That is, not as he conceived it. One of his elementary books, published 1803, was called *The Mother's Book, or Hints to Mothers on Teaching their Children to Observe and Talk.* But this book was nearly all of it written by Krüsi, and its fundamental idea—that of using the human body as the basis for the first lessons in sense-impression—Krüsi owed to Basedow. Parts 1-6 are by Krüsi; part 7 and the introduction are by Pestalozzi; 10 parts were proposed, but only 7 were published. The separate parts—called "Exercises" in the book—are:—

1. Observation, and naming the parts of the body; 2. Their position; 3. Their connection; 4. Which parts are single, double, etc.; 5. Characteristics of each separate part; 6. Comparison of parts; 7. Function.

The three remaining exercises were to have been:—

8. What belongs and is necessary to the *care* of the body; 9. Various uses of the special parts—5; 10. Summary and description.

Pestalozzi seems to have thought that his fellow-workers understood his ideas better, and were more capable of carrying them out than he was himself. But he saw later they were not, as the note in Letter X. and the Preface to Ed. 2 shows. "We were too different," he says. None had had his experience; none followed so heartily his way of experiment and observation. This, then, is not his conception of the *Mother's Book*; it is only a part, and an unsatisfactory part of what he proposed. He often indicates his notion of it, especially in Letter X.—"The first course in the *Mother's Book* is an attempt to raise sense-impression to an art, and to lead the child by form, number, and speech to a comprehensive consciousness of all sense-impression, the more definite concepts of which will constitute the foundation of his later knowledge." "I have impressed the first ten numbers on the child's senses," etc. These quotations show the difference between his conception of the *Mother's Book* and the portion published.

This book was attacked and criticised more than any other of his elementary books, and perhaps justly. It was natural to suppose that the body, so near to the child, would interest it, and attract its early observation. But to see ourselves as others see us is a late acquirement; its own body, as seen externally, the child observes less than many other things entirely outside it. If we may judge from its own drawings, its fixed notion is that the eyes are at the top of the head; it does not see or feel and is unconscious of the brain and bone above them. Thousands of children's drawings repeat and confirm this. I have seen the eyes placed so high that a line, representing either eyelid or eyelash, had to be put outside the outline of the head itself. The child conceives of the arm as rounded, because its smooth action is *felt* within, not *seen* without, and the inner feeling is stronger than sight. Naturally, then, the child does not accurately observe its own body, as seen from without, very early.

Here are two criticisms on the book: "The lessons on the body treat the over-abundant material with almost anatomical exactness and completeness. What can the poor mother and children make of these long sentences, difficult for them to understand, and impossible to remember? "The right cheek, or jowl, lies beneath the right eye and the right temple, in front of the right ear on the right side of the nose, the mouth and the chin." (Ex. 2.) "The ten fingers of my two hands have twenty-eight joints; ten at the top, eight in the middle, and ten below. Twenty-eight phalanges; ten at the top, eight in the middle, and ten below; and twenty-eight knuckles—ten at the top, eight in the middle, and ten below." (Ex. 4.) The French journalist, Dussault, ridicules this. "Pestalozzi takes a world of trouble to teach a child that his nose is in the middle of his face." But, strangely enough, the child does not *know* this simple fact; and if he did, he could not clearly express it. The child may be surprised and stimulated to observe more carefully, when it realises that it does not know it. Further, accurate description of even the most common and best known objects, is difficult for children and others. The form or model in the *Mother's Book* is not the best for this. But to be obliged to describe accurately demands careful observation and the right use of words. The idea is not complete till it can be expressed in some way. We cannot tell if it is complete, nor can the child or student, until it is expressed. Pestalozzi's *Mother's Book* is an attempt to raise sense-impression to an art. "Hints on teaching children to observe and talk," is its second title. In the introduction he says: "Mother, you must learn by the clue given by my method or my book, to choose a *few* essential objects out of the ocean of sense-impressions, in which your helpless child is swimming. This is essentially necessary—and, mother, never neglects, while using the exercises in observation and speech, to dwell indefatigably and stedfastly upon each separately, as well as upon the book as a whole, until the child understands the object and its parts according to the point of view of every exercise, perfectly and accurately, and has learned to express himself not only clearly, but with absolute fluency."

Here is criticism of another kind : The *Mother's Book* " gave a false impression of his method," says de Guimp. " People did not sufficiently understand that these series of statements were to result from the child's own observation and experience ; they only saw in them a lesson to be learned by heart, mechanically. And thus, not without some show of reason. Pestalozzi's method has been blamed for a defect which is precisely the defect it was intended to cure." (pp. 246, 247.) A book or manual for the teacher, scientific without being didactic—one that the uninstructed might use as well as the instructed, he had not discovered. Possibly, *Spencer's Inventional Geometry*, or *Huxley's Biology* are nearer what he sought. If you are to teach without knowledge—and it is possible—if you are to lead others to learn as you learn yourself, then real knowledge of the method is necessary, that is practical knowledge of the "physical mechanism," or the mental organism, psychology ; and this depends on *actual observation*, not on books. He says in the Preface, " I cannot prevent the forms of my method from having the same fate as all other forms, which inevitably perish in the hands of men who are neither desirous nor capable of grasping their spirit." To grasp the spirit is the great difficulty ; it is easier to learn than to observe how we learn ; it is a further difficulty to perceive the causes which prevent another learning. Until the value of observing the outer is appreciated, observation of the inner may be disregarded. If these long sentences are to be repeated without clear sense-impression at first—and the teacher who does not grasp the method is sure to undervalue, and even ignore this—then the mere repetition becomes as bad as the worst parrot-like repetition Pestalozzi denounces. But if the facts are really clearly impressed on the senses, it will be well for the child to form its own expression, for that will indicate the state and growth of its thought. At first, all there is in objects is not seen ; thought, expression, and observation, alternate and help each other, as thought and act alternate in experiments, and lead finally to complete thought—the imperfect expression guides the teacher. Pestalozzi has some faith in the "mechanical," perhaps derived from the allied province of "activities" where it is necessary. His children—so Herbart and others testify— could draw very wonderfully, but they were drawing for hours daily. Here the repetition exercises told ; but to repeat mere formulas of words is quite another thing.

This book probably suggested to Froebel his *Mutter und Koselieder.*

⁶ Ed. 1, p. 196. " What does it say of him as a reasonable being struggling upwards towards inner independence and self-ennoblement ? "

⁷ Ed. 1, p. 212. " To fall is to move downwards without or against your will."

⁸ " *A legacy.*" Pestalozzi left a work in MS. called *The Natural*

Schoolmaster, written between 1802–1805, which contains several exercises of the kind referred to. He gave it to Krüsi, who published it, or a selection from it and other works, under the title of *A Father's Lessons on the Customary Use of Words, a Legacy from Father Pestalozzi to His Pupils*, 1829. The manuscript, in Pestalozzi's handwriting throughout, is in Morf's possession. It is printed in Seyffarth's Ed., vol. 16. Pestalozzi began this before the *Mother's Book* was published. After talking to the child about his physical impressions, he thought it would be well to talk about his moral impressions, and he took words for his text.—The "moral lesson" and its Socratising was as regular with us as the "object lesson," but I never hear of it now.

[9] Ed. 1, p. 212. "I should try to connect truth, correct sense-impressions and pure feelings with every word describing human action or condition."

[10] Ed. 1, p. 213. "But if the State allows the proprietor or itself a power opposed to this purpose, then special actions of the rich and powerful, springing from this, will rouse, as far as they are felt, feelings never to be quite extinguished in the human breast, of its original equal rights in the division of the land; and if they become universal, will produce revolutions, so long as men are men. The evils of this cannot be mitigated or remedied except by turning them back to the limits of the purpose for the sake of which," etc.

[11] Ed. 1, p. 216. "To teach the humble folk to talk, but have made the speechless people learn isolated, abstract words by heart."

[12] Ed. 1, p. 216. "To keep their lowest classes always lowest and always stupid."

[13] Ed. 1, p. 217. "'Yes! yes!' say the clergy. 'When they come to us they understand not a word of our teaching.' 'Yes! yes!' say the magistrates, 'even when they are right it is impossible for them to make their rights intelligible to man.' The lady complains loudly and piteously, 'They are hardly a step higher than cattle; they can be used for no service.' Thick-heads that cannot count five, find them stupider than themselves, and rogues of many kinds call out, each with his own gesture: 'Well for us that it is so; were they different, we could neither buy so cheap, nor sell so dear at the market.'

"Friend! this is the way all the people in the stalls of the Great European Christian Theatre talk of the people in the gallery, and they cannot speak in any other way, because, for more than a century, those in the gallery have been made by them soul-less, as no Asiatic and heathen people ever were. I once more explain it. The Christian people of our part of the world have sunk so low because for more than a century, in our lower schools, empty words have been given an importance to the human mind that not only over-powered attention to the impressions of nature, but even destroyed the inner susceptibility to such impressions in men. I say again, while men did that, and degraded the Christian people of Europe to a people of words and chatter, as no people have ever yet been degraded, they *never taught them to talk.* It is no wonder that the Christianity of this century and this land looks as it does; on the contrary, it is wonderful that good human nature, in spite of all the bungling arts that are tried in our word and clapper schools, has still preserved so much inward strength as we always find in the midst of the people. Yet, praised be God! The stupidity of all these ape-like arts finds at last a counterpoise in human nature itself, and ceases to be harmful to our race when its apeings have reached the highest point that we can bear. Folly and error," etc.

Karl Riedel's comment on this is worth repetition, even here where we are so often told that we have got beyond Pestalozzi and need his method no more :—

"Seldom has all word-teaching, all weakness in school teaching been so boldly and frankly criticised as here by Pestalozzi with all justice and noble wrath. Parents, teachers, teachers' trainers and school inspectors should never forget for one instant that only by instruction founded upon the Pestalozzian principle of sense-impression and self-activity that avoids every uncomprehended or superfluous word can 'word and clapper' schools be set aside. This cannot be too often repeated."

[14] "Word and clapper folk"; words and empty phrases; "sounding brass and tinkling cymbals."

[15] Seyffarth ends Letter VII. here; his Letter VIII. begins with *Form.*

[16] Pestalozzi summarises here his meanings of "Anschauung." All knowledge arises from—

(1) Impressions made by all that comes *accidentally* into contact with the five senses. The objects are *in no order*, but in natural confusion. The action on the mind is limited and slow. There is but little if any active living interest in the mind. No attention.

(2) *Attention.* Teachers call *attention* to what they consider important, and so arouse *consciousness*, and deepen the impression. There is order in the presentation, and the thought is connected. The *Art of teaching guides* the selection, and exercises the thought.

(3) *Spontaneous efforts.* But what the teacher presents does not always absorb the whole attention, sometimes not at all. The child has its own interests. Some knowledge it strongly desires, and therefore will seek this of its own free will, and throw its whole soul into the search. The will, stimulated by *self-activity of all the faculties*, prompts to *spontaneous* efforts. This is a step towards moral self-activity and independence.

(4) *Necessary work.* Man must satisfy his wants and wishes, he must work, he must know and think that he may *be able to do.* This is especially considered in Letter XII. To know, Anschauung is necessary, and *knowing and doing* are so intimately connected that if one ceases, the other ceases also. Anschauung and Fertigkeit, observation and experiment, seeing and doing, impression and

expression united, lead to clear ideas, generalisations and education.

(5) *Analogy* and *Subjective observation.* The unseen is understood by its likeness to the seen. We classify and know by analogy. What we can remember we compare, reason about, judge and generalize. " The *results of sense-impression are changed into the work of my mind and all my powers.*" This wider meaning includes the whole psychological sequence.

Pestalozzi's Anschauung covers as much or more than Wordsworth's " imagination":

> " Which in truth
> Is but another name for abstract powers
> And clearest insight, amplitude of mind
> And Reason in her most exalted mood."—*Prelude.*

Prof. Ruskin has always insisted on the value of seeing. "The sight is more important than the drawing." (*Elements of Drawing.*) Compare one of his many passages. "How many manner of eyes are there? You physical-science students should be able to tell us painters that. We only know in a vague way the external aspect and expression of eyes. We see, as we try to draw the endlessly grotesque creatures about us, what infinite variety of instruments they have; but you know far better than we do how those instruments are constructed and directed. You know how some play in their sockets with independent revolution,—project into near-sightedness on pyramids of bone,—are brandished at the points of horns, studded over backs and shoulders,—thrust at the ends of antennæ to pioneer for the head, or pinched up into tubercles at the corners of the lips. But how do the creatures see out of all these eyes?

"No business of ours you may think? Pardon me. This is no Siren's question—this is altogether business of ours, lest, perchance any of us should see partly in the same manner. Comparative sight is a far more important question than comparative anatomy. It is no matter, though we sometimes walk—and it may often be desirable to climb—like apes; but suppose we should only *see* like apes or like lower creatures? I can tell you the science of optics is an essential one to us, for exactly according to these infinitely grotesque directions and multiplications of instrument you have correspondent not only intellectual but moral faculty in the soul of the creatures. Literally, if the eye be pure, the body is pure; but, if the light of the body be but darkness, how great is that darkness." (*The Eagles Nest,* 1887, pp. 127–8.)

[17] The five paragraphs which follow are not in Niederer's version of *The Report of the Method.*

[18] "Measurement." Compare this with what Prof. Ruskin says on our public schools of art system. "The first error in that system is the forbidding accuracy of measurement, and enforcing the practice of guessing the size of objects. . . . the student finishes his inaccurate drawing to the end, and his mind is thus during the whole

process of his work accustomed to falseness of every contour.   Such a practice is not to be characterised as merely harmful—it is ruinous." *Laws of Fésole*, Preface, pp. vii., viii. Pestalozzi, however, carried measurement to extremes, until form was lost. The Author of *The Two Paths* would not agree to this. One of Pestalozzi's strong points is, that in teaching the child, we should follow the natural course of the race. The *Laws of Fésole* are so called because they are "founded on principles established by Giotto in Florence, he receiving them from the Attic Greeks through Cimabue, the last of their disciples." Pestalozzi's principle is admitted here as the foundation of teaching art. It is not generally admitted, and is applied less frequently, perhaps not even in these *Laws of Fésole.*

[19] These measuring-forms are the squares in Buss's A B C of Form, (*The Method*. Appendix): "measuring sub-divisions of the square" are those underlying the general form. The child is to be so familiar with the measure-forms that they become a kind of instinct.   Then they are needed no longer; without this help he can represent all proportions and express himself clearly about them. Froebel adopts these measured squares to get over the difficulty children have of measuring for invention, but we hear nothing about abandoning them later.

[20] "First oval, half oval," etc. In Letter III. ovals or "elongated forms of the circle" are not mentioned at all.   What he means by "oval" is not clear, but Herbart explains it.   "Pestalozzi also has taken up the ellipse in the *A B C der Anschauung*. He calls it somewhat erroneously the oval" (Herbart, *Päd. Schriften*, vol. ii. p. 142).   Pestalozzi has not understood or appreciated this form or its allies, nor its parts.   His description "elongated form of the circle" shows this. He mentions it and leaves it. It seems to me that the oval is the fundamental form of all living things, and until some line of graduated curvature, such as the quadrant of the ellipse, is added to elementary lines, and the ellipse or oval, to our general forms, an A B C of Form is impossible, useless, injurious. Pestalozzi's failed partly because he did not see this, as I have tried to show in a paper on "*Neglected Elements in Art Teaching*" (Trans. Teachers Guild, 1887).—I did not know when that was published that Pestalozzi recognised the ellipse or oval at all.   Biber says nothing about it. The entire absence of satisfactory accounts of Pestalozzi's work drives us to the original works.

LETTER VIII.

[1] Fractions Table. Pestalozzi has three tables, (1) Table of Units, which is not referred to here, and possibly did not yet exist, consisting of twelve rows of twelve rectangular spaces; in each space of the first row is one stroke, in each of the second two strokes, and so on, up to twelve strokes. (2) Table of Simple Fractions, and (3)

Table of Compound Fractions, as here described.   The plate gives the left hand half of the third table.

[2] Pestalozzi's "narrow sense" seems wider than this. He has reduced *form* to the square only.   He never really saw the value of the oval and ellipse.   He can teach number by these measure-forms, but he cannot reverse the process and teach *form* by them, nor by number nor by words. His "Elements" have not the same foundation as his "Anschauung, Psychology, and Prototype."   What value there is in them rests on these principles, not on the harmony which he endeavours to establish between these elements.

[3] Ed. 1, p. 271. "Here too we can say with decision, this reckoning is an exercise for the reason only, and is in no way a mere work of memory and no routine-like help to trade.   It is the result of the clearest, most definite sense-impressions, and leads easily, by simple evidence, to truth.

LETTER IX.

[1] "Educational" here should be "Instructional."

Except in this case we have translated *Unterricht* by instruction. It is Pestalozzi's usual term.   *Erziehung* (education) he made the current term it is now, but it often has not his meaning. Instead of "drawing out," it frequently means "cramming in."

[2] Ed. 1, p. 277. "Because it opened the mouth of the obvious stupidity of a monkish and feudal world to express abstract ideas, that the most perfect wisdom of the most intellectual life of our race can never solve."

[3] *Zungendrescherei*, literally tongue-threshing.   Tongue-twisting or turning sophistry ; twisted words or twisted talk.

This is one of his many characteristic words, not easily translated. Like *Maulbrauchen*, Letter I.

LETTER X.

[1] If this passage is from *The Method* it is not to be found in the Niederer version. When he referred to the Report in Letter I., he said, "six months ago," here "more than a year ago." But *Wie Gertrud* was not published till October, 1801."

In this letter we have said "the art of sense-impression (or *observation*)," to distinguish it from sense-impression, but Pestalozzi uses "art of sense-impression" only. "What Pestalozzi meant," says J. H. Fichte, is "that only can become the pupil's, or even the man's, true mental possession which he has raised for himself to a perfectly clear mental picture (*Anschauung*), that is, has thought out and has reproduced out of himself from his own knowledge through the self-activity of his mind. It is only then that it becomes one with his consciousness. It is become evident, real, to him a conviction which is theoretically and practically at his command at any moment of

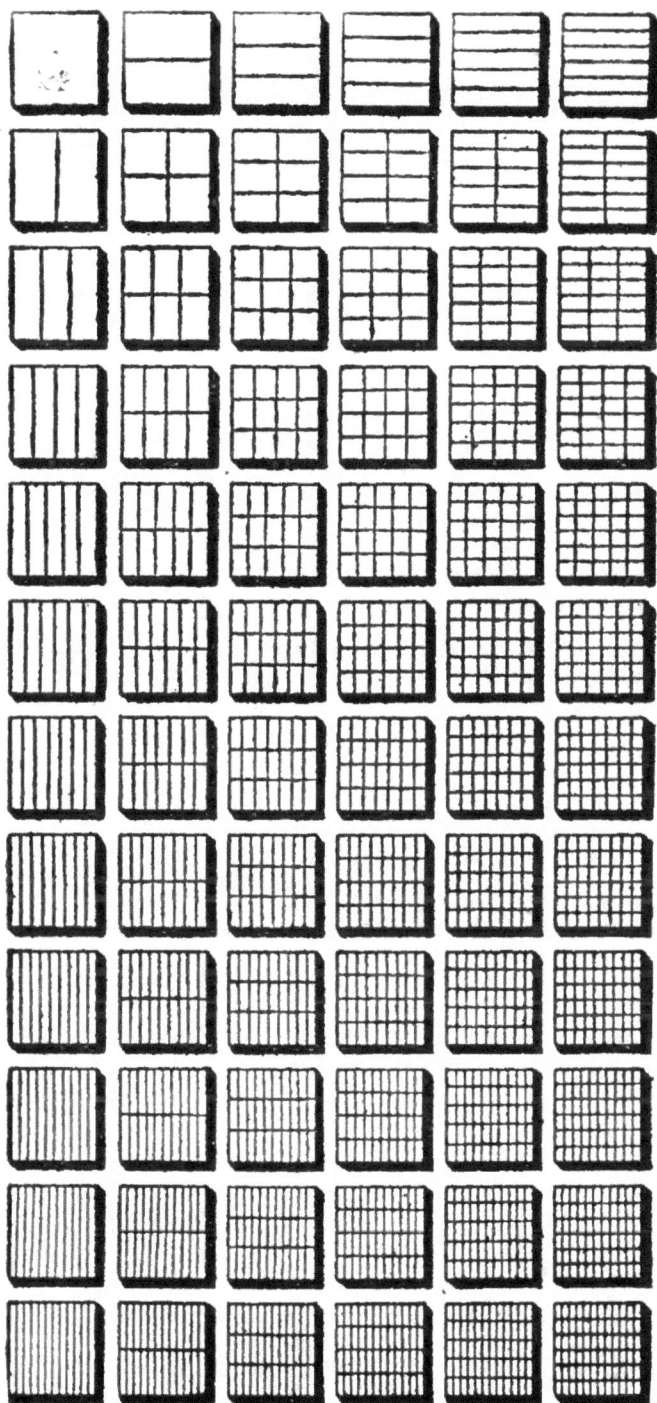

PART OF PESTALOZZI'S TABLE OF COMPOUND FRACTIONS.

his life " (*Deutsche Vierteljahrsschrift*, No. 127, 1869). " This is really what Pestalozzi meant by his art of sense-impression," Richter adds (*Exkurse Wie Gertrud*, p. 187).

² Ed. 1, 289. " Number also in itself, without a foundation of sense-impression is a phantom for our mind. The child must know its *form* before he is in a position to consider it as a *number-relation*, *i.e.*, as the basis of a clear consciousness of few or many."

³ Ed. 1, p. 301. " My grammar is only a series of methods for leading the child by every kind or change of word-combination from vague sense-impressions to clear ideas."

⁴ Ed. 1, p. 303. " But I am convinced by experiments, which lie at the base of this statement, and have come with decision to reject all half measures, and to put aside all text-books for elementary instruction which are based on the supposition," etc.

⁵ Ed. 1, p. 304. " And since all instruction books which are written in the usual grammatical way assume this, I would, had I influence, act quite mercilessly towards school libraries, or at any rate towards those elementary books which are meant for the youngest children."

⁶ Ed. 1, p. 305. " Will there be even a few who wish, with me, that I may succeed in checking and putting an end to the mad trust in empty words that is enervating our generation, by making word and sound unimportant to the imagination of men, and in restoring to sense-impression that preponderance over word and sound in instruction that obviously belongs to it ? "

⁷ Ed. 1, p. 305. " Yes, friend, there will long be few, very few. The babble of our time is so closely connected with the bread-getting, and the ordinary association of tens and hundreds of thousands together, that it must be long, very long, before the men of our time can take that truth " etc.

⁸ Ed. 1, p. 306. " Such pupils never dream that they are dreaming and sleeping ; but all wakeful men round them feel their presumption, and—if they are kind—look on them as night wanderers," etc.

⁹ Ed. 1, p. 307. " I well know that the one good method is neither in my hands nor in any other man's, but with all the power lying in my hands I try to approach this one true good (method)."

¹⁰ Ed. 1, p. 307. " I have one rule in judging all others. '*By their fruits shall ye know them.*' "

¹¹ Ed. 1, p. 308. " Can be nothing but developed faculties and clear ideas. Oh, if starting from this point of view, they would ask themselves at every step, ' Does it really further this end ? ' "

¹² Ed 1, p. 310. " In this way and no other can the child be led to definitions which give him ideas of the thing to be defined. For definitions are only the simplest and purest expression of clear ideas, but, for the child, definitions contain actual truth only so far as he has a clear, vivid background of sense-impression."

¹³ Ed. 1, pp. 314–316. " You must distinguish the laws of nature

from her course, that is, from special workings and statements about these workings. In respect to her laws she is eternal truth, and for us the eternal standard of all truth. But in respect to her course and the statements about her course she is not satisfactory to the individual of my race; she is not *all-satisfying truth.* Careful of the whole, she is careless of the single creature and particularly of man, whose self-dependence she will lessen by no kind of guardianship.

"In this aspect and no other, be it understood that she is careless and blind, and that she requires that the guidance of our race should be taken out of her hands. But in this respect it is quite true and urgent for my race. When you leave the earth to nature, she bears weeds and thistles, and when you leave the training of your race to her, she carries it on no further than to a confusion of sense-impressions, necessary for your first lessons, but now unfit either for your own power of comprehension or for that of your child. Therefore it is neither to the forest nor the meadow that the child must go to learn herbs and trees. Trees and herbs stand not there in the orders which are most suitable to make the essentials of every relationship visible (*anschaulich*) to him, and through this first impression of the thing itself to prepare him for general knowledge of the subject."

LETTER XI.

[1] Ed. 1, pp. 322–324. "Now my method gives this passage a kind of truth which I could not imagine then; it is now incontestable. In it I take no share in all the strife of men, I teach through it neither truth nor error. It spreads its influence not one step beyond what is undeniable, it touches on no opinion that is disputed among men, it is not the teacher of *truths*, it is the teacher of *truth*; and combines the results of physical necessity, at which the mechanism of my Art is aiming, with the complete certainty of my judgment.

"Friend, there is no presumption in my heart. Throughout my life I have wished for nothing but the salvation of the people, whom I love, and whose misery I feel as few feel it, because I have suffered with them as few have done before. However, when I say there is a mechanism which results from physical necessity, I do not therefore say I have developed all its laws; and when I say there is a rational course of instruction, it does not follow that I have fully stated this course. In the whole account of my doings, I have tried far more to make the security of my principles clear than to set up the very limited action of my own little individuality as a standard of what may and must come from the full development of these principles for the human race. I do not know myself, and I feel daily more and more how much I do not know."

LETTER XII.

[1] Ed. 1, p. 332. "I see in it the ideal of the lost innocence of my race, but I see in it also the ideal of the shame which the memory of

R

this lost holiness always awakens in me, so long as I am worthy, and so long as I am worthy ever revives within me the power of seeking what I have lost and of saving myself from ruin. Friend, so long as man is worthy of the sublime characteristic of his race, speech, so long as he uses it with a pure desire to ennoble himself through it, it is a high and holy thing. But when he is no longer worthy, when he uses it with no pure desire to ennoble himself, it will be to him and for him the first cause of ruin, a wretched promoter of much misery, an inexhaustible source of unspeakable illusion and a lamentable cloak for his crimes. Friend, it is true—terribly true—the depravity of language grows with the depravity of man. Through it the wretched become more wretched; through it the night of error becomes still darker; through it the crimes of the wicked still increase. Friend, the crimes of Europe are still increasing through idle talk. We cannot guess to what this ever-increasing list of publications will lead a generation whose weakness, confusion and violence have already reached the stage we see."

This passage has been extended but not much altered in the second edition.

² After Anschauung, the most difficult word to translate is FERTIGKEIT, which literally means (1) *promptitude* or *readiness;* (2) *readiness and skill in performing some action.*

It is not easy to find a satisfactory English equivalent in this sense. The following quotations given in Grimm, in addition to one from *Wie Gertrud*, will make the meaning quite clear. (The English equivalent in each case is in italics.)

"Da nemlich, es kurz zu sagen, diese Reinigung in nichts anders beruhet als in der Verwandlung der Leidenschaften in tugendhafte Fertigkeiten." "As, to put it shortly, this purification consists of nothing less than the transformation of the passions into *habits of virtuous action.*" (Lessing.)

"Ihr alle reimt mit gleicher Fertigkeit." "You all rhyme with equal *facility.*" (Gellert.)

"Die Eigenschaften, die Fertigkeiten des Lichts rege zu machen." "To bring the properties, the *capabilities* of light into play." (Goethe.)

"Er besitzt eine ausserordentliche Fertigkeit in Geigen." "He possesses extraordinary *skill* in fiddling." (F. C. T.)

"Fertigkeiten" we have generally translated "activities," but several other equivalents are used, *e.g.* (1) acts, actions; (2) powers of doing, skill, practical skill, technical skill; (3) practical ability, abilities, faculties, capacities;—*e.g.* (1) "We are far behind the greatest barbarians in the *A B C of acts or actions (gymnastics)* and their skill in striking and throwing," etc. "These contain the foundations of all possible *actions* on which human callings depend." (2) "The people do not enjoy in regard to culture in skill (technical education) one scrap of that public and universal help from government that each man needs. In no way do they enjoy the culture of those *practical abilities.*" (3) "The abilities (capacities, talents, etc.) on the possession of which depend all the powers of knowing and doing (*Können*) that are required of an educated mind and noble heart, come as little of themselves as intelligence and knowledge." "*Powers of knowing and doing.*" "Can" and "ken" are derived from the same root as the German *können* and *kennen*; the present tense "can" is the preterite of the obsolete verb meaning *know*, so that its real meaning is *I have known* or *learnt*, and therefore *am able to do*. I *ken*, therefore *I can*; knowledge and skill are inseparable. See Murray's Dictionary.

This whole series of meanings, as with Anschauung, are connected. "Knowing and doing are so closely connected that if one ceases the other ceases with it." Doing has a double function; by doing thought is expressed, and by doing thought is also gained and made clear. It is Anschauung, by experience, through the sense of touch or active movement; impression and expression combine. The whole psychological sequence of Pestalozzi is impression, clear idea or knowledge, and expression. Observe, think, do, and know. One kind of Anschauung, he says, Letter VII. is obtained "by working at one's calling." He connects observation and experience.

³ Ed. 1, p. 335. "Thought and action should stand in such close relation to each other, that, like spring and stream, if one cease the other ceases with it."

⁴ Ed. 1, p. 336. "Mechanical laws." "The mechanism of nature."

⁵ *Abrichtungsverderben*, degeneracy or decadence caused by artificial or circus training; that is, training possible but not in harmony with the true nature of the creature trained.

⁶ This entire passage and the beginning of the next is altered in the later edition. We give it here as it stands in the first edition, and also fill up the "great gap" once more.

Ed. 1, p. 324. "The individual man has not lost the consciousness of these important requirements for his development. His natural instinct, together with the knowledge he possesses, drives him to this path. The father does not leave his child wholly to Nature, still less the master his *apprentice, but governments make infinitely more mistakes than men.* No corporation is influenced by instinct, and where instinct does not act truth enjoys but half its right.

"It is a fact that no father is guilty towards his son, no master towards his apprentice, of that which the government is guilty towards the people. The people of Europe do not enjoy in regard to their culture in skill (*Fertigkeit*=technical education) a vestige of that public and general help from government that each man needs in order by wise care of his own business to attain inward satisfaction. In no way do they enjoy the cultivation of their *practical abilities*, except indeed for the purpose of human slaughter; for military organization devours all that is due to the people or rather what they owe to themselves. It devours all that is ground out of the people, all that can be ground out of them in an ever-increasing ratio. Their practical abilities are neglected because the government does not fulfil the promises which were made in order to grind the people. But this which the government withholds from them, is of such a nature that if it were only granted the extortion would become just and the misery of the people, as a consequence of this justice, would be changed into contentment and happiness. But now they snatch the bread from the widow, who is taking it out of her own mouth to give it to her babe. They snatch it, not intending to use it for the people, but in order to make their injustice and worthlessness lawful and legal. In the same spirit, at one time, they snatched bread from the widow and orphan to make jobbery ecclesiastical and canonical. The same methods served for both, for the jobbery, spiritual extortion, and for the injustice, worldly taxation, both in the name of the public welfare—the one for the salvation of the soul, the other for the happiness of the body—both notoriously work against salvation and against happiness.

"The people of Europe are fatherless and wretched. Most of those who stand near enough to help them have something else to do than to think of their welfare. In the stable, and with dogs and cats, you will be led to believe that many of them are humane, but they are not humane to the people; they have no heart for them. They live on the revenues from land, but in constant forgetfulness of the conditions that produce these revenues. They do not realize how the people are degraded by the ever-increasing extortion and the *confusion caused by it*, nor how *practical honesty* is constantly decreasing as well as a *want of a sense of responsibility* in using public property. They are responsible for the dreadful increase of physical enervation of men and classes who are *de facto*, if not *de jure*, free from responsibility. They, receiving revenues, wash their dirty hands. It is this which degrades and perplexes human nature and robs it of its power of enjoyment and its true humanity. They do not realize how great the universal pressure of work has become. They do not realize how the difficulty increases day by day of getting through the world with religion and honour, and of leaving the children behind provided for according to their circumstances. Least of all do they realize the disproportion between that which they grind from the poor of the land, and that which they leave in his hands wherewith to earn what they grind from him. But, dear friend, whither is my holy simplicity leading me?"

[7] Ed. 1, p. 341. "The culture of the physical faculties, that the state should assiduously and might easily give to the people, like the culture for special purposes, depends, like all culture, on a profound mechanism—on an A B C of the Art; that is, on general rules of art by following which the children can be trained by a series of exercises, proceeding gradually from the simplest to the most complicated. These exercises must certainly result in affording daily increasing ease in those faculties (*Feri*) which need improvement.

But this A B C is *not found*. Of course we seldom find what nobody seeks. It was so easy to find. It must begin with the simplest expressions of the physical powers, which contain the principles of the most complicated human practical ability (*Fert*)."

[8] Ed. 1, p. 343. "But these are of no use to the principles of jobbery and injustice that form the basis of our public revenues, and are not easily compatible with the distinctly nervous state of the gentry, who *take the biggest slice* of the results of the jobbery and injustice."

[9] Ed. 1, p. 345. "These considerations must determine the power of applying our activities. Every influence that in the application of our powers and faculties turns us away from the centre point."

[10] Ed. 1, p. 346. "Every kind of instruction that bears within itself the seeds of such evil for short-lived men must cause the more terror to every father and mother who have their children's lifelong peace of mind at heart, since we must seek the sources of the infinite evil of our *sham enlightenment* and the misery of our *masquerade revolution* in errors of this kind, since they have existed for generations both in the *instruction* and *non-instruction* of our people."

[11] Ed. 1, p. 347. "And on its lines a sense-preparation for physical instinct will be laid, which will promote the wisdom and virtue of our race."

[12] Ed. 1, p. 347. "In this way the only form of education suitable to the human race is developed which can be recognized as a means of training virtue."

[13] Ed. 1, p. 347. "Therefore it is that as definition before sense-impression makes men presumptuous fools, so explanations about virtue before the exercise of virtue make them presumptuous villains. I do not believe I am contradicted by experience. Gaps in the sense-cultivation of virtue cannot well have other results than gaps in the sense-cultivation of knowledge."

LETTER XIII.

[1] Ed. 1, p. 353. "It is not a simple result of natural instinct, but yet it follows the same course of development."

LETTER XIV.

[1] Ed. 1, p. 370. "Friend, if my method here satisfies a want of my race, its value surpasses my every hope, and it does."

[2] Here the second edition ends. In the first edition a long passage follows from a letter addressed to Pestalozzi by Dr. Schnell, of Burgdorf. We give it here, for it weakens Pestalozzi's masterly conclusion.

Ed. 1, 383–390. "I must add to this passage, that explains exactly the sanctity of religion, yet another, written by a man whose head and heart are alike dear to me, describing the external origin of religion, so far as it is an affair of nations and external human associations. Dr. Schnell of Burgdorf wrote to me a few days since:—

" ' Man reflects much sooner upon that which he sees and handles than upon those feelings which lie undeveloped in his inmost soul, and which only now and then glide over the background of his consciousness like formless shadows. He must, of necessity, learn to know the physical world before he can attain to knowledge of the intellectual world.

" ' His reflection will be awakened, as soon as he becomes self-conscious, by unusual natural phenomena, such as earthquakes, floods, thunder, etc., and his propensity to *try to get to the bottom of everything* leads him to reflect upon the *causes* of these phenomena before he knows their nature; but these reflections lead him no further than to *personifications* of these causes. It lightens because Zeus willed it, etc. In this way man refers every kind of phenomena to its special author, overseer, or god, who divide the kingdom of causes among them, at first peaceably, afterwards by force.

" ' But the human mind, according to its nature, ever trying to reduce multiplicity to unity, did not long find pleasure in polytheism. Man began to look upon nature as a gang of under-workers in the great workshop, and now inquired about the *master.* As imagination had led him so far, it now led him further. It showed him an image representing this master and called it *Fate*—an idea expressing neither more nor less than a *senseless supreme will,* a personified caprice, that can give no reason for its decrees except its own authority: This is my absolute will and command.

" ' And this is the *supreme* cause, the *one* god to which *human* reason points; and when reason finds its goal, imagination must furl her wings, because she can paint no picture without borrowing colours from the palette of experience ; for to mix colours different from those on this palette is beyond her skill.

" ' Man was obliged to stop at this stage of education, until by constant examination and inquiry, he discovered that all the phenomena of nature stand in more or less close relationship, and depend more or less upon each other. He saw one weight sink while another rose, and began to find order and harmony, where before he saw nothing but disorder and confusion. From this time forward he no longer looked upon the changes and phenomena around him as the play of accident, or as the effect of the capricious decrees of a mighty being, but as the harmonious action of a machine, *moving according to definite laws, towards a definite, though to him unknown, end.* Now he knew the whole clock as far as—mainspring and dial—the cause and purpose of movement.

" ' The idea of *rule, of law,* to which his reason led him through inquiry, seemed to fit an inner feeling that had often before disturbed him, but which he could not express because words were wanting to him. Now he had made this feeling clear to himself with the objects of the material world, the symbol led him to the thing itself, and he ventured to apply what he had found in the known world, to a *visionary unknown* world. If he wished to act, or acted, he felt every time that a judgment, not to be silenced, would be spoken of his action in his soul, that would not always agree with the judgment that his reason pronounced upon the success or failure of the purpose for which he had acted. He was fully conscious that this feeling might be powerless to determine him against his will for or against the perpetration of any action; but nevertheless it happened that disobedience to the word of this inner voice awakened an enemy in his own heart that the friendship of the whole world could not lay to rest. He applied his newly-found idea of a rule, a law, to this unknown something, and he saw that this guess had not deceived him; for he found the command of this inner voice just as absolute a command as he had found that law absolute, which directs the changes of the seasons; but he found that his desires were not so absolutely submissive to this command as nature is submissive to her laws. He said therefore, to himself,—

"'Nature *must* obey her laws; she has no will. But I need not obey the law in my breast unless I wish. Herein I am my own judge and so far a nobler being than all nature.

"'With this knowledge, a new sun rose over a new world for our race. Man saw himself on the boundary between the physical and the spiritual world, and found himself a citizen of both—of the one through his body, of the other through his will. He found that the laws of these worlds are at bottom *one and the same law,* because both command *order* and *harmony;* and that their apparent difference only comes from the difference of the natures through which they command. Natures, gifted with knowledge, ought to obey the law, and they will wish to obey it, because they must know that it leads them to peace with themselves—to their own end. But natures not gifted with knowledge must obey, because they have no purpose of their own, and if they are not driven, they must stand still. . . . And now Thy creatures need only raise their eyes from nourishing earth to the eternal heaven, and they found Thee, known and yet unknown, to whom no work is discordant. . . . And Thou seest with joy, author of every law of the physical and the spiritual world, *in this glance of Thy creature,* that this work too is good, because even by it, he raises himself from the dust of the earth and longs for freedom and for Thee, and has recognised the purpose of the material world as a means to Thy end in the moral world,'" etc.

AUTHORITIES.

It has not been possible to give authorities for notes except where they are quoted entire. We have consulted and are indebted to the following editions of Pestalozzi's: *Wie Gertrud ihre Kinder lehrt,* Ed. 1, Gessner, Zürich, 1801.—*Padagogische Bibliothek,* Albert Richter, Leipzig, 1880. This is the text we have generally followed. Seyffarth, *Pestalozzi's sämmtliche Werke,* vol. XI. Brandenburg, 1872.—*Pädagogische Klassiker* III., Karl Riedel, Wien, 1877.—*Ausgewählte Schriften berühmter Pädagogen*, IV., Dr. K. Aug. Beck, 1887.—*Universal Bibliothek*, Leipzig, 991, 992, 40 pf., a small popular edition without notes.

Dr. Darin *Comment Gertrude instruit ses infants*, Ed. 2, Paris, 1886. Also the following biographies, etc., Biber, E., *Henry Pestalozzi and his Plan of Education, being an account of his life and writings*, London, 1831.—R. de Guimps, *Pestalozzi, his Life and Work. Translated from Second Edition by J. Russell, B.A.*, London, 1890.—Morf, *Zur Biographie Heinrich Pestalozzi's*, Winterthur, 1868-1885.—Guillaume, J., *Pestalozzi, Étude Biographique*, Paris, 1890. *Pestalozzi Blätter*, Zürich, 1878-1892—Herbart, *Päd. Schriften*, 1880.—J. P. Rossel, *Allgemeine Monatschrift für Erziehung und Unterricht*, Aachen, 1828, etc., etc.

SUPPLEMENTS TO THE METHOD.

The supplements omitted are not necessary, as their character can be inferred from the book, nor have we given all Pestalozzi's examples.

Supplement No. 2. A collection of words almost alike, which receive a variety of changes by small additions. These must have the effect of giving certainty to spelling—a result that could hardly be so easily gained in any other way. All combinations of letters, grammatically possible, have been used as series of syllables and words. Here is an example:—

ein	eint	eine	einen	einet	einern
bein	meint	deine	deinen	meinet	beinern
dein	neint	meine	meinen	weinet	steinern
sein	scheint	seine	seinen	scheinet	kleinern, etc.

The use of these words in language, may at the same time be learnt in a way pleasant to the children and adapted to their intelligence.

For instance, ine (ein) is put upon the board as the principal sound, and while I add to it I say, "What I have bought is? *m*ine (m-ein). But with a *w*: "What do we squeeze out of grapes?" *W*ine (W-ein), etc.

No. 3 is a guide to lessons upon the relations of numbers according to regulated steps.

The various relations of the numerical system must be brought home to the sense-impression of the children by means of real objects. I find the letters on the reading-board the handiest.

At first, I put one letter on the board, and ask, "How many are there?" The child says 1. I add another, and ask—

$$1 \text{ and } 1 \text{ are? } 2$$
$$2 \;\text{ ,, }\; 1 \;\text{ ,, }\; ? \; 3$$
$$3 \;\text{ ,, }\; 1 \;\text{ ,, }\; ? \; 4$$

Only very few are wanted at first, until by very easy exercises the increased power of the child demands gradually more and different numbers. Then we take the added letters away one by one, and ask—

How much is 1 less than 20? Ans. 19.
" " 1 " " 19? " 18.
I go on with—What are 1 and 2? 3
" " 3 " 2? 5
" " 5 " 2? 7 etc.

Then back again. 2 less than 99 are? 97
2 " " 97 " ? 95
Then 1 and 3 are? 4
4 " 3 " ? 7 up to 100 and back again.
Then 2 " 3 " ? 5
5 " 3 " ? 8 up to 100 etc.
Then 1 " 4 " ? 5
5 " 4 " ? 9 up to 100 etc.
Then 2 " 4 " ? 6 etc.
Then 3 " 4 " ? 7 etc.
Then 1 " 5 " ? 6 etc.

I go on further to
2 and 2 are? 4. How many times 2 make 4?
4 " 2 " ? 6. How many times 2 make 6?
6 " 2 " ? 8. How many times 2 make 8?
And so on up to 100 and then backwards.
2 less than 100 are? 98. How many times 2 make 98?
2 " " 98 " ? 96. How many times 2 make 96?
In the same way I go on—
3 and 3 are? 6. How many times 3 make 6?
4 " 4 " ? 8. How many times 4 make 8? etc.

No. 4.	Gold-finch	Silver-gilt	Almond-tree.
	" mine	" mine	" scent.
	" dust	" ware	" flavour.
	" fish	" plate	" oil.

(A selection from many examples.)
No. 8. To make signs is to make something understood by gestures without words.
To extend is to make longer.
To stretch is to make longer.
To spread is to make broader.
(All the other examples, " to go," etc., are in Letter VII.)

NOTE TO "THE METHOD."

The Society of Friends of Education was founded by Stapfer, June, 1800, to make Pestalozzi's views better known. A Commission was appointed from among its members to examine and report. At their request he gave them " *An Account of the Method.*" They visited his school and presented their Report at a general meeting of the Society, Oct. 1, 1800.

The "Report or Account of the Method," which Pestalozzi made for this Society, is the first systematic statement of his views.

When he left Stanz, he was not sure of his principles. In this Report, "Anschauung" and his great principles first appear; but the *A B C of Anschauung* is not here. That and his *Elements* first appear in *Wie Gertrud*, and the attempts to correlate and unite them also.

When he wrote this Report, he was quite alone. It is entirely his own work: it gives us the condition of his mind a year after he left Stanz. The observations made there have germinated and developed: this is their first expression. It comes between the *First Letter from Stanz*, and *How Gertrude Teaches her Children*; these three works complete his writings at this important period of his own development. After this, until we come to the *Swan's Song*, there is nothing of equal value, nothing quite free from the influence of helpers who had never been at Stanz.

The Report is quoted several times in *Wie Gertrud*; it is the germ of that work; to add it here was necessary to complete the work of this period, and also to show how the idea "germinated" in him. "It sets forth," says de Guimps, "his doctrine with a clearness and precision that are hardly to be found in any other of his writings" (p. 184). He forgets that he has only just said, overleaf, "He was not yet clear himself as to what his method really was, and could hardly have given an explanation of it." He was, in fact, seeking a principle (p. 182). These statements can be reconciled if applied to 1799, but not to 1800. "Unfortunately," says de Guimps, "this document was never published, and has remained unknown. It is wanting even in the collection published by Seyffarth at Brandenburg, which is the most complete edition of his works. Niederer, we believe, incorporated it in his *Notes on Pestalozzi*, Aix-la-Chapelle, but this book is no longer to be found."

But de Guimps is mistaken. The first edition of his Life of Pestalozzi was published in 1874, Seyffarth had reprinted *The Method* only the previous year, 1873, while Niederer had published it in 1828 in the *Allgemeine Monatschrift für Erziehung und Unterricht*, with other works of Pestalozzi. These works had also been published separately, but de Guimps did not know this in 1874, when his first edition was published; in Edition 2 he adds an appendix, but does not correct the text, and his note is not quite accurate. He says, that Seyffarth (vol. 18) contains some special works here first published; among them "*The Method.*" This is the Report presented by Pestalozzi to the Society of the Friends of Education in 1800, referred to by us in its proper place" (p. 431). Now this Niederer version of the Method referred to in the appendix is not the same as that quoted by de Guimps (p. 184). He has not discovered this. He gives the *conclusion* of the Report, but his last two paragraphs are at the *beginning* of Niederer's version its second and third paragraphs. There are other differences. There is evidently then another copy. This is confirmed by *Wie Gertrud*: some of the quotations given there are not to be found in this version of

Niederer's. In Letter VII. there is a long quotation beginning, "Grant the principle" (p. 116.) This is not in Niederer's version; so that, although it is signed by Pestalozzi, is in his own handwriting, and is undoubtedly genuine, it is not the version quoted in *Wie Gertrud* nor by de Guimps. It may be the first draft. The question arises, If no account was published, how did de Guimps obtain an abstract and quotations for his first edition? This is answered by referring to Morf, vol. I. p. 228. Morf has given an abstract and quotations, and de Guimps has copied them. The one quotation he gives, which is not in Morf, is taken from *Wie Gertrud*, Letter IV.

Seyffarth also has not seen that there are *two* versions of the "*Account of The Method.*" He says in the Preface to *Wie Gertrud*, Pestalozzi made "a Report which was afterwards published by Niederer, 1840, in the *Pestaloggische Blätter*—unfortunately with Niederer's revisions. Morf gives a summary of it." Seyffarth does not know apparently that Morf's version is entirely different from Niederer's. It is strange that this first *Account of the Method* is not known to Pestalozzi's editor and biographer, and has never been, so far as we can learn, reprinted.

It seemed probable to us that Pestalozzi's version of *The Method* might have been published at the time it was presented. Dr. Schnell, Prefect of Burgdorf, published a pamphlet in 1800 which gave a more complete exposition of Pestalozzi's views than the Report contained. The Society also appealed publicly for subscriptions. Possibly the Report was printed and circulated. Mr. Morf evidently knew, we wrote to him and he replied,

" In answer to your letter of June 23rd, allow me first to remind you that in dealing with those portions of Pestalozzi's work which he edited, Niederer left nothing untouched, he gave his own colour to everything. He lived in the firm belief that he understood Pestalozzi better than Pestalozzi understood himself. The quotations that I give, vol. I. p. 228 and seq., are taken from the original document of June, 1800. It was printed in the newspapers of that date."

At present, we have not been able to get at these newspapers, but we may suggest to the Editor of *Pestalozzi-blätter* that it would be well to reprint it. The *Augsburger Zeitung* and *Deutscher Merkur* (Wieland Editor) took up his cause.

Mr. Morf does not settle one point of importance. Did the diagram of (Buss's) *A B C der Anschauung* appear in the newspapers? Seyffarth excludes it, and the sentence preceding it. If this diagram is really Buss's, it could not have existed when Pestalozzi wrote the Report. If it is not in the versions from which Morf copies, it seems clear that Niederer has not left this untouched. The A B C is probably not Pestalozzi's own production, for Buss says (Lett. III.) he could not draw, and that for months he could not understand him. But he gave Buss some lines as a pattern.

INDEX.

Trieste

Trieste Publishing has a massive catalogue of classic book titles. Our aim is to provide readers with the highest quality reproductions of fiction and non-fiction literature that has stood the test of time. The many thousands of books in our collection have been sourced from libraries and private collections around the world.

The titles that Trieste Publishing has chosen to be part of the collection have been scanned to simulate the original. Our readers see the books the same way that their first readers did decades or a hundred or more years ago. Books from that period are often spoiled by imperfections that did not exist in the original. Imperfections could be in the form of blurred text, photographs, or missing pages. It is highly unlikely that this would occur with one of our books. Our extensive quality control ensures that the readers of Trieste Publishing's books will be delighted with their purchase. Our staff has thoroughly reviewed every page of all the books in the collection, repairing, or if necessary, rejecting titles that are not of the highest quality. This process ensures that the reader of one of Trieste Publishing's titles receives a volume that faithfully reproduces the original, and to the maximum degree possible, gives them the experience of owning the original work.

We pride ourselves on not only creating a pathway to an extensive reservoir of books of the finest quality, but also providing value to every one of our readers. Generally, Trieste books are purchased singly - on demand, however they may also be purchased in bulk. Readers interested in bulk purchases are invited to contact us directly to enquire about our tailored bulk rates. Email: customerservice@triestepublishing.com

You May Also Like

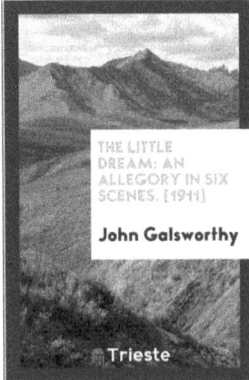

The Little Dream: An Allegory in Six Scenes. [1911]

John Galsworthy

ISBN: 9780649637270
Paperback: 50 pages
Dimensions: 6.14 x 0.10 x 9.21 inches
Language: eng

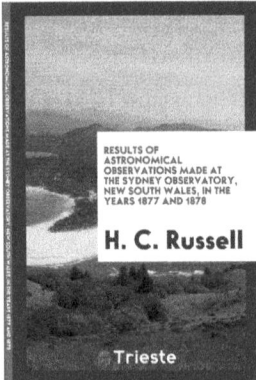

Results of Astronomical Observations Made at the Sydney Observatory, New South Wales, in the Years 1877 and 1878

H. C. Russell

ISBN: 9780649692613
Paperback: 120 pages
Dimensions: 6.14 x 0.25 x 9.21 inches
Language: eng

www.triestepublishing.com

You May Also Like

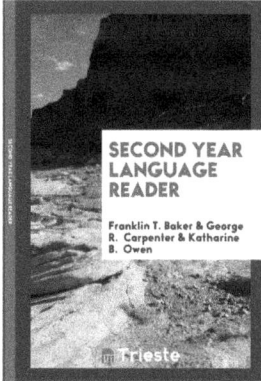

Second Year Language Reader

Franklin T. Baker & George R. Carpenter & Katharine B. Owen

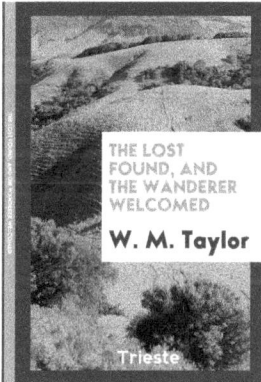

ISBN: 9780649587667
Paperback: 176 pages
Dimensions: 6.14 x 0.38 x 9.21 inches
Language: eng

The Lost Found, and the Wanderer Welcomed

W. M. Taylor

ISBN: 9780649639663
Paperback: 188 pages
Dimensions: 6.14 x 0.40 x 9.21 inches
Language: eng

You May Also Like

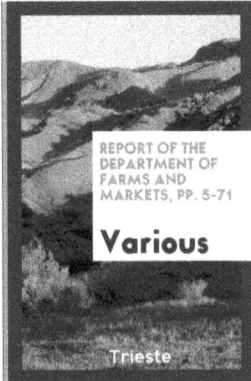

ISBN: 9780649333158
Paperback: 84 pages
Dimensions: 6.14 x 0.17 x 9.21 inches
Language: eng

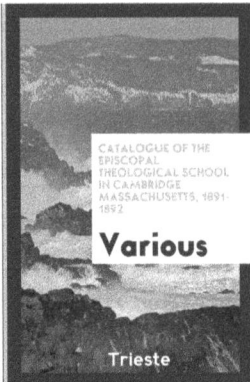

Report of the Department of Farms and Markets, pp. 5-71

Various

ISBN: 9780649324132
Paperback: 78 pages
Dimensions: 6.14 x 0.16 x 9.21 inches
Language: eng

Catalogue of the Episcopal Theological School in Cambridge Massachusetts, 1891-1892

Various

You May Also Like

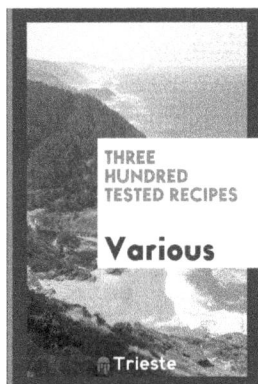

Three Hundred Tested Recipes

Various

ISBN: 9780649352142
Paperback: 88 pages
Dimensions: 6.14 x 0.18 x 9.21 inches
Language: eng

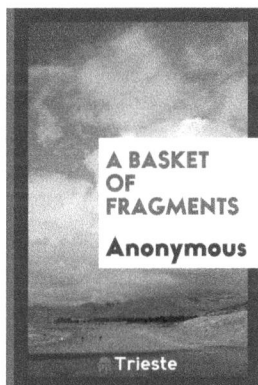

A Basket of Fragments

Anonymous

ISBN: 9780649419418
Paperback: 108 pages
Dimensions: 6.14 x 0.22 x 9.21 inches
Language: eng

Find more of our titles on our website. We have a selection of thousands of titles that will interest you. Please visit

www.triestepublishing.com

9 780649 607969